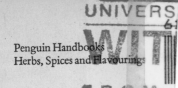

Penguin Handbooks
Herbs, Spices and Flavourings

Tom Stobart, O.B.E., is not only an expert on cookery, but also a well-known photographer and mountaineer. As a member of the successful Hunt–Hillary expedition in 1953, he filmed *The Conquest of Everest*, and other expeditions have taken him in search of the Abominable Snowman, to the Antarctic and to Africa and Northern Australia with Armand Denis. Recently, he has directed and photographed the *Master Chefs*, a series of films showing famous dishes being prepared in their local settings. Among his other publications is *Adventure's Eye*.

Tom Stobart

Herbs, Spices and Flavourings

Illustrations by Ian Garrard

 Penguin Books

Penguin Books Ltd, Harmondsworth,
Middlesex, England
Penguin Books, 625 Madison Avenue,
New York, New York 10022, U.S.A.
Penguin Books Australia Ltd, Ringwood,
Victoria, Australia
Penguin Books Canada Ltd, 2801 John Street,
Markham, Ontario, Canada L3R 1B4
Penguin Books (N.Z.) Ltd, 182–190 Wairau Road,
Auckland 10, New Zealand

First published by The International Wine and Food Publishing Company 1970
Published in Penguin Books 1977

Made and printed in Great Britain by
Hazell Watson & Viney Ltd, Aylesbury, Bucks
Set in Monotype Bembo

Acknowledgements

I should like to express my thanks to the following for the help they have given me during the writing of this book:

Mrs Khayat, Mrs Eve French and Mr David E. Provan of Beirut, Lebanon; Mr A. C. Thimiah of Coorg and other friends and planters in India; Messrs Volkart in Tellicherry; Mrs C. Baptista of Bombay; the Ministry of Agriculture and other friends in New Delhi; Mr C. Kondoyiannis, agriculturalist to the Greek Embassy in London; Mr W. B. Boast and the scientists at the British Sugar Corporation; 'Grey Poupon', 'Amora' and the Fédération des industries condimentaires de France; Mr D. J. Oliver and the scientific staff of Reckitt Colman Ltd, Norwich, England; Mr Lea of Lea and Perrins Ltd, Worcester, England; Frau Stähli and other friends at the Swiss Cheese Union in Bern; Chef Roy of the Hôtel du Nord, Dijon; Dr W. T. Stearn of the British Museum (Natural History), London; Professor V. H. Heywood, Dr J. McNeill, Dr J. B. Harborne and Miss Fiona Getliffe of the Hartley Botanical Laboratories, Liverpool University; Miss P. M. North of the Pharmaceutical Society of Great Britain; Mr Tony Pueyo of Tarragona, Spain; E. & A. Evetts of Ashfields Herb Nursery, Market Drayton, Shropshire; Mr and Mrs Nils Hogner, Litchfield, Connecticut; and the many other friends and people whose names I never knew in many countries of Europe, Africa and Asia. Also, I should like to mention the authors of the dozens of books I have consulted on one point or another.

Since I have not agreed with everyone whom I have consulted, I alone must take the responsibility for anything I have said and especially for any over-simplifications I may appear guilty of in the eyes of scientific specialists.

Environmental Soc.

Contents

Black and White Illustrations

Colour Plates

Plate VIII   Mushrooms and Toadstools: 1 Death Cap
(Poisonous), 2 Boletus edulis, 3 Birch
Boletus, 4 Oronge (Caesar's Amanita), 5 Fly
Agaric, 6 Paddy Straw Mushroom, 7 Black
Truffle, 8 White Truffle, 9 Morel.

Introduction

The History of Flavourings

I once helped to dig up two earthenware jars still containing the remains of food some four thousand years old. I was the guest of an Italian cave exploration group in the Sardinian mountains and the jars had been found by scratching under a crust of stalagmite in a corner of one of the caverns. The place was deep inside the mountain, damp as a tomb and with the rocks covered in a film of slimy mud. It was hard to believe that anyone had lived here because they liked it. Perhaps it had been only a refuge for times of danger and the food an emergency store. Perhaps the owner had been killed and this was why he had not returned for the jars he had hidden there.

Over the centuries the contents of the jars had degenerated into an unrecognizable brown powder, though the laboratories in Milan might just be able to say what it once had been. One could not taste it, but could only speculate on what exactly people living so long ago had enjoyed eating, and what their food had tasted like.

However, speculations do not last long when one is cold and wet. It was November, and the mountains outside were thick in mist and dark. It was well past dinner time, and ahead lay the cold scramble down the screes and the cheerless drive in wet clothes back to a hotel from which the kitchen staff would have long since departed for bed.

But this was Sardinia. Just outside the cave, on a limestone ledge overhanging the river which emerged from the rock like the Styx, there blazed a huge aromatic fire of rosemary and ilex branches. Beside it, on wooden spits, sizzled two whole lambs tended by an old shepherd in white pants and a Garibaldi hat. The local refrigerator salesman, a jolly fellow, fat but energetic for all that, had come up after work with several other friends to see that we were properly looked after. He had himself carried an enormous flagon of wine up the steep slope and appeared already to have got quite a lot of it inside him. His rich Italian voice was blasting Verdi into the darkness around the flickering perimeter of firelight as he cut up a huge loaf and an almost equally large sheep's milk cheese with his sheath knife.

We ate with our hands, rolling up our sleeves to let the fat drip down our bare forearms. The lamb tasted of the rosemary smoke, the bread of brick ovens; the wine was rough but good. There were salty black olives plump with oil, and the cheese tasted of sheep. The firelight glowed on the happy faces: it was quite as wonderful as any banquet with cut glass glittering under the candelabra.

This is, generally, the kind of rough gastronomic experience on which this book is based. Although sometimes I have drunk great wines and eaten the most sophisticated food, more often I have dined in peasant houses, in the desert or on such Sardinian mountainsides. However, as it is peasant cooking which makes the greatest use of herbs and spices, perhaps this has been an advantage after all.

When the feast was over, as I reclined Roman fashion on a rock and watched the steam rise from my wet trousers, I could not help wondering if the people who had hidden those food jars four thousand years ago had not also eaten their meals in just this fashion. And their food, too, must have tasted of rosemary: they could scarcely have avoided it.

Nobody knows when man first started cooking – or indeed *how* – without lighters or matches, fires, at first sight, do not seem all that easy to make. Yet often in the Himalayas, surrounded by dripping pines and rhododendron bushes, when everything was soaked and I was the mug trying vainly to make a fire with paper and matches, I have watched with amazement the ease with which the hillmen take a piece of flint and steel, together with a small bag of dried moss tinder and, sheltering under the homespun blanket, their only clothing, in a moment strike and catch a spark in the moss and blow up the makings of a fire in their cupped hands. And what did they do before the age of flint and steel? I guess they also had their methods.

As to the first use of flavourings, again something that happened before recorded history and probably before cooking on fire, it is tempting to think that a man of more than average intelligence at some time tried tasting plants, gradually eating more of the ones he liked until he made sure they were not poisonous. But it is more likely that the idea of flavouring arose less purposefully than that. After all, any dumb beast will select by instinct the plants it likes and which are good for it. This we say is 'by instinct' but it had nevertheless to be learned. When man first learned to cook he must have already been eating herbs. Even carnivorous animals sometimes eat herbs: a dog eats grass. We accept evolution, we can hardly not, but the implications are rarely thought out in concrete terms. Considered personally, for instance, it means that you can boast an unbroken chain of successful ancestors right back to primeval blobs. You would stamp on them today. It means that out of the millions of baby fishes which failed to make the grade because they were snapped up by something bigger or stranded in a pool, your ancestors were *always*, in every generation, the lucky and successful ones who got away and survived at least long enough to produce your multi-great-grandparents. They were also the ones who avoided the poisonous plants. In all the millions not one missed the mating. And what a remarkable thought, that if one could travel back in time through a sufficient number of great-grandmothers – each with the intimate physical relationship which exists between parent and child – there would have been strange little creature grandparents, the like of which we have never seen, laying eggs and eating herbs and why not the herbs they liked the taste of?

Much later on, of course, the search for good herbs, fruits, roots and berries (which dried we call spices) became purposeful. I have heard the view expressed that herbs came into cooking by way of medicine, but it is probably the other way round. The brilliant unknown writer of the Hippocratic treatise on ancient medicine, himself ancient to us since he was writing about four hundred years before Christ, was of the opinion that medicine itself arose in the first place with cooks in the kitchen. This seems very likely.

It is only a step from noticing that people who are unwell do not relish the same foods as they do when they are fit to preparing deliberately comforting brews.

Many herbs also came into use in connection with ceremony, magic and religion: parsley, bay and hyssop, for instance, have strong magical connections. Bay was supposed to keep away lightning, and the Roman Emperor Tiberius wore his crown of laurel during thunderstorms – no more stupid than not walking under ladders.

Obviously, herbs must first have been used in the places where they grew wild. They may sometimes have been transported to other regions as dried herbs, but we usually think of a herb as something which can be grown in our own locality and which if not actually indigenous has been introduced and then perpetuated. Many of the herbs used in Britain were originally brought in by the Romans. The stock may sometimes have died out and the herb been forgotten for a time only to be re-introduced later. In North America and other parts of the world colonized from Europe, most of the herbs were established in their new home by the settlers. Occasionally they found species, growing wild, which were closely allied to or identical with those which they used in the home country. New herbs were also picked up and taken into use from the indigenous inhabitants – from the North American Indians, for instance, the bergamots – but these have not become of general use in cooking.

Spices on the other hand could not be grown at home. The word 'spice', covering dried roots, bark and berries, came from the same source as 'species', meaning 'classes of object', and referred to any dried aromatics, nearly all parts of plants which grew in the tropical East. As trade goods of enormous commercial value they have had a long and very bloody history.

Spices were brought to the eastern Mediterranean and into Europe for at least five thousand years along the caravan routes which passed through the Middle East. Their origin might be anywhere from China south to Indonesia, southern India or Ceylon. Very often the people receiving them knew nothing about this origin and thought that they came from Arabia, a belief encouraged by the traders who carried and delivered them. The classic route crossed the river Indus at Attock, just below its junction with the Kabul River and then went on through Peshawar, over the Khyber Pass, through Afghanistan and Iran and eventually south to Babylon on the Euphrates. From there it went west to the eastern Mediterranean and eventually to Europe. However, the route varied considerably over the centuries depending on which country in the Arab and Persian world happened to be in power. It was also subject to competition by sailing ships plying up the Persian Gulf and Red Sea. Sometimes new pressure was put on the route by rising powers; there were often heavy taxes on merchants and at other times the routes were unsafe or fell into disrepair. The spices would then find other more profitable and convenient lines of entry.

Even after the spices had reached the Mediterranean the trade was still controlled by yet more towns and groups of merchants. At one time it was the Phoenicians; at another, the Arabs; and later the Italians in Venice, Amalfi, Genoa – they all grew rich in turn on the trade in spices. The efforts of one country to break the stranglehold on the trade held by another were responsible for intensive interest in finding a sea route to the East via the Cape. Once this had been done, an era began with further bloody competition among the English, Dutch, French and Portuguese. Whole books have been devoted to the history of the spice trade, and for further details one of these will have to be consulted. Space does not permit it here, and one could not follow the story without maps and some knowledge of ancient and medieval history. From our point of view, however, we can take it that all the common spices have been available to cooks in the Mediterranean area since the beginning of written records, although until fairly recently they were exceedingly expensive. Pepper, ginger, cloves, cinnamon and nutmeg for instance, may be found in the cooking of almost every country in the world today except in that of very primitive people.

The only spice to have come from the New World is allspice, except for paprika, chilli and sweet peppers, which also originated in America (and were therefore unknown in Europe and Asia before Columbus) but can be grown in Europe. The flavourings vanilla and chocolate were also brought by the Spaniards from America.

The Importance of Flavourings

Very often the secrets of the great chefs have been tiny amounts of unusual flavouring added in unrecognizable quantity. To do this requires not only imagination, but a good knowledge of the possibilities. A composer must know the sounds and characteristics of all the instruments of the orchestra in order to achieve effects which are subtle or unexpected.

There is at present a lively new interest in foreign cooking. Although in any one region the number of flavourings in common use is often limited to a group which together takes on a regional character, the total number of flavourings is over a thousand. Anyone seriously interested in foreign cookery could well use eighty-five common spices, fifteen green and ten dried herbs, a few salad herbs and a large collection of miscellaneous articles ranging from wines, vinegars and oils, to capers, fruits, nuts and anchovies.

If the original cook, the experimentally-minded cook and the possessor of foreign cookery books should know their spices, then we ought not to forget the gastronomically-minded traveller who is not prepared to sit in ignorance of what he is eating. For shock treatment he might try the direct non-stop flight from Rome to Bombay. Given that there are onions, garlic, tomatoes, a chicken and rice available to a cook at either end of the flight, what a fantastic difference there will be in the taste of the dish a cook at each end will turn out! Experienced travellers can tell blindfolded what part of the world they are in simply by tasting the cooking. A Frenchman would even know if he was in Normandy or Provence. Distinctions are, in fact, so characteristic that one may regard cooking as necessary geographical information. For instance, I was recently entertained in Landi Kotal at the top of the Khyber Pass. Even though I had left Peshawar only a few hours previously and was still in Pakistan politically, I could tell from the food that I had suddenly left the Indian sub-continent and was entering the Middle East as represented by the Iranian plateau. There were also certain elements coming in from Central Asia, and I should probably have guessed at a trade connection even if I had not already known that there were links due to ancient caravan routes.

Food is a subject much neglected by serious historians and geographers, but because it is both basic and a living tradition it can in fact be very revealing. People in general are rather conservative about what they eat and particularly so about their flavourings. The flavourings which have come to be used in any area are dictated by the climate, history and trade links. People naturally tend first to use what can be grown and produced in their own area, then to add dried 'spices' which are easy to transport. Historical accidents, migrations and conquests have also a lot to do with the style of cooking and the preferred flavourings. In the end, in any one period of history, people seem to settle on their own selection and very often there is a touch of genius in the combinations which they decide should be used together.

In cooking as in almost everything, there are, at present, the rumblings of revolution, and changes are rapid. It commonly happens that when different cultures are brought into close contact, the forced mating produces a new hybrid vigour, new invention and explosive innovations. Air transport has brought people into closer contact. People take holidays abroad and become interested in foreign cooking. They read foreign cookery books, cookery now being a respectable hobby and relaxation for the educated as well as being the number one do-it-yourself occupation. More efficient methods of preservation and storage and the possibility of bringing perishable things quickly by air from one place to another nurture this interest. There have also been considerable emigrations. For instance, the arrival of immigrants in Britain from both the East and West Indies has already had a profound effect on what is available from the shops and markets. One can buy not only flying fish and squid in small towns which until recently had never heard of such exotic ingredients, but even fresh flavourings, like green ginger and fresh coriander which have not been sold in England for centuries.

Indeed, from the beginning of the nineteenth century, when many herbs were on sale, the number was steadily reduced to a dismal four – mint, thyme, sage and parsley –

and even today these can be bought only with some difficulty.

But a revival is beginning. There are new openings for originality and variety. Of course, there are hideous possibilities if everything is thoughtlessly and ignorantly mixed together. Perhaps it has once more become necessary to *think* about flavours. Also, as we are in an era of accepting foreign dishes, there must be a consideration of what dishes will go together in a satisfactory menu. America has perhaps already acknowledged this culinary invasion, because it has been accepting people from all over the world and has, in fact, developed from them. Its size and greater variety of climate offers a vast assortment of foods.

Stuffy gourmets may view such a new situation with a certain amount of horror. They may consider the best French cooking to have reached perfection and that any changes would be retrogressive. This is a dangerous assumption. No doubt the first person who put saffron in bouillabaisse got the chop from his contemporaries, and in any case cooking is a living art in France as elsewhere, and so in a continual state of evolution.

The Origin of this Book

I come to this subject as a traveller who has lived in a number of different countries. My homes have usually been somewhere not far from the Mediterranean, my preference.

Interspersed with delightful and well-fed rests in Cyprus, Spain or Italy there have been long journeys, frequently in uncomfortable conditions and extending over nearly seventy different countries. I have had to camp or sleep out in the wilderness and cook my own food as part of my work. When I started as a traveller, I was not greatly concerned whether I ate steak or sawdust, providing I could keep alive and get where I wanted to. Indeed, as a student with very little money I can remember grudging what I spent on food and wishing it were not necessary to eat at all. This did not prevent me from discovering that chives could be bought very cheaply in the Tirolean markets and that they would improve a diet of bread and soft lard, which was all I could afford in the mountains. It also did not prevent the enjoyment of a good meal whenever the opportunity offered. But at length there came the time when I no longer considered a 'Hillary Special' very funny. This is a sort of legendary soup invented by or for Sir Edmund Hillary on Everest. The recipe is tea, dried milk, sugar, *tsampa* (a kind of gritty Sherpa breakfast cereal) and a can of sardines with the oil. All this stirred together would produce what some people said was a balanced diet, while others considered it a kind of nightmare fuel properly served from a bowser. Then there was that splendid opinion offered to the press by another tough member of the same expedition, the late Tom Bourdillon: 'The only important thing about food is that there should be some!'

The other side of the argument, however, was expressed to me in forcible terms by an (if possible) even tougher Australian: a drover in northern Queensland. He had come on my camp at dawn and allowed his mob of cattle to graze while he stopped for a 'cuppa'. It was then that he discovered that I did not know how to bake my own bread and that I slept without sheets or pillow. He con-considered that I was exceedingly stupid and dirty to rough it in a sleeping bag, and a raw amateur to live on biscuits. In fact, in traditional Australian, I was *bloody* inefficient.

I do not suppose that really Sir Edmund's potage or the Australian drover influenced me much one way or the other. I always enjoyed cooking and, as experience grew, it did not seem necessary to go without good food anywhere, provided one knew what was in the local market and planned the cook box and the canned food very carefully. I have, for instance, made a quite recognizable 'lobster Newburg' within ten miles of the foot of Everest, and would never in these days think of setting out for any really wild place without some herbs in screws of paper and a knob of garlic in my pocket.

So I became interested in herbs and flavourings, particularly because even old yak is vastly improved by herbs, garlic and a dash of burgundy. My first collection of wild Himalayan herbs was made as long ago as 1946, but it was destroyed when the roof of a hut fell in during an earth-quake. I also became passionately addicted to the markets and bazaars in the countries I was visiting – and what picturesque places. I needed a book of reference to which I could refer, but could not find one. In the end I was compelled to open my own card index – the best way to file notes made on the backs of old envelopes – and start collecting information myself from all sorts of sources. Whenever possible I went through the bazaars and bought samples which I took to the local agricultural experts. I also visited herb gardens and spice plantations, questioned planters and merchants and read many specialized books.

Over ten years I amassed a huge tattered card index of data derived from various sources. Friends and acquaintances took me round markets and bazaars and acted as interpreters, while patient stall holders weighed out unprofitably small quantities of practically everything they had in the shop.

I think particularly of two very fat and shy Gujarati ladies who conducted me for a whole morning around the back streets of Bombay, and who gradually became quite relaxed as they propounded the secrets of their famous regional pickles. But information on spices came from people in places as far apart as Zanzibar and Meshed, Beirut and Singapore, from planters in Sylhet, Coorg and Ceylon; on herbs, from people from Sweden to Spain and Bessarabia. It came from housewives, chefs, people in commerce, ministries of agriculture and universities, as well as from reading. In the end my card index had become so large, tattered and dog-eared, that I felt it had to be turned into a book.

Such an interest in local food proved to be exceedingly useful for reasons other than cooking. Very often one has little in common with peasants in remote places, but food is a basic subject for discussion with everyone. Even in the most xenophobic countries it is only necessary to express an interest in the local dishes to find oneself taken behind the walls and into people's houses. They can see that you are human. You do not set yourself apart by eating in the big international hotels; indeed, you flatter them by appreciating their cooking. There are, of course, the few occasions when one's motives are misunderstood. Ethiopians, I found, considered that the only thing of interest that a man could find in the kitchen was a woman. So I was sometimes turned out, but not very often. Most often I made friends, and as it is customary to thank one's assistants for their help in the introduction, may I do it now if any of them should chance to read this book.

The Scientific Basis of Flavouring

What we know of the taste of food is largely its smell: that is, the sensations are detected mainly in the nose and not in the mouth. Since smell and taste are usually regarded as the most primitive animal senses (after touch), it is rather surprising that we do not yet understand their scientific basis in the way we do that of sight or hearing. It may be impossible to describe colours or sounds accurately in words, but we can do so in terms of wavelength and amplitude. Such descriptions would mean something to a scientist and would in theory, at any rate, make possible an accurate reproduction. One can, however, describe a smell or a taste only vaguely in terms of other tastes and smells, and as a personal experience.

One of the most astonishing things about smell is the incredibly small quantities of an odiferous substance needed to produce the sensation. How little actual matter can be left on the ground by the foot of the animal which the bloodhound is tracking. How little material from the tiger a mile or so away is blown down wind into the deer's nostrils. What we do know is that there seems to be no simple relationship between types of smell and the chemical structure of the substances which give rise to them. There are other odd facts. The sense of smell is more acute in moist than in dry conditions. It needs a movement of air in the olfactory passages, which is one reason why we hold the nose when taking nasty medicine. For this reason also, food becomes tasteless when we have a bad cold.

The true tastes detected in the mouth are in fact very few in number, namely sourness, sweetness, saltiness, alkaline and metallic tastes, pungency (pain?), bitterness and astringency. These we might, if we were limiting the meaning of words by definition, regard as the only true tastes. The rest is smell.

These mouth-detected true tastes are very important in cooking because they are basic. They have to be properly adjusted in a dish. However, our sensitivity to them is influenced quite sharply by temperature. For instance, our sensitivity to both sweetness and sourness is reduced by cold, which is why ice-cream has to be so heavily sweetened and sweet wine is less sweet when chilled. The sensation of saltiness on the other hand is increased by cold – at least by moderate cold – as anyone who has tasted a cold stock will probably have noticed. These points become very important when we are adjusting dishes such as mousse or cold consommé, which are chilled after making.

There are other less direct effects of temperature on flavour. The use of a deep freezer is becoming more and more common and although we regard this as a means of preservation it also has some permanent effect on flavour. Perhaps the reason is mechanical. During freezing, ice crystals are formed which rupture cell walls and release flavour constituents otherwise trapped inside. For instance, food containing pepper will have the peppery taste increased when reheated after being deep-frozen. Therefore, if one is in the habit of making a double quantity of dishes, one to be eaten and one for the deep freezer, one should not necessarily make them identical.

The effect of heat during cooking is something of a paradox because it both increases and destroys flavour. Two processes are going on: in one the flavouring substances are being released as the tissues and cell walls are broken down, and in the other the more volatile aromatic substances, particularly the essential oils (*see* Oils), are being driven off by the heat and dispersed into the atmosphere. A cook is therefore always walking on a tightrope and should not lean too much towards one side or the other. Long slow cooking will usually release the aromatic substances without driving too much away into the atmosphere. If the lid of a casserole is sealed with paste, there is the maximum retention of aromatics. Fast boiling drives off the more volatile flavourings, but may increase the overall taste by concentration.

Heat also changes the flavour of foods by encouraging chemical reactions and the breakdown of one substance into another. This book does not deal with this aspect of flavour creation just as it does not deal with the basic flavours of the substances being cooked. But to give only one example, there is a strong difference in taste between fried and boiled meat, and so a great difference in a stew if the meat has been fried before stewing. This is the result of the products formed at the different temperatures to which the meat has been subjected.

Another chemical reaction which frequently results in change or loss of flavour is oxidization by the oxygen in the air, especially when the reaction is assisted by enzymes in the food or by micro-organisms. That exposure to air produces changes, is everybody's experience. Many foods become discoloured on their cut surfaces: there are also changes of flavour in food such as in onions which have been cut up and left standing for some time. As a general rule, changes due to exposure to air are undesirable. Exposure to air also produces loss of flavour due to evaporation of the more ethereal substances. Therefore, flavouring substances should, wherever possible be stored whole and not ground and kept in airtight bottles or jars. They should also be dry, because damp conditions encourage the growth of moulds and other micro-organisms which usually lead to bad flavours.

The flavours of herbs change during drying, some herbs more than others, particularly if the methods used are inefficient. Modern commercial methods of drying herbs make it possible to dry some of those which formerly could not be satisfactorily dried by older methods. The new methods avoid the production of a hay-like taste and retain much more of the original flavour.

The main flavouring substances contained in the natural products are usually known, but the chemical names need not concern the cook. A few chemical groups such as sugars and essential oils have separate entries in this book.

One mechanism which should be understood is involved in some items, such as mustard and bitter almonds, which develop their flavour only after mixing with water. They contain bitter compounds related to sugars known as glucosides together with enzymes which cause these glucosides to react with water. Enzymes, which are responsible for many changes we make use of (for instance fermentation), are organic catalysts: that is, they promote a reaction without themselves getting used up in the process. They are exceedingly important in almost all life processes. Many of them are delicate: they behave almost as if they were alive and are destroyed by heating. One therefore could inadvertently prevent the development of flavour by blanching, roasting, or mixing with boiling water.

Flavours are also developed during many pickling and maturing processes in which yeasts, moulds and bacteria play a part. Anchovies, vinegars, capers, cheeses – one could give many examples. One often buys these things ready made, but if called on to make them oneself, one should not be frightened by such mysteries. People have been handling processes they did not understand for thousands of years, and though it helps to understand what is going on, it is not strictly necessary. In practice it is mainly a question of managing the conditions – the amount of salt or vinegar and the temperature.

Scientific, Popular and Foreign Names

The purpose of names is essentially to enable two people to be certain they are talking about the same thing. Popular names are not certain, so scientific names are given, together with the botanical family to which the plant belongs.

Families are large groups having characters broadly in common, and there are some strange bedfellows. For instance, it is curious that the orange, lemon, curry leaf and rue should be related. A list by families is given as an appendix.

The first part of the scientific name is the name of the genus, and when this is common to two plants it shows an even closer relationship. For instance tarragon, wormwood, southernwood and mugwort all belong to the same genus (*Artemesia*).

The second half of the scientific name is the specific name and applies to that one kind of plant and no other. A species may breed with the same species, but sometimes there can also be crosses between different ones (donkey× horse = mule). These are called hybrids. Some plants hybridize easily, for instance the mints, and this is confusing.

Within the species there are often natural varieties (*vars.*) and varieties produced by cultivation (*cultivars.*). These often look wildly different, to casual observation more different than species. Common examples are cabbage, sprouts, cauliflower and kohl-rabi. When plants have been in cultivation for a long time they sometimes change so much that it becomes impossible to be certain of the wild ancestor: often it is thought the wild ancestor may have become extinct.

As if this were not already confusing enough for the layman, the scientific names themselves are not fixed but are continually being changed as the science advances. Not only do plants get their specific names changed but also they get shifted from one genus, even from one family, to another. Some names are disputed. So it depends on what author is followed, how old the book is and what botanical name is given. This has led serious botanists to quote not only several scientific names but also the initials of the authors. For instance, L. stands for the Swedish botanist Linnaeus, the father of scientific naming and classification. We give a few alternative names, such as may be in older books.

Now why is this of any interest to cooks? The reason is that while there may be a little confusion in the scientific names, and some doubt about what is what, when it comes to popular names the confusion is quite incredible. For instance, the word 'pepper' is applied to several quite different things. Similarly there is confusion among caraway, cumin and nigella. The botanical names straighten out such difficulties.

We have also given the names of many items in French, German, Italian and Spanish, and where necessary in other languages. Here again one must be careful because in many countries there are dozens of local dialect names for the same thing, and worse, the same word can mean different things in different places. One Italian book I consulted would give half a page of dialect names to one plant and so many obviously could not be included in this book. So we have selected a few common versions which may help a traveller. In the last resort it is the scientific names which are the most useful since these are international. These, together with the pictures should go a long way towards the identification of flavourings in foreign restaurants, shops and markets. At least I hope the reader will be considerably better-off with this book than I was without it.

Synthetic and Harmful Flavourings

There seems to be a general idea that all herbs are good for you and all spices are bad. This is silly – spices are only dried parts of tropical plants. Many herbs have marked physiological effects and large quantities, for instance, of rue or wormwood would be bad for you – indeed poisonous. This does not mean that there is any harm in ordinary flavouring quantities. Some spices also have physiological effects. For instance, ginger makes most people sweat, and cloves or cinnamon are also valuable as intestinal disinfectants. On the other hand, large quantities of nutmeg are poisonous – lesser quantities will make you drunk. None of these is poisonous in small quantity in the way, for instance, that the fungus *Amanita phalloides* or the beautiful oleander are poisonous. These are killers even in a tiny quantity.

Dangers in herbs and spices can, however, arise when the flavourings are unnaturally concentrated. Extracts of chillies, for instance, can easily raise blisters, and enthusiasts with juice extractors could overdo the herb extracts of even the healthy and wholesome parsley. A few things, such as bitter almonds or peach leaves, would be poisonous when raw. But, on the whole, all of these are harmless in moderation.

It is not necessarily the case that substitutes or synthetic flavourings are so harmless. The trouble with all artificial substances is that they should not logically be used in food until it is absolutely certain that they are harmless: but, nobody can be absolutely certain that they are harmless until they have long been used. It therefore happens that some flavouring and colouring substances, which are initially regarded as perfectly safe, gradually come under suspicion. One example would be coumarin, a substance responsible for the smell of new-mown hay and present in many herbs, such as sweet woodruff. This can be extracted from tonka beans or made synthetically, and was much used as a flavouring in ice-cream, which, of course, is consumed mostly by children. Now it is forbidden in many countries. Another item which has come under suspicion is cyclamate sodium, a much recommended artificial sweetening used in soft drinks and squashes – again much consumed by children. The fact is that although there are no doubt a lot of potentially harmful substances present in small quantities in many of the foods we eat, they are not likely to harm us in a diet which has plenty of variety. When, however, they are concentrated and overdone or we introduce entirely new synthetic flavourings, there is liable to be some danger of excess or long-term harmful effects. Some countries have much tougher food laws than others. France, for instance, sets a very high standard. I personally ban almost all extracts or synthetics from the kitchen unless I am very certain of what they contain and know that they have been safely used over a very long period. They are in any case most often crude and inferior, and on these grounds also should be avoided by serious cooks.

Flavouring in Practice

The art of creating flavour is neglected, probably because it cannot be turned into glossy colour photographs or demonstrated on television. It gets relegated to the 'pinch of salt', the 'grate of nutmeg', the 'half teaspoon of cinnamon' or the 'garlic if liked'. Yet flavour, with texture, is the cornerstone of good cooking and cannot be achieved by slavish uncomprehending measurement.

I have been lucky to watch many of the finest chefs at work, and they seldom measure the flavourings they add. Eye, taste, instinct and experience determine how they flavour the dish. This is something a cook must cultivate. Flavour has to be developed by basic good cooking and a balance struck between the various added flavours which are blended together or placed in antagonism.

This is difficult. Ingredients vary. Those people who cook a dish for the first time especially to honour guests are being optimistic. A recipe is only a guide, a point from which to start. The good cook, like any artist, must back a personal opinion after some careful study and practice. The recipe is then taken into the repertoire – the music can be played with certainty and interpreted to give a good performance.

The amateur must, however, find this a council of perfection. Chefs seem to taste their creations only at points they know to be critical. Most of us cannot practise a dish so often and have to proceed by tasting at intervals, which is often not satisfactory – especially in the early stages of a dish before the flavours have gone together – and quite impossible when for instance, seasoning a terrine of raw pig's liver. On the other side of the picture, my aunt Molly, a splendid cook, even tastes the water for saltiness before putting in the vegetables. The main thing is to be thoroughly alerted to the world of seasoning and flavour and then one will find one's own method.

As to quantity: obviously the amounts one uses have a direct relationship with the quantity of food in the pot, and one would not measure the salt in pinches when seasoning a whole ox. One does, however, see cooks becoming more cautious when reaching the point of perfection – very often with salt. This is a mistake and almost always results in undersalting.

The reason is twofold. To begin with, most people think of flavouring and seasoning in terms of school arithmetic, of adding – say, one clove of garlic, then two, then three, then four . . .

Although it is rather obvious that when one gets to twenty, a garlic clove or so is not going to make as much difference as it did when one started. In other words, the more one adds, the less critical the extra additions become.

Conversely, when dealing with small quantities, a small change makes a big difference, and so the smaller the quantity the more critical the addition becomes. There is, for instance, a big difference between a quarter and a half a clove of garlic in a pâté – in fact, the same difference mathematically as between 10 and 20. Two times in each case. But whereas many cooks will jump from $\frac{1}{4}$ to $\frac{1}{2}$ a clove with no thought, the jump from 10 to 20 will cause hysterics.

Actually the jump from 10 to 20 is *less* in result than from $\frac{1}{4}$ to $\frac{1}{2}$ because if it takes a small thump to start a donkey, he will not (even if he does not go stubborn) go twice as fast if you thump him twice as hard, poor beast. He soon reaches his maximum speed.

So to produce the same sort of increase as between $\frac{1}{4}$ to $\frac{1}{2}$ a clove of garlic, one might have to go not double from 10 to 20 but more than double, say from 10 to 25 or 30.

And in the end, no matter how many more cloves one added, there would be no change. The palate would be saturated. So one has a law: the smaller the quantity of flavouring the more critical its adjustment.

Perhaps the most difficult taste to adjust is one in which one has three conflicting elements such as salt, sugar and vinegar in a salty sweet-sour combination such as in the piquant peanut sauce for Indonesian *sate*. It is easy to sweeten a sour dish to the point of perfection, but, when the third element, salt, is added, it changes the relationship of the other two and for anyone interested in flavouring such a problem is fascinating.

And now a final practical point. The flavouring shelf should be within easy reach of the stove, not at the other end of the kitchen, and although houseproud cooks may opt for a set of matching jars, naturally with labels, I have found that this is a mistake. I like glass bottles so that I can see what is inside (though one should not use clear glass for long storage) and I like them to be of all different shapes and sizes so that I do not have to read the labels and can recognize the bottles even if they are standing behind others on the shelf. It is a truism in the kitchen that the more time one saves the more time one has to cook.

Growing Herbs

Apart from appearance and texture, the flavour of many herbs is changed or degraded by drying, and as all fresh herbs are not to be bought in shops, the only solution is to grow them oneself.

Gardening notes have been given in the text. They are very general because so much depends on soil and climate. Keen gardeners are probably going to have their local gardening books anyway.

Personally, I am not a very keen gardener because I do not have the time and am usually away from home when important operations need doing. In my experience, however, the books always give instructions for growing *prize* herbs, and this for the cook is quite unnecessary. All we want is a piece of the herb when we want it, and it does not matter if it is a fully-grown fine plant or a clump of young leaves seeded by accident in a corner, although it is quite true that most herbs have their very best moments for gathering usually just before flowering.

I sow and stick in herbs all over the place in the flower beds with some reference to whether they like shelter, full sun, partial shade, lime, and so on, but not otherwise being fussy. I usually find that by chance I have put in some of the cuttings, plants or seeds in places they like. There they are allowed to establish themselves. In the other places they either do not thrive or die out. Now with annuals or biennials it is usually enough to let some plants set seed and give them a good shake when the seed is ripe. They will come up in the same place next year.

Perennials are no further bother once established, and can also occasionally be allowed to set seed and produce new plants.

By this lazy method a number of herbs are soon established in the garden without trouble. There may be a few which require a battle. The point for the cook is that most herbs are decorative and should be allowed to grow where they want to grow not where *you* want them to. Isn't this a basic difference in outlook between a cook and a real gardener?

And now, at the end, I feel that I ought to do what I was no doubt expected to do at the beginning: define a flavouring. Unfortunately, it defies definition. On tasting any well-flavoured dish, it becomes apparent that its flavour depends not only on the small quantities of herbs, spices and special bits and pieces added to the basic mixture, but on the basic mixture itself and especially on the balance and quality of the ingredients.

The important point is not necessarily what a flavouring *is*, but that one has an awareness of the harmony of ingredients and of those special flavourings which complement the basic ingredients. One must know which dishes need the addition of herbs and spices, as opposed to those to which any addition would be unnecessary – even a sacrilege. Almost all foods have some flavour of their own, and different methods of cooking also produce different flavours. Oils, fats and even water lend special flavours to cooking. In Rome one can see smart women dressed in mink coming to certain fountains with bottles to collect water which has a special reputation in cooking. A friend of mine who keeps a fine restaurant, swears that the fame of one of his specialities depends on using bottled mineral water instead of ordinary water in its preparation. Is this a flavouring? Whether they are right or wrong – and I suspect they are right – they care, which is the basis of all work above the average and even all genius.

So, in the end, wanting a definition to decide what is and what is not a flavouring I have put into this book just what I felt might be useful, though considerations of length have made it necessary to delete a number of the more unusual items. Other disputable things, such as strongly flavoured salad herbs and oil seeds, have stayed in.

Flavourings have the great merit of being cheap, and with them one can play tunes on even the commonest everyday ingredients. But attention! There are two proverbs for consideration. There is the English, 'Enough is as good as a feast', and the Rumanian, 'Too much is better than not enough'. One can disagree with both, but in cooking both prove perhaps that the final arbiter of taste is the individual. One must trust one's *own* palate and approach all foods and flavourings with curiosity and inventiveness. In these days when there is a strong pressure towards uniformity, those to whom cooking is not a chore, but a creative occupation and means of expression, are very fortunate. Fortunate also are the friends they entertain in their houses.

An Alphabet of Herbs, Spices and Flavourings

Ajowan

Ajwain, Bishop's Weed, Omam, Omum

GER: Ajowan
IT: Ajowan
BOT: Carum ajowan (Ptychotis ajowan and Carum copticum)
FAM: Umbelliferae
Plate II, No. 9 and Ill. 20, No. 4, page 268

Ajowan is a spice seed closely related to caraway and cumin. It is grown in India and to some extent in Egypt, Persia and Afghanistan. It looks roughly like large celery seed, but tastes rather brutally of thyme as it contains considerable amounts of the pungent oil of thyme. An extract of this oil is thymol which is chemically related to carbolic (phenol) and is powerfully germicidal. Ajowan water is locally used for 'gippy tummy' and cholera. One is never quite sure, in Indian cooking, whether an ingredient is added for flavouring or for medicinal reasons. Often it is both. Since Indians eat large quantities of pulses (*dhal gram, channa*) as a source of protein, they are more than a little concerned with spices that prevent wind.

Ajowan is used in many Indian savouries – *ompadi, namkin boondi, sev* and so on – to impart a thyme-like flavour and is often mentioned in less westernized Indian cookery books. In our kitchens it is almost unknown but is occasionally useful as a source of a crude thyme substitute. However, it lacks the subtlety of thyme, and so although thyme could possibly replace ajowan in Indian recipes, the contrary is not recommended except in emergency. The dry seed keeps indefinitely.

Alexanders*

Allisanders, Black Lovage

FR: Ombrelle jaune
GER: Gelbolde
IT: Macerore

Alexanders is a heavily built umbelliferous herb, growing up to four or five feet high under suitable conditions. It has yellow-green flowers, black fruits and some resemblance to celery in both appearance and flavour. The original home of this plant was the Mediterranean, but it has long been naturalized in Britain where it is local on wasteland and

*In the United States the name alexanders is sometimes used for the indigenous wild angelica.

SP: Esmirnio
BOT: Smyrnium
olusatrum
FAM: Umbelliferae
Ill. 6, No. 6, page 97

cliffs near the sea. For the garden it can be raised in any sunny bed either from the plants or seed sown in March and April.

Alexanders as a vegetable and herb is out of fashion, but at one time it was much used in the same way we use celery today. Celery displaced it.

It is possible that some people with large gardens will find alexanders worth growing for the flavour (somewhere between parsley and celery) or for the sake of variety.

Allspice

Jamaica Pepper,
Myrtle Pepper

FR: Piment jamaïque,
Poivre aromatique,
Poivre de la Jamaïque,
Toute-épice
GER: Jamaikapfeffer,
Nelkenpfeffer
IT: Pimento
SP: Baya o fruta del
pimiento de Jamaica
BOT: Pimenta dioica
(Pimenta officinalis)
FAM: Myrtaceae
Plate I, No. 1 and
Ill. 18, No. 4, page 244

This spice comes from a tree native to the West Indies and Central and South America. It is now grown in many tropical countries, but flourishes so profusely in Jamaica that this island produces most of the world's supply. The tree has purple berries. These are picked while still green and then dried in the sun. They turn brown, and this is the familiar allspice of the kitchen, looking like large brown peppercorns.

Allspice is not, as some think who only buy it ground, a compound of several spices, although its taste is very like cloves, cinnamon and nutmeg mixed together. It is a useful spice and should, like other spices, be stored whole rather than bought pre-ground. When a light mixed spicing is required, one or two corns can be easily powdered in a mortar. Cloves and cinnamon are more difficult to pulverize.

Allspice is used in almost every country. Ground, it is used in cakes, and is one of the common pickling spices: it is, for instance, a usual spice in Scandinavian raw marinated herring. It can also be used in curries and pilau though it is not one of the traditional Indian ingredients. It is much used in the Near and Middle East and is a spice which most cooks will want to keep on the shelf.

There are several aromatic garden shrubs popularly called 'allspice' – the Carolina allspice, Japanese allspice and wild allspice or spice bush – but these have nothing to do with Jamaica pepper.

Almond

FR: Amande

The nuts are the seed of a tree related to the peach, and the fruits look rather like small green peaches. The almond tree is a native of the eastern Mediterranean regions and has been cultivated in southern Europe and the Middle East for

GER: Mandel
IT: Mandorla
SP: Almendra
BOT: Prunus amygdalus
(Amygdalus
communis)
FAM: Rosaceae

Sweet Almond
FR: Amande douce
GER: Mandelsüße
IT: Mandorla
SP: Almendra dulce
BOT: Prunus amygdalus,
var. dulcis

Bitter Almond
FR: Amande amère
GER: Mandelbittere
IT: Mandorla
SP: Almendra amarga
BOT: Prunus amygdalus,
var. amara
Cuddapah Almond
BOT: Buchanania
lanzan, Buchanania
latifolia
FAM: Anacardiaceae

many centuries. Today it is grown in almost all warm temperate climates, but Spain and Italy are particularly large producers.

The fruit of the almond (which surrounds the nut) is tough, fibrous and inedible when ripe, but it is a local delicacy when young and the stone is still soft. It has then a pleasantly sour taste and is often eaten with salt as an apéritif. It may be eaten almost anywhere around the Mediterranean in early summer.

There are many varieties of almond – Jordan, Valencia – such names are commonly used, but these distinctions concern size and shape. The distinction that concerns us is the fundamental flavour difference between sweet and bitter almonds.

SWEET ALMONDS are a flavouring of the most refined kind. In early medieval European cooking, a milk of almonds was a common ingredient. In the East, many delicate sweet dishes are flavoured with sweet almonds or tropical *cudappah* almonds. Sweet almonds are also an important ingredient in a number of soups and fish or meat dishes – either whole, ground, fresh, roasted (which changes the flavour) or fried. This use of almonds is particularly common in food of Arab origin, yet one finds them used on the one hand in Spanish food (e.g., roasted for Romesco sauce) and on the other hand in the mild forms of curry and pilau out of northwest India, Pakistan and Kashmir. They are also much used in the Levant. Chicken stuffed with a lightly spiced mixture of rice and almonds is commonly eaten in the Near and Middle East. In the United States, they are often included in seafood recipes, such as those for soft-shelled crab.

In using sweet almonds it is safer to grind one's own in a nutmill, for the ground almond sold in shops is often adulterated with cheap nut flour and spiked with a dash of bitter almond. Bitter almond will spoil the taste of any dish in which only sweet almonds are intended.

BITTER ALMONDS have quite another taste with no similarity whatever to sweet almonds. The powerful taste occurs not only in bitter almonds but also in the kernels of plums, peaches, cherries and other related fruits, as well as in peach leaves and cherry-laurel leaves (*Prunus laurocerasus*) as practical sources. There are also bitter almond essences of varying degrees of crudity, as well as ratafias made from bitter almonds or the fruit kernels we have mentioned. These are known as noyau (with variations in spelling) and are made in many parts of the world.

The flavour of bitter almonds is due to substances formed when the nut is mixed with water. Then an enzyme promotes a reaction between the water and a glucoside (a bitter substance related to sugar) which the kernels or leaves contain, and two new substances, neither present in the living plant, are formed. These are benzaldehyde (or oil of bitter almonds) and hydrocyanic acid (prussic acid, present in quantities of two to four per cent). Both taste of bitter almonds, but hydrocyanic acid is a deadly poison. Luckily it is also very volatile and vanishes into the air when heated, but raw sources of bitter almond flavour are likely to be poisonous and should not be taken in quantity.

A bitter almond flavour is commonly used in sweet dishes and biscuits. In fruits such as plums and cherries, where the taste occurs naturally in the stones, it can be intensified by crushing a few stones to expose the kernels before cooking. Much less usual is the flavour of bitter almonds with meat. Roast pork or chicken dishes are very interesting with bitter almond, but the perfuming needs to be done with the subtlety of a Chinaman. When achieved it is delicious.

Besides 'oil of bitter almonds' there is 'sweet almond oil'. This is not an essential or flavouring oil, but a fatty oil used particularly in confectionery. It can be expressed from either sweet or bitter almonds; in fact, it is mostly made from bitter almonds. Whatever its source the flavour is mildly nutty, sweet and not bitter. But, of course, if the residue left after pressing bitter almonds is mixed with water, then the bitter almond substances will develop, and oil of bitter almonds can be recovered by steam distillation. This is the basis of good almond essence.

Those interested in the reactions which produce the bitter almond flavour should compare mustard in which a similar reaction occurs. If bitter almonds – like mustard seeds – are roasted before being broken, then the enzyme is destroyed and the bitter almond taste will not develop. Poor samples of sweet almond sometimes contain a few bitter ones amongst them, so this is a useful fact to know.

TROPICAL ALMONDS (Country, Java, Malaysia, Malabar almonds etc.). True almonds do not grow in the tropics and in these regions many nuts with some resemblance to almonds are given the name and may also be mentioned under their local names in books on Indian, Malaysian and Vietnamese cookery or in the cooking of former colonial countries. Badam is the common name for such almonds in India and further East. The French call them *badamier*.

CUDDAPAH ALMONDS or CHIRONJI NUTS. References to chironji nuts are often mentioned in books on Indian cookery, but one can always substitute sweet almond as the Chironji nut itself is regarded as an almond substitute.

Aloe

FR: Aloès
GER: Aloe
IT: Aloe
SP: Aloe
BOT: Aloe barbadensis
FAM: Liliaceae or Agaraceae
Ill. 2, No. 3, page 45

Aloes, with their rosettes of fleshy but leathery sword-shaped leaves (looking a bit like an aspidistra) are familiar as greenhouse or ornamental plants. They come mainly from Africa and the West Indies, and some species contain an intensely bitter honey-like sap, which turns black when boiled down. It is used in small quantities in *fernets* and bitters and, by tradition, is used to discourage small children from biting their nails. It is best to buy aloes from the druggist rather than to experiment with the plants from the garden, as some species are very poisonous.

Ambergris

FR: Ambre gris
GER: Ambra (graue)
IT: Ambra grigia
SP: Ámbar gris

This substance is called 'grey amber' because like amber it is found washed up on beaches and was once thought to be of similar vegetable origin. It is enormously valuable, bringing a small fortune to any beachcomber lucky enough to find some.

Ambergris is in fact not vegetable, but semi-digested squid from the intestines of sick sperm whales (cachalot). Whalers find it sometimes when they cut up their catch. It is variable in appearance but is generally grey, black or marbled, fatty and putty-like. It sounds horrid but has a sweet earthy smell and later develops a whiff of violets. It also has a 'musky note' of squid and is used in perfumery.

Ambergris was a common flavouring in kitchens of the wealthy in the sixteenth and seventeenth centuries and was highly regarded as a restorative (often mixed with chocolate). It is occasionally mentioned in more recent recipes for

ratafias. Some authorities say it is still used in Eastern cookery, but I have not come across this myself. I doubt whether many people will want to try it, now that they know its origin, but it dissolves in alcohol and may be bought as an essence.

Powdered amber was also used in ancient cooking. This of course is fossilized resin.

Anchovy

FR: Anchois
GER: Anschovis
IT: Acciuga, Alice
SP: Anchoa, Anchova
SC: Engraulis
encrasicholus
FAM: Engraulidae

The anchovy is a small fish, with a dark blue back and silver underneath, found in the Mediterranean and on the Atlantic coasts of southern Europe. (What is called the Norwegian anchovy or *kilkis* is another fish.) Although they will grow to eight inches long, the usual size is nearer three inches. Fresh anchovies are often on sale in Mediterranean fish markets and the Atlantic coasts of Spain and Portugal. The fresh fish is excellent, with white flesh and good flavour, but it gives no indication whatever of the special anchovy flavour which develops after curing. This special flavour, together with the red-brown colour, is formed after several months of pickling in salt and is the result of fermentative changes. The preparation of salted anchovies and other fermented fish products has been understood for thousands of years in the Mediterranean area. (*See* Fishy Flavours.)

For people who live where anchovies are landed (they are fished with lights in quantity from March to September), curing is simple. In the local markets, wide straight-sided lidless glass jars made especially for the purpose are sold. After buying the jar, one visits the beach to find a flat stone that will just fit into the top. The fresh anchovies have to be cleaned by removing the head and entrails (fishmongers' daughters will usually oblige). The anchovies are now packed firmly in layers in the jar, each layer being well-sprinkled with coarse salt, the weight of the salt being usually about a quarter of that of the anchovies. When

---

Ill. 1 Some members of the Allium family: 1 Japanese Bunching Onion or Welsh Onion, 2 Shallot, 3 Poor Keeper Onion, 4 Good Keeper Onion, 5 Leek, 6 Top Onion, 7 Chive, 8 Garlic.

salting is completed, the stone is placed on top. This acts as a weight to keep the fish sunk below the surface of the brine, which will gradually form as the salt extracts the juices from the fish. Often a mouldy crust grows on top but this can be removed later and is of no importance. The anchovies will be ready after a few months and will have acquired the typical anchovy colour and flavour. They can then be split without difficulty into two fillets and the backbone removed.

Anchovies made in this way are the plain salted anchovies, the best to use in cooking after de-salting them a little in water. Unfortunately, they are difficult to obtain in northern Europe and North America where anchovies canned in oil are more commonly stocked. A third form of anchovy is dry salted, but this usually acquires slightly rancid flavours which might possibly be needed in some local dishes but which most people will not find particularly pleasant. As for the anchovy pastes, sauces and essences, these are almost always inferior in flavour, oversalted – to preserve them – and coloured with such things as Armenian bole (a red clay). In Victorian England it was common practice to lard meat with anchovies, and to use anchovies almost as if they were a kind of salt, because in small quantities they blend well into almost any savoury background and give a richer flavour without being obvious or prominent. Anchovy sauce and anchovy butter were popular accompaniments not only to fish dishes but even to beef and mutton. I have recorded a recipe labelled discreetly 'haggis (English)' which contains anchovies as part of the spicing for the oatmeal and lights. They also went into pork pies.

Those people who like anchovies will have no difficulty in finding dozens of ways of eating them. There are recipes coming from all parts of Europe. Not only anchovy fillets marinated in oil but also de-salted fillets are a common hors d'oeuvre to be eaten with bread and butter. From Belgium and Holland I use a recipe for anchovy fillets marinated in wine vinegar with thin slices of onion and slivers of lemon rind. They make a delicious accompaniment to vodka. In Italy, I have eaten anchovy fillets spread with a tomato sauce flavoured with white truffles. In England, there is anchovy toast and in France *anchoïade* and *beignets* of anchovies de-salted and fried in batter. Anchovies go well with cheese and in Italy are frequently used as a garnish for pizzas, in which the garnish adds important islands of flavour, and in dishes such as *crostini di mozzarella* or *provatura* cheese. Anchovies go with black olives and capers as in the *tapénade* of the South of France in which they are all pounded into a 'spread' with brandy, mountain thyme, bay, and a dash of wine vinegar. Anchovies and garlic together make up the famous *bagna cauda* of Piedmont which consists of anchovies and finely chopped garlic melted in a mixture of butter and olive oil. This highly indigestible sauce is kept warm at table either in a communal dish over a small spirit lamp or in individual earthen pots with a night-light underneath (but the words do not mean 'hot bath'). Pieces of raw vegetables, particularly cardoon, are dipped into this sauce which is traditionally perfumed with slices of white truffle, though in my own opinion this is a waste of truffle.

A jar of plain salted anchovies, which keep almost indefinitely provided they remain covered by liquid, should be on the shelf in every kitchen. Even the liquid is used as a flavouring. It is unfortunate that they are at present difficult to get but perhaps persistent demand would alter the situation.

Angelica
Garden Angelica

FR: Angélique
GER: Angelika,
  Brustwurz,
  Engelwurz
IT: Angelica
SP: Angélica
BOT: Angelica
  archangelica
  (Angelica officinalis,
  Archangelica
  officinalis)
FAM: Umbelliferae
Ill. 11, No. 5, page 144

Wild Angelica
FR: Angélique sauvage
GER: Wilde Engelwurz
IT: Angelica selvatica

A giant member of the parsley family, this hardy annual, biennial or triennial stands up to seven feet and has a very thick, hollow stem and white flowers. It is grown from seed and really fresh seed is essential for germination. Preferring rich damp soil and some shade, it dies after seeding.

The origin of angelica is given as either northern Europe or Syria. Whichever is correct it grows wild today locally from the Alps and Pyrenees to Lapland, the Faroes, Iceland and Siberia.

Angelica does not seem to be very ancient as a flavouring herb (probably fifteenth century). It was introduced into England at about the beginning of the sixteenth century. Today it is grown commercially, mainly in Germany and France.

Nobody knows just why this herb is connected with angels in almost every European language. Old books credit it with power against 'the evil eye', and say it cures

SP: Angélica silvestre
BOT: Angelica sylvestris

American Angelica
BOT: Angelica
    atropurpurea

a number of diseases. It is still used, medicinally, mainly as a digestive.

Although angelica is best known in the form of the candied young green stems used for decorating cakes and trifles, all parts of the plant – stem, leaves, seeds and root – have some purpose in cookery. It is eaten cooked as a vegetable in some countries – for instance in Greenland, Sweden and Finland, and the Faroes. The raw blanched young shoots may also be used in salads. Some advocate angelica leaves in chopped herb mixtures or in a court bouillon for fish and shellfish; others, that it should be served as a sweet after boiling in sugar. A most excellent use is as a flavouring for rhubarb or in orange marmalade. It is an ingredient of many liqueurs and apéritifs, the flavour being introduced either by maceration or in the form of the essential oil: absinthe, anisette, vermouth or even gin may all contain angelica.

Angelica has a strong and penetrating taste, which some have described as 'musky', but it varies considerably with climate. There are many people who violently dislike it so, if used, it must be with discretion.

In Britain and continental Europe, the allied wild angelica grows in damp woods and flowers in July and August. In America, the wild species is American angelica, sometimes wrongly called alexanders. Neither of these species has so good or strong a flavour as the true garden angelica. Japanese angelica comes from yet another species and is very strongly flavoured.

Angostura Bitters
Angostura Bark,
    Cuspara Bark

Angostura is the old name for the Venezuelan town on the Orinoco River now called Ciudad Bolivar. It gave its name to angostura bitters, which was originally a medicine for fever invented by a Doctor Siegert during the last century. His recipe has become the famous angostura bitters of today. These bitters are made in Trinidad and are said to consist of cinnamon and cloves, mace and nutmeg, orange

Ill. 2   Flavourings: 1 Arabian Coffee, 2 Cocoa Branch With Fruit, 2a Fruit Opened, 3 Aloe, 4 Cassava Root, 4a Cassava Leaf.

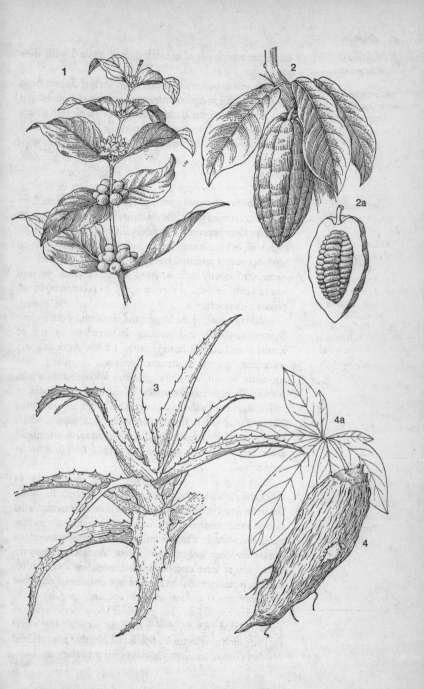

and lemon peel, together with prunes crushed with their stones, quinine and rum.

Angostura is an excellent aromatic bitters and apart from its use in pink gin and champagne cocktails can be used to give a touch of aromatic bitterness to iced fruit dishes, ice-creams and cups. It is also a good cure for hiccups, sprinkled generously on a slice of lemon which has been covered with sugar.

Anise
Sweet Cumin

FR: Anis
GER: Anis
INDIA: Saunf
IT: Anice
SP: Anís
   Matalahuga or
   Matalahúva
BOT: Pimpinella anisum
FAM: Umbelliferae
Plate II, No. 4 and
   Ill. 11, No. 2, page 144

The plant is an annual growing about two feet high. Like coriander, the leaves at the base are lobed, but further up the stem they become more finely divided. The flowers are yellowish-white. Anise, for leaf, can be easily grown from seed in a warm position, but in northern latitudes seed will ripen satisfactorily only in good summers. Since the seed can so easily be bought there is really no point in trying to produce it oneself.

Anise is a native of the Levant and was used by the ancient Egyptians, Greeks and Romans. It spread to the rest of southern and central Europe in the Middle Ages and was sometimes grown in Britain. Today it is grown commercially in suitably warm climates all over the world, particularly in Southeast Europe, North Africa and India.

The flavour of anise seed is sweet and quite characteristic. The essential oil is mainly anethole, a substance which occurs in equally large quantities in star anise, as one might guess, and to a lesser extent in cultivated fennel (but not in wild fennel).

Anise is used in flavouring sweets and creams; also in cakes and bread in eastern and northern Europe. Probably the most important gastronomic use is in various alcoholic liqueurs and cordials which are flavoured either by macerating the anise in alcohol, or by steam distillation of the seed to produce 'oil of anise'. Most Mediterranean countries have at least one drink dominated by this flavour, though it will usually be derived not only from anise but also from fennel and star anise. In France, especially in the south, are the drinks that go under the generic name of *pastis* (*Pernod*, *Ricard*, *Berger* etc.) as well as the sweet liqueurs such as anisette. In Spain and North Africa there is another crop of similar anise-flavoured preparations. Then, going east, one bypasses Italy, where anise-flavoured drinks are less popular, but in Greece we are back in business once more with ouzo, and in the eastern Mediterranean countries the popular version is rather similar and called *arrak*. The love of anise-flavoured drinks has also emigrated to Latin America.

Anise drinks are a convenient way of introducing the flavour of anise into cooking as well as into the cook. Some chefs put a few drops of *pastis* into the garlic and parsley butter for snails, and with olive oil it marinates the Mediterranean rock fish before they are turned into a *soupe de poisson*. Then there are, for instance, the many *spécialités Ricard* – in which this pastis goes into dishes based on chicken, partridge, crayfish, salt cod, mullet and mackerel: anisette is part of the flavouring for the sauce for *homard Courchamps* and *Pernod* in Oysters Rockefeller. It is delicious in dishes of chestnuts and it also improves dried figs. When I lived in Majorca, village friends used always to give me, for Christmas, cakes of minced figs flavoured with anisette and dried in leaves of fig or vine (Catalan: *Pa de figues*).

To the East, aniseed is also an important spice. In India it is used in certain types of curry, particularly in vegetable and fish dishes from Bengal and is commonly chewed after meals (as also is fennel seed) to sweeten the breath and aid digestion. Aniseed for this purpose is usually slightly roasted, which gives it a nutty taste. A not so hygienic habit is handing dirty change in a saucer of seed. One is supposed to take a pinch to chew as one leaves.

Green anise leaf is less used than the seed, but some people use it as a flavouring herb or in salads. An almost classical French use is finely chopped leaves sprinkled on young carrots, but in my opinion young carrots which have not been scraped require no addition other than melted butter.

Anise-pepper
Chinese Pepper
Chinese: Faah Jiu
Japan pepper

This spice is little-known in the West, although it is important in China, and is made by drying the red berries of a small, feathery-leaved, spiny tree. The flavour is hot and aromatic. Anise-pepper is one of the ingredients of Chinese

GER: Anispfeffer
IT. Pepe d'anice
BOT: Xanthoxylum
    piperitum
FAM: Rutaceae

five spices and is commonly used with fish and other strongly-flavoured ingredients.

Areca Nut

GER: Arecanuz
INDIA: Supari
IT: Noce di areca
BOT: Areca catechu
FAM: Palmae (Arecaceae)
Ill. 17, No. 3, page 229

The habit of chewing betel is very common in Asia and wherever there are Indian colonists. Betel chewing is as habit-forming as smoking, and one of the chief ingredients of such chewing mixtures is the areca nut, which is a stimulant.

The areca nut grows on a palm, originally from Malaysia and is recognized by the tall, very slender vertical trunk.

The nuts grow in loose bunches of a hundred or more. Inside a fibrous cover is a kernel the size of a walnut. The bunches are cut either when green ('tender nuts') or when orange yellow or scarlet and ripe. There are thus two quite distinct types of product.

The unripe tender nuts (India: *chikni*) are taken out of the husks, boiled to remove the tannin and then dried in the sun. The ripe nuts (India: *chali*) are dried, husk and all, until the kernel becomes loose. After that they are husked.

When whole, the areca nut looks something like a nutmeg; when cracked in two (unless it has been boiled) it is creamy white inside, veined with intricate folds of brown. It is exceedingly hard, and must be chopped into small pieces before use. Areca nut has little flavour and is strongly astringent, but it is a very important article in the East, and travellers or shoppers in Indian shops are certain to come across it.

Asafoetida

Asafetida,
    Devil's Dung,
    Stinking Gum

FR: Assa foetida,
    Férule perisque
GER: Stinkasant,
    Teufelsdreck
IT: Assafetida
SP: Asafétida
BOT: Ferula asafoetida,
    Asafoetida narthex

This is an exceedingly interesting flavour when used in minute quantities. In bulk it has a quite ghastly stink, a little like bad garlic (due to the presence of smelly sulphur compounds). It was a favourite flavouring in Roman times when, under the name of *silphium*, *laserpitium* or *laser*, it entered into many recipes. The best was said to come from a plant which then grew plentifully in Cyrenaica. This plant was so important that it was even depicted on coins, but it was already extinct by Pliny's time and has never been certainly identified. An inferior type of *silphium* then came from Persia and Armenia, and this is almost certainly what

FAM: Umbelliferae
Plate I, No. 8 and
   Ill. 11, No. 6, page 144

today we call asafoetida. That the Cyrenaican type was similar is only a reasonable conjecture.

Asafoetida is derived from several species of the genus *Ferula* – the giant fennels – of which there are some fifty in southern Europe, western Asia and North Africa (some are poisonous). They are closely related to the hog fennels, but are not to be confused with garden fennel though of rather similar appearance.

Ferula asafoetida is a huge evil-smelling perennial, with yellow flowers, growing from six to twelve feet high. A smaller species, also a source of asafoetida, is *Ferula narthex* which reaches only eight feet. Both are native to Persia and Afghanistan, and sometimes make dense 'forests' in suitable situations. When the stems of these plants are cut to the root, a milky juice flows out which dries into the solid, resin-like mass which we know as asafoetida. When fresh it is pearly, but it darkens with keeping. The whole plant, incidentally, is locally used as a vegetable, and the centre of the large stem is regarded as a luxury. The common giant fennel (*Ferula communis*), grown as a foliage plant in gardens, is said to be poisonous.

Asafoetida can be bought in solid wax-like pieces or perhaps more conveniently as a powder from shops specializing in Indian spices. It can also be bought from druggists as an extract. Minute quantities of asafoetida can be used particularly with fresh and salted fish to which it gives a delicious flavour.

In the East this spice is more commonly used, and one will need it particularly in Indian recipes from Maharashtra and Gujarat – recipes for vegetables, pulses and pickles – though rarely if ever in North Indian cooking or with meat. In fact, it is part of the special magic which has enabled Indians to solve the problems involved in trying to create tasty vegetarian dishes.

Asafoetida is a much neglected flavouring in European cooking, though used sometimes in France. It should certainly be tried if one does not know it already.

Ash

FR: Frêne

The shoots and 'keys' when young can be used in salads – dressed with oil and vinegar. In France, the leaves are sometimes used to make a fermented drink – *frenette*. If first

GER: Esche
IT: Frassino
SP: Fresno
BOT: Fraxinus excelsior
FAM: Oleaceae
Plate VI, No. 3

boiled till tender in plenty of water to remove bitterness, the keys make an excellent pickle in salted spiced vinegar.

In Italy, both the leaves and the fruit are infused to make a tea (one tablespoon to a cup of boiling water), which is refreshing as well as diuretic and mildly laxative. The use of herbs in country medicine frequently overlaps with their uses in the kitchen.

Avens
Geum, Herb Bennet,
  Wood Avens

FR: Benoîte
GER: Geum,
  Nelkenwurz,
  Sumpfnelke
IT: Cariofillata
  or Ambretta
SP: Gariofilea
BOT: Geum urbanum
FAM: Rosaceae
Ill. 5, No. 3, page 83

The avens, native to Europe, is commonly found wild in woods and shady damp hedgerows in Britain and is also found in Asia. It does not grow wild in North America.

The flower has five yellow petals appearing from above as if separated by the green sepals. The plant grows to about twelve inches high. The roots have a sweet smell of cloves and, according to old herbals, were used to flavour ale and prevent it souring, which suggests the presence of bacteriostatic substances that inhibit the multiplication of bacteria without killing them completely. Cloves produce the same reaction.

Avens was considered essential in Tudor kitchen gardens and may be found mentioned in old recipes. The young leaves can be used in salads.

Balm
Balm Gentle, Balm-mint,
  Lemon Balm,
  Melissa, Sweet Balm

FR: Baume, Citronelle,
  Mélisse
GER: Bienenkraut,
  Honigblume, Melisse,
  Zitronenmelisse
IT: Melisa (or) Melissa
SP: Balsamita major,
  Toronjiña, (or)
  Toronjil
BOT: Melissa officinalis
FAM: Labiatae
Ill. 13, No. 1, page 168

Balm should not be confused with barm (yeast). The word balm is a shortened form of balsam, and many other herbs and trees get the word 'balm' popularly tacked on to their name. Lemon balm is native to southern Europe and has been in cultivation for over two thousand years. It was first introduced to Britain by the Romans.

The plant grows over two feet high, has oval leaves with slightly serrated edges and small whitish or yellowish flowers borne in clusters. It is perennial, but dies down in winter. It is easily grown, spreads quickly and can be raised from seed, by planting out young plants, or by root division. Each plant needs at least a foot of space around it.

Balm has a pleasant lemon scent and is useful chopped and combined with other herbs, e.g. in omelettes. In Belgium and Holland, it is said to be used in pickled herrings and eels, although the recipes which I have from these countries make use of lemon peel. Some use it in salads. It is also the basis of the famous melissa cordial or *eau-de-melisse des carmes* and comes into the composition of several liqueurs. Lemon balm is a pleasant aromatic plant, greatly loved by bees (indeed the name *melissa* comes from the Greek for bee) but is otherwise not of great culinary importance, though delicious in long white-wine cups and iced drinks. In Spain balm – always fresh if possible – is used in soups, sauces and green salads, but also with road birds, game and fish. It is also used to flavour milk – '*leche perfumada con melisa*'.

Basil, Sweet

FR: Basilic commun
GER: Basilienkraut,
   Basilikum
IT: Basilico
SP: Alabega, Albahaca
BOT: Ocimum basilicum
FAM: Labiatae
Plate III, No. 3

Since basil is one of the great culinary herbs, it is rather to the shame of English cooks that in the Ministry of Agriculture bulletin on herbs it should be omitted as being 'now of little or no importance'.

Basil probably came from India to Europe overland via the Middle East. It arrived in Britain in the sixteenth century and reached America in the seventeenth, so its use in the West is comparatively recent. In India, basil is little used in cooking, but a type of basil (*Ocimum sanctum*) is the holy *tulsi* which Hindus regard with such reverence that when the British wanted to find something on which Hindus (who have nothing equivalent to the Bible) could take an oath in court, *tulsi* was one of the items chosen as of sufficient holiness.

In the West, basil is the symbol of fertility. Boccaccio tells the story of Lisabetta, whose tears watered the pot of basil in which she had buried the head of her lover. (Keats' *Isabella* or *The Pot of Basil* is another version.) In a quite different vein the Flemish doctor, Van Helmont (1577–1644), who was one of the fathers of experimental science, believed that if crushed basil were left in the cavity between two bricks, it would turn into scorpions! The old wives' tale must have originated not in Belgium but in southern Europe where one can usually find small scorpions under stones if one looks for them.

Basil is an annual and, being a warm country plant, it will stand no frost. It is exceedingly variable but typically grows to about two feet high and has light green, silky and tender leaves sometimes about the size of a beech leaf but often much smaller. Also, the plant breeders have been at work, and there are now even lettuce-leaved varieties. The flowers are small and creamy white.

Basil may be sown in a light rich soil or compost, either under glass or in the garden when all danger of frost is past. It can be grown in a sunny sheltered place if protected from cold winds. Plants should be twelve inches apart, and it may be trained to a bushy form by pinching out shoots. But such old basil which has been grown in what are, for it, rather adverse climatic conditions is usually rank and tough. Worse, it loses its most delicate sweet scent and acquires strong overtones. It is much better to sow in succession – perhaps in boxes – and to use only young plants. In Genoa, Italy, where basil is grown extensively, it is forced in greenhouses under tropical heat and humidity, and always pulled when only about six inches high. It is then sold in the markets in bunches with the roots still intact and bound up in green leaves or grass and paper. This is because it rather quickly wilts. Basil is an exception to the general rule for labiate herbs: it is best grown quickly in soft conditions and used young. Other members of this family develop a better flavour when they have to fight for a living. If limited to one home-grown, fresh herb, I should select basil, sow it frequently in a box protected by glass, and never grow large plants. The flavour of fresh basil is slightly like that of cloves, but this description does not do it justice. Its smell is so sweet and strong that it perfumes the whole garden, when picked. The flavour of dried basil on the other hand is not comparable: it tastes a little like curry and cannot ever replace the fresh herb. Basil can be kept for a short time in a polythene bag in the refrigerator and is also suitable for quick freezing in polythene bags after it has been blanched momentarily in boiling water. However, I prefer the Italian method of preserving it in oil. If the leaves are dirty, wash and dry; otherwise pack the leaves straight into a clean dry jar, sprinkling a good pinch of salt over each layer. When the jar is full, fill up with olive oil to cover. Close well. This will keep indefinitely in a cool store cupboard or refrigerator and preserves most of the fresh flavour, even though with time it will blacken. It is splendid for making *pesto* (*see* below).

Although in English and American markets basil as a fresh herb is nowadays very uncommon, it is traditional in turtle soup and was certainly used in the past. All books quote the famous seventeenth century Fetter Lane sausages. However, it cannot be regarded as a typical ingredient of northern European cooking. In northern France one finds that basil is seldom used, perhaps because the use of fresh herbs in regional cooking depends rather on what can be easily grown in the climate. Because basil likes warmth, if one wishes to find real 'basil country' one must go south to the Mediterranean – particularly to the Ligurian coast of Italy.

Perhaps the most delicious use of basil is in *pesto Genovese*, which in various forms is found all along the Riviera coast from Genoa to Provence (where it is called *pistou*). The basis is always basil, with garlic, salt, olive oil, Parmesan and sardo (hard Sardinian sheep's milk) cheese, pine nuts and often skinned walnuts – all pounded together to a thick sauce. Needless to say some bowdlerized recipes in English books suggest leaving out the garlic. In southern France *pistou* is used in soup; in Italy *pesto* with plenty of olive oil is used as a sauce for spaghetti or *trenette*. Basil, like garlic, leads to passionate addiction, and the two combined provide what in my opinion is the sauce for spaghetti quite beyond all others. Unfortunately *pesto* is local, but it is easy to make, and one can buy it canned or preserved in glass jars. These are scarcely passable substitutes for fresh *pesto*, but perhaps are better than no *pesto* at all.

Basil has a great affinity with tomatoes. Where I lived on the Italian Riviera the common snack consisted of a crusty roll split and filled with sliced tomato, salt, olive oil, and a few leaves of fresh basil – no butter of course – just squashed to make the oil and juice impregnate the bread. Tourists should avoid hotel sandwiches and try this (with a bottle of red wine) having started the day with a visit to the market. Basil is delicious in a tomato salad dressed with salt and olive oil. Incidentally, chopping basil rather spoils the flavour, and it is better to shred the leaves with the fingers.

Basil goes in tomato sauces – any dish of tomatoes. It also goes with sweet peppers and aubergines; with fish of any kind but especially with red mullet; in meat dishes with wine and garlic, and with chicken; pounded with butter, as a herb butter with steak; with eggs (e.g. *oeufs mollets à la crème aux fines herbes*); and even with shellfish. I often

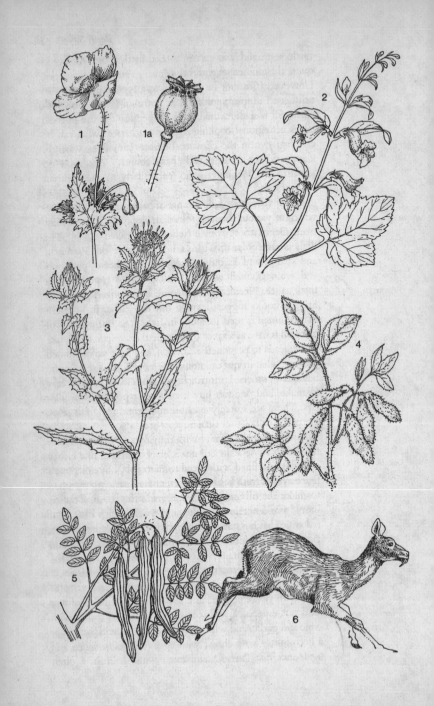

include a few leaves in my pâté. Indeed, an addict will use basil in almost anything.

Outside Europe, basil and its near relatives are occasionally used in India (*babuitulsi*), and in Malaysian cookery (*selaseh*), and the seeds of one type – gelatinous after soaking – are also used in drinks.

Finally there is basil vinegar – made by macerating the leaves in wine vinegar. This is a good herb vinegar for use in winter.

BUSH or DWARF BASIL grows not much over six inches high and is mainly a decorative plant. There are horticultural varieties with different coloured leaves and it can be grown into a bush by 'pinching out'. The flavour is inferior to that of sweet basil.

LEMON BASIL and ITALIAN or CURLY BASIL are both ornamental though quite wholesome. The so-called wild basil is not a basil but a relative of calamint which itself is sometimes called basil thyme. It is also fragrant and wholesome to use in cooking if liked, but is nothing like sweet basil in flavour.

Bay
Sweet Bay,
  Sweet Laurel

FR: Laurier
GER: Lorbeer
IT: Alloro, Lauro
SP: Laural
BOT: Laurus nobilis
FAM: Lauraceae
Plate III, No. 3

The bay is a small tree, usually grown as a bush, although it can reach sixty feet in height in perfect conditions. It has tough leaves, and in warm climates produces berries resembling small olives in appearance. Although rather like the common Portugal laurel, bay leaves are more glossy and have a characteristic sweet balsamic scent when crushed. Trees should be planted either in late September or early April. They require a sheltered, sunny position and will not usually survive in the northern parts of Britain or America. Bay trees are often grown in tubs which should be filled with equal quantities of sand, loam and peat, topdressed with well-rotted manure and never allowed to dry out.

Bay is said to have come originally from Asia Minor, but was established all round the Mediterranean at a very early date. It was the laurel of the 'crown of laurel leaves',

Ill. 3 Flavourings: 1 Poppy, 1a Poppy Seed Capsule, 2 Sesame, 3 Safflower, 4 Soy Bean Pods Growing on Plant, 5 Horseradish Tree, 6 Musk Deer.

symbol of wisdom and glory in ancient Greece and Rome, worn by victors and emperors, and popularly supposed to keep away lightning.

As a culinary herb, bay may be used either fresh or dried. The fresh leaves are rather bitter, as well as strongly scented. Some people prefer bay after it has been wilted for a few days. Then the bitterness has gone, but the scent remains strong. Very old dried bay leaves, as are so often sold, lose their strength and are of no use whatever.

Bay is used all over the world but is quite essential in French and Mediterranean cooking – indeed, in all good continental cooking. It is a traditional part of the bouquet garni and goes into marinades, court bouillon, pickles and olives. It is even packed round liquorice and in boxes of dried figs to discourage weevils. Indeed, if bay has only a short entry here, it is quite out of proportion to its culinary importance; it seems to go into almost everything. No kitchen should exist without bay leaves, and they should be used as a matter of habit.

Besides its use in savoury dishes, bay may be used boiled in the milk to flavour creams and custards. This will give a dominant flavour of bay, one used more commonly in the past than it is today. Bay berries are pressed or distilled to give a thick greenish oil used in some liqueurs.

Bay should not be confused with the cherry laurel (*Prunus laurocerasus*) as it is in some books. This has a bitter almond flavour. (*See* almond.)

Many books on Indian cookery give bay as being equivalent to *tej pat* (*see* cinnamon). In fact, bay leaves are not traditional in curries.

Beer

FR: Bière
GER: Bier
IT: Birra
LATIN: Cerevisia (from Ceres goddess of the harvest)
SP: Cerveza

One of the oldest clay tablets from Babylon, dated about 6000 B.C. shows the making of ale. Crude alcoholic drinks made from fermented grain – wheat, barley, rice, maize, millet etc. – are still home-made in many countries. One may be forced to drink them in rural areas as far apart as Zululand and Nepal. The appearance is usually like dirty bath-water and the flavour like sour yeasty porridge. If, however, such crude ales are left to clear, and if, as was the practice in the olden days, they are flavoured with aromatic or bitter herbs, such as alecost (costmary), ground ivy, nettles, dandelion or mixed herbs (gruit), then there is a great improvement. Today, ales are almost universally flavoured with hops which some say were originally added as a preservative.

Hops have been in use since at least 600 B.C., but their introduction to European beer dates from much later. The taste for Flanders *bere* or *biere* came to England with soldiers returning from the Hundred Years' War (1338–1453), and although they are an indigenous wild plant in parts of Britain, hops were not cultivated here until 1525. It is therefore more correct to refer to the earlier drinks without hop flavouring as 'ales' and keep the word 'beer' only for the more modern drink.

The important thing in following a recipe calling for beer is to find one that has the correct degree of bitterness – strongly or mildly hopped – and sweetness, as these qualities must be correctly judged to conform to the type used for the dish in its country of origin.

Beer is used in the cooking of northern Europe, just as wine is used in the vine growing countries, but is much less flexible and enters into a much smaller variety of dishes. One might mention German beer soup, made with a dark lager, and the well-known carbonnade of beef, a delicious beef and onion stew of Flemish origin which must be made of Belgian beer called *La geuze* – sour without prunes or if *Carbonade Walons* with *Diest Moire* – sweet and black with prunes. In other words the type of beer used is critical. In England it is locally common to cook shin of beef in dark mild ale.

Whole books have been written on the art of using beer in cooking. This entry will serve its purpose if it draws attention to the interesting possibilities. It is a neglected field in England and America.

Bergamot

FR: Bergamote
GER: Bergamott
IT: Monarda
SP: Bergamota
FAM: Labiatae
Ill. 13, No. 7, page 168

The bergamots are North American aromatic herbs of the mint family.

Wild Bergamot is from southern Canada and the northern United States. The flowers are purple or red, it is two to three feet high and the leaves are pleasantly lemon scented.

Red Bergamot is also known as fragrant balm, bee balm,

Wild Bergamot
BOT: Monarda fistulosa

Red Bergamot
BOT: Monarda didyma

Lemon Bergamot
BOT: Monarda citriodora

red balm, Indian's plume or Oswego tea, after the Oswego Indians who used it. At the time of the Boston Tea Party, Oswego tea was used by the colonists who wanted to boycott British goods. It was brought to Europe where it is now often cultivated as a decorative garden plant and used in perfumery.

Lemon bergamot is also North American and has aromatic properties similar to the wild and red bergamots.

The bergamots are of little importance in cooking, but are always mentioned in herb books. The leaves may be put into soft fruit drinks and iced cups. They may also be used to make herb teas which are supposed to be both relaxing and soporific.

Do not confuse with the Bergamot orange (*Citrus bergamia*) grown particularly in Sicily and Southern Italy, a small citrus fruit with very characteristic perfume. The skin yields an essential oil and is also candied.

Betony

FR: Bétoine
GER: Betonie
IT: Betonica
SP: Betónica
BOT: Betonica officinalis
(Stachys betonica,
Stachys officinalis)
FAM: Labiatae
Ill. 13, No. 6, page 168

Betony is a herb of hedge banks, woods and heaths. It grows wild in England, Wales and other parts of Europe and Asia Minor and is a rare escape in the United States. In appearance it is rather like a deadnettle, with aromatic purple red flowers densely grouped at the top of the stem and a few lower down in the axils of the leaves.

Formerly, betony was used as a substitute for tea and as a flavouring in various herb beers. It was listed as essential in Tudor herb gardens. Today it has little culinary importance and is grown mainly as decoration.

It may be of interest that the *chorogi* (Chinese or Japanese artichoke) is a close relative (*Stachys Sieboldii*).

Bitter Flavours

Bitterness is not a flavour but a true taste; that is, along with sourness, saltiness, sweetness, astringency, metallic tastes and pepperiness or pungency, it is detected in the mouth and not by the nose.

Of all tastes, bitterness can be detected in the smallest amount. It is also very often not liked, especially by children, and this is possibly due to the fact that many poisonous plants are intensely bitter. Perhaps our dislike is a primitive defence.

Although bitterness can be somewhat masked (druggists use raspberry and cocoa), it cannot be counteracted by sugar or anything else in the same way as sourness. Some substances can be simultaneously sweet, sour and bitter. Bitterness increases the effect of sourness and is also more pronounced when dishes are cold than when they are hot. In this it is similar to saltiness but the opposite of sweetness and sourness. Unwanted bitterness can only be removed by extracting a part of the bitter principle by boiling and throwing away the water. This procedure is often resorted to, for instance, with bitter oranges used for marmalade or in cooking bitter greens.

The addition of any bitter-flavoured ingredient must be done with care, but when correctly adjusted bitterness makes food more interesting and sharpens the appetite. Bitter plants, such as dandelion and chicory, are often put into salads, although most of the bitter salad plants have had their bitterness much reduced by horticultural selection or blanching. Bitter oranges are interesting and are preferred to sweet by many, not only in marmalade but also in sauces. Many of our most refreshing fruits, such as the grapefruit and pomelo, are naturally slightly bitter, and sometimes the addition of a touch of bitters or bitter peel can improve fruits which are without natural bitterness. The main use of bitter substances, however, is in drinks, both in refreshing ones or in those intended to promote an appetite or encourage a failing liver. Hops in beer, quinine in Indian tonic water, bitters in gin, wormwood in vermouth, angostura bitters, *amer picon, fernet branca,* literally hundreds of commercial apéritifs and bitters of different formulae in France and Italy and some quite devastatingly bitter gentian drinks such as *suze* and *enzian.* Commonly used bitter substances are gentian root, quassia chips, aloes, dandelion, and quinine. These are all intensely bitter. Of the more aromatic and pleasantly bitter ingredients available in the kitchen, one might list preparations such as angostura bitters and orange bitters together with bitter orange peel and hops. Perhaps one should add wormwood, which is easily grown in the garden and perfectly wholesome in small quantities. One or two of these may be kept handy in the kitchen for adding bitterness when necessary.

Bog Myrtle
Candle-berry,
  Sweet Gale

FR: Galé odorant,
  Myrte des marais,
  Poivre de Brabant
GER: Gagel (strauch)
IT: Mirica
SP: Mirto holandés
BOT: Myrica gale
FAM: Myricaceae
Plate V, No. 5

Bog myrtle is a common plant of wet moors in the nor-thern countries of the northern hemisphere. It is a small shrubby plant with a reddish stem growing two to seven feet high. The male and female catkins are usually borne on separate plants and appear before the leaves. The leaves have a pleasant aromatic smell vaguely like bay and in ancient times were used all over northern Europe to flavour beer. In China, they were dried to make a tea. In the past, 'sweet gale' was an important plant and in Britain there were laws to prevent the bushes being destroyed.

The characteristic smell is due to a wax secreted by glands under the leaves. The fruits are particularly rich in this wax, and if they are macerated in hot water the wax will float to the top. In times past it was used to make candles which gave off a sweet smell as they burned, hence the name candle-berry, which is applied to this plant and other related species.

According to one authority the small two-winged fruits are used in France and Sweden to flavour soup. I myself can remember an old Northumbrian cook using both the fruits and leaves in meat stews. People who live near bogs in which this plant grows should experiment with it as the results are interesting and it is a true flavouring of peasant food.

Borage

FR: Bourrache
GER: Boretsch,
  Gurkenkraut
IT: Borragine
SP: Borraja
BOT: Borago officinalis
FAM: Boraginaceae
Plate IV, No. 3

Borage is said to have come from the Middle East, but today it is one of the more common wild flowers in southern Europe and can be found on chalk downs in southern England, where it was introduced by the Romans.

The plant is an annual, three feet high and covered with coarse irritating hairs which give a hoary appearance to leaves and stem. The flowers are a beautiful Mediterranean sky-blue. Borage can be grown with ease from seed in all temperate or warm climates and prefers a well-drained calcareous soil and sun.

The blue flowers are sometimes used for decoration or are candied, but it is the leaves, with their flavour of cucumber, that are of most importance. The commonest use of borage leaves is in drinks to which they give a cooling taste of cucumber. It should always, if possible, be a part of the 'garden' in a Pimms. The young leaves and flowers are sometimes used in salads, but although the taste is excellent, the leaves must be chopped finely if they are to be eaten raw, as their hairy texture makes them unappetizing when whole. Borage, like cucumber, is delicious with yoghurt or in cream cheese. In parts of Italy (Liguria) – where borage grows in wild profusion – the leaves are used as a stuffing for ravioli or boiled as a spinach. They may even be fried in batter. In other parts, it is unknown.

Borage is locally on sale in markets, and it wilts almost immediately it is picked. It can be dried, they say, but this is a herb to be grown for decorative effect in a garden and used fresh during the hot summer weather.

Ill. 9, No. 7, page 123
Plate V, No. 7

Many relatives of borage, such as comfrey (*Symphytum officinale*), viper's bugloss (*Echium vulgare*) and anchusa (*Pentaglottis sempervirens*) are also edible and may be used in similar ways. German cookery books mention a comfrey butter from Bavaria, and the roots are a flavouring for country wine. Various other related plants are known as alkanet and were used as a dye.

Bouquet Garni

This is the internationally used French name for what in English we also call a 'bundle of sweet herbs' or a 'faggot of herbs'. The herbs are tied together so that they can be removed at the end of cooking or when sufficient flavour has been imparted to the dish. The same result is obtained by tying the herbs in a piece of muslin, and this allows spices, orange peel or garlic to be included. In peasant cooking the herbs are often just thrown in. It is correct however to remove these signs of good cooking. The cook who does not habitually use some sort of bouquet garni is probably not worthy of being called a cook, and it really will not do to substitute commercial 'mixed herbs' or powdered bouquet garni from a packet.

The classic bouquet garni consists of three stalks of parsley to a small sprig of thyme and a small bay leaf. In Provence, it would also include a piece of dried orange peel. These proportions must, however, be flexible because in herbs we are not dealing with a standard commodity. A glance through the literature also reveals a surprising number of mixtures which could be called a bouquet garni. '2 sprigs of parsley, one of orange or lemon thyme, and a bay leaf'. Or '2 sprigs of parsley, one of sweet marjoram, one of winter savory, and one of lemon thyme', even 'a few sprigs of parsley, a sprig of thyme, a sprig of marjoram, a bay leaf, a sprig of basil, a celery leaf, a small piece of cinnamon stick, a clove of garlic, a small blade of mace, and a pod of red pepper'. This last seems over-elaborate and is from a Victorian recipe.

The bouquet garni is essentially one of the things this book is about. It is something one must experiment with if one wishes to create dishes with one's own individual stamp.

Brooklime

Water Pimpernel,
Water Purpie (Scotland)

FR: Beccabunga,
    Cresson de cheval
    (chien), Véronique
    cressonnée
GER: Bachbunge
IT: Veronica or
    Beccabunga or
    Erba grassa
SP: Becabunga
BOT: Veronica
    beccabunga
FAM: Scrophulariaceae
Ill. 16, No. 4, page 216

In Britain, this wild salad plant is common in ponds, streams and marshy places. It has small blue flowers and rather large, smooth, round, fleshy leaves, which can be mixed like watercress in a green salad.

As with watercress or any other wild salad plant which grows in water, it is necessary to make sure that the water is not contaminated with sewage. In many countries it is unwise to eat water-growing plants in restaurants, although I have on occasion eaten plants from the Nile without suffering any unpleasant consequences. I did it only from curiosity and was probably just lucky. Incidentally, the common habit in the East of washing salad vegetables in dilute permanganate and potash to clean them is virtually useless.

Bulrush

Cattail (U.S.A.),
    Reedmace

FR: Jonc des marais
    (des chaisiers)
GER: Binse,
    Rohrkolbenschilf,
    Seesimse
IT: Stiancia or
    Mazzasorda
SP: Enea, Junco
BOT: Typha latifolia

The bulrush commonly grows at the edges of ponds or lakes in northern latitudes. Its great club-like flower heads are well known to most people, but few realize it is edible. Young sprouts and shoots are eaten as a wild salad. The 'mace' when still green can be boiled for a vegetable, the pollen used to flavour pancakes, a flour made from the peeled roots, and the softer fleshy swellings from which the sprouts spring used in winter as a vegetable. The tender white inside parts of the new shoots (when they are about two feet high) make an excellent salad, either raw or cooked. This is a well-known spring food amongst the Don Cossacks in Russia. For further reading on bulrushes and

FAM: Typhaceae
Plate VI, No. 1

other wild foods, I recommend Euell Gibbons' *Stalking the Wild Asparagus*. This should not be confused with the other more grass-like plant, also known as bulrush, the club-rush (*Scirpus lacustris*).

Burnet
Garden Burnet,
  Lesser Burnet,
  Salad Burnet

FR: Grande pimprenelle,
  Pimprenelle commune
  des prés
GER: Großer
  Wiesenknopf,
  Pimpinelle
IT: Pimpinella
SP: Pimpinela or
  Salvastrella
BOT: Poterium
  sanguisorba
FAM: Rosaceae
Ill. 10, No. 2, page 136

The salad burnet was an essential kitchen garden herb in Elizabethan England and was taken to America by the early colonists. Today it is mainly used in France and Italy.

It is native to Europe, growing particularly on calcareous soil, and common in southern England on chalk downs. It is a small perennial with rather characteristic little toothed leaves growing in pairs. The stem grows to about a foot high, and the flower head is a sort of greenish 'bobble' feathered with long purple-red stamens. The leaves smell rather like cucumber when crushed. This is a useful plant to be able to recognize and really cannot be confused with anything poisonous. It is also easy to cultivate in the garden as it is hardy and will grow in almost any soil. It is raised from seed or by division of clumps.

Burnet is a classical ingredient in several butters and sauces, such as *ravigote* and *chivry*, in which it is used finely chopped and fresh (although it can be quick frozen). The leaves are also used like borage, to flavour cooling drinks, and are sometimes infused to make 'burnet vinegar'. As a salad plant burnet is excellent, though unless the leaves are very young they are inclined to be tough. Leaves of burnet are frequently found in the collection of mixed green salad leaves sold in Italian markets. It is part of the charm of such a salad (consisting entirely of green leaves dressed simply with fine olive oil, salt and wine vinegar) that one should come on leaves of varying toughness, flavour and bitterness.

GREAT BURNET (*Sanguisorba officinalis*), in Britain a rarer plant of damp meadows, is often confused with the salad burnet. Though somewhat similar in appearance, it is a larger plant growing two feet high, the flower head being a more colourful crimson-purple bobble. This plant used to be called bloodwort and was employed to stanch wounds on the battlefield. It grows over a great deal of Europe and Asia, but is not indigenous to North America.

Some old recipes for burnet vinegar involved the use of pounded burnet seed. It is often difficult to tell which burnet is being referred to in these old recipes, and there is confusion with yet another kind of burnet, the burnet saxifrage.

BURNET SAXIFRAGE (*Pimpinella saxifraga*) is another wild plant of chalky soils but belongs to the parsley family (*Umbellifereae*). It has white typically umbelliferous flowers and although the lower leaves are vaguely like those of the salad burnet, the leaves further up the stem (as with coriander and other members of this family) are a different shape and much more finely cut.

The burnet saxifrage is known in France as *pied de bouc* or *boucage* (in Italy, *pie di becco*) and is one of the very old cordial herbs. It was used even in ancient Greece. This plant does not grow wild in America, but there is another species of wild burnet found in the eastern states and cultivated in the South. Burnet saxifrage has also a big brother, the greater burnet saxifrage (*Pimpinella major*) which grows in damp meadows and shady hedgerows in Britain. Great burnet and greater burnet saxifrage should not be confused with the great burdock (*Arctium lappa*) which has edible roots of which the Japanese *gobo* is a cultivated form.

Calamint

FR: Calament
GER: Bergminze
IT: Calaminta
SP: Calamento
BOT: Calamintha
    ascendens
    (Calamintha officinalis)
FAM: Labiatae
Ill. 15, No. 6, page 201

Calamint grows wild in waste places on chalky soil over much of Europe including the southern part of Britain. It grows one to two feet high and the flowers are purply-blue and rather like catmint. The leaves are aromatic, a little like peppermint. It is a medicinal herb, but is occasionally used in cooking.

Calamint should not be confused with basil thyme (*Acinos arvensis*, formerly *Calamintha acinos*) nor with the lesser calamint (*Calamintha nepeta*), which in North America is called field balm, though both of these herbs may be used as a flavouring if liked. Further confusion may come from the fact that in some older books savory is listed as *Calamintha hortensis* and winter savory as *Calamintha montana*.

Calamus
Sweet Flag,
    Sweet Grass,

This is a marsh plant common in the entire northern hemisphere. It grows wild in Britain (although not native here) and throughout the United States. The plant grows

Sweet Rush, Wild Iris

FR: Calamus, Jonc
odorant, Lis des
marais, Roseau
aromatique
GER: Schilffeder,
Schilfrohr
IT: Calamo Aromatico
SP: Cálamo aromático
BOT: Acorus calamus
FAM: Araceae
Ill. 4, No. 6, page 70

in shallow water on the edges of pools and sluggish streams. It stands about four feet high; the leaves have crinkly margins and are scented when rubbed. First record of its cultivation is from Poland in the thirteenth century.

All parts of this plant are sweet and aromatic and the roots were at one time candied to make a strongly pungent sweetmeat in both England and America. It is used as a flavouring, particularly in liqueurs. The very young leaf buds can also be eaten as a salad. Older rhizomes are often fibrous.

Camomile
Chamomile

FR: Camomille
GER: Garten Kamille,
Hundeskamille,
Magdblume,
Mutterkraut
IT: Camomilla,
Camomilla Romama
SP: Camomila,
Manzanilla
FAM: Compositae

Sweet Camomile
BOT: Chamaemelum
nobile (Anthemis
nobilis)
Plate V, No. 4

Wild or German
Camomile
BOT: Matricaria recutita
(Matricaria
chamomilla)

Both sweet and wild or German camomile grow wild over much of Europe and temperate Asia, in Britain are local. They have run wild in the eastern parts of the United States. Sweet camomile is a perennial, but wild camomile (or, as it is sometimes called, 'scented mayweed') is an annual. Both can be easily grown in the garden and for commercial purposes a double-flowered form of the sweet camomile is usually grown. There is no agreement as to which of these plants is the true camomile or which of the two is the more effective.

Camomile tea, made from the dried flower heads, is a very ancient remedy and is still on sale in the markets of the less pill-conscious countries. It sometimes enters into the composition of vermouths and apéritifs, but is not used to flavour the very dry sherry known as Manzanilla (the Spanish name for camomile); the sherry is called after a place.

Body and hair lotions were once made from sweet camomile, and a wine and sugar mixture which had been impregnated with the flowers produced a remedy for kidney and bladder ailments. Also, in Tudor times lawns of camomile were sown and there is still such a lawn in the grounds of Buckingham Palace.

Candlenut

MALAY: Kemiri or
Buah kĕras

Candlenuts are hard-shelled seeds from a handsome tree native to Malaysia and the Pacific Islands, but now cultivated in other hot countries. The popular name has been given because the oily nuts when threaded on to the mid-

BOT: Aleurites
   moluccana
FAM: Euphorbiaceae
Ill. 17, No. 7, page 229

rib of a palm leaf, are used as a primitive candle. The nut is cultivated for its oil, which is used for making paints, linoleum, soap and other products. The residue, after the oil has been expressed, and the fresh nut are poisonous (as are many Euphorbias), but after some time the poison disappears.

Candlenuts are commonly used in Indonesian cooking (sometimes roasted) where, with unusual spices such as galangal and lemon grass, they play a part in curries which differ considerably from the better-known curries of India. Use macadamia nuts or blanched almonds which local people prefer.

Caper

FR: Câpre, Câpre
   capucine Fabagelle,
GER: Kaper
IT: Cappero
SP: Alcaparra, Tápana,
   Tápara
BOT: Capparis rupestris;
   Capparis inermis (no
   spines), Camparis
   spinosa (spiny)
FAM: Capparidaceae
   (Capparaceae)
Ill. 10, No. 5, page 136

The caper is a small bush with tough oval leaves. The flowers, the size of a wild rose, are white or pink with four petals and a tassel of long purple stamens. They are most beautiful but have a very short life. Flowers that open in the morning, are gone by the afternoon and the famous quotation from Ecclesiastes, 'The flower shall wither, beauty shall fade away', may well refer to the caper which grows, amongst other places, wild in the Holy Land. Since capers often grow on old walls and ruins – they were once common on the Colosseum in Rome – there is something melancholy about them. Today one also finds them growing in Majorca in the gutters and on the rubble of new hotel developments.

Capers have been used as a condiment for thousands of years. They grow wild all around the Mediterranean basin. I have found them in Cyprus, on the shores of the Dead Sea and on archaeological sites as far east as the edge of the steppes in north-eastern Persia. One wonders if they were wild or brought to these remote places by people in the past, for in these days the natives there do not always know how to use them. Capers also grow wild in North Africa, well down into the Sahara and here, for survival, their leaves are always turned edgeways to the hot sun. In these very hot places the plants are also armed with spines, although the types grown commercially further north, for instance in southern France, are not.

One country where capers grow wild in profusion and are much used is Cyprus. Here, one will be offered not only the pickled buds but also the small gherkin-shaped fruits (these are found in Spain as well) and even whole sprigs of pickled leaves (complete with prickles!). This is rough but delicious peasant food. The best capers (*non-pareilles*) come from southern France, particularly near the mouth of the Rhone and further east in the Var; but Spain, Italy and Algeria also produce large quantities of capers, as do California and other places with a Mediterranean climate. However, the cultivation of capers is rather difficult, and gathering them requires much hand work. Ideally, the buds must be picked every morning just as they reach the proper size. After being wilted in the air for a day, they are put in casks of strong salted white vinegar or are dry-salted. The best capers are graded and packed in bottles, and their quality is usually indicated by the price you have to pay for them. In the Mediterranean countries, where capers are an everyday commodity, they are also sold loose in the markets. Though usually of inferior quality, often over-large or dry-salted, they are cheap.

The taste of fresh caper buds is not promising, and the characteristic flavour comes only after they have been pickled, due to the development of an organic acid – capric acid – which, when strong, smells unpleasantly of billy-goats. A small trace of capric acid, in spite of (or perhaps because of) this goaty taste, is an important flavouring occurring in many other foods. Although there are many caper substitutes (broom buds, marsh marigold buds, caper spurge [possibly poisonous] and so on), most lack this essential flavour, but pickled green nasturtium seeds are excellent.

Capers are essential in the kitchen. Keeping them presents no problem if one always retains the liquid until the bottle is finished. Capers must not dry out, and one must never add extra vinegar as this spoils them. If they are always carefully removed from the bottle, leaving the pickling liquid behind to cover those that remain, there should be no trouble. The liquid is used at the end.

Although in English cooking the common use of capers is only in caper sauce (usually eaten with boiled mutton), other important uses are in *tartare*, *remoulade*, *ravigote*, *gribiche* and sometimes *vinaigrette* sauces. They are combined with pickles (chopped), with anchovies and with herbs, and grated lemon rind is often an improvement not given in the books. As one would expect, capers are most used in the cooking of the regions where they grow. They go very well with fish. Caper sauce may be eaten with salmon or turbot, but cheaper fish are particularly liable to be cooked or garnished with capers; whiting, for instance, (*merlans à la bretonne*) or skate (*raie au beurre noir*) or conger (*congre sauté aux câpres*). They are particularly used with salt cod in Mediterranean areas where this is commonly eaten on a Friday, and many people buying their salt cod (already soaked) will also buy capers to go with it (e.g. *morue à la provençale*, with garlic, capers and olives).

Again, in meat dishes, capers have a place, particularly in dishes which might otherwise be too oily. In some of these dishes the sauce is greatly reduced, and the capers are almost dry and on the verge of being fried. When bitten into the sour salty caper in which the flavour has been enclosed, gives an explosion of new taste in the mouth with an effect which is interesting and refreshing. There are dishes of dry casserolled chicken or rabbit, often containing black olives as well as capers.

Capers play their part in butters (e.g. Montpellier butter), salads, hors d'oeuvre (e.g. *tapénade*), decoration (in which their strong flavour can be a mistake) and with Liptauer cheese.

Caper Spurge

IT: Catapuaia
BOT: Euphorbia lathyrus
FAM: Euphorbiaceae

This family includes such economically important plants as castor oil, rubber and cassava, as well as dogs mercury (*Mercurialis perennis*), many spurges well-known as weeds and the spectacular cactus-like euphorbias of the desert regions of America and Africa.

Spurges often contain a white milky latex and are exceedingly poisonous. (Castor oil seeds are extremely poisonous.) Dogs mercury and the common tropical decorative plant, *poinsettia*, are no exception. For this reason, perhaps, although the little green seeds of the caper spurge (which look rather like capers) are said to be good when pickled, authorities give this plant as poisonous. It is safer to avoid eating plants from this family altogether unless they are well-known as esculents.

Caraway

FR: Carvi, Cumin des prés
GER: Kümmel, Mattenkümmel, Wiesenkümmel
IT: Carvi, or Comino dei prati
SP: Alcaravea, Carvi, Kummel
BOT: Carum carvi
FAM: Umbelliferae
Plate II, No. 2 and Ill. 11, No. 3, page 144

This biennial grows over two feet high with typically umbelliferous creamy-white flowers and feathery leaves. It prefers a semi-shaded position and a moderately heavy soil, but there is not much difficulty in growing it, and it will self-sow if the seed is not collected. For leaf, it can be sown almost any time during the summer, but germination is rather slow.

Caraway grows wild in Europe and temperate Asia (Persia, India, Turkey and North Africa) but is not native to Britain. It has naturalized itself in North America. The wild seed is smaller than the cultivated seed but has a stronger flavour. Caraway has been used since ancient times. It was used by the Romans and is well established in most European cooking. It is grown commercially in Holland and over most of Europe, Russia, the Balkans and North Africa. A little is grown in England and the United States.

The young green leaves of caraway have a mild flavour, something between parsley and dill and quite unlike the pungent taste of the seed, though the flavour changes as the plant gets older. In the Middle Ages (and to some extent today [e.g. Norwegian Karvekål-suppe]), caraway leaves were used chopped in soups and salads exactly as we use chopped parsley or chervil. The spindly tap roots are also eaten cooked as a vegetable in some countries and are excellent.

Caraway seed was important in English cooking in Elizabethan times, but its use has declined. It was used with fruit, in cakes and bread, much as it is used in southern Germany and Austria to this day. Roast apples were always served with caraway and Falstaff was invited to 'A pippin and a dish of caraways' by Master Shallow (*Henry IV* pt. 2).

Children may have traumatic memories of 'seed cake' and many adults dislike it. In Austria, where they seem to use it in everything, constant vigilance is necessary. I can well remember sitting on the edge of my bunk in a mountain hut at two in the morning and trying to pick the caraway seeds out of the bread by the light of a candle. This impossible task was a prelude to almost every ascent I made in the Austrian Alps during my apprenticeship as a mountaineer. Perhaps it is due to old associations that I now enjoy the flavour.

Whether one likes caraway or not it is a useful spice

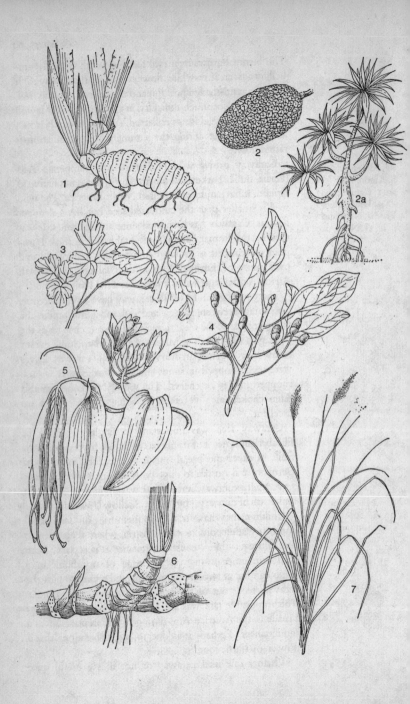

when used in unrecognizable amounts in savoury dishes. Caraway is a very German taste, and Germany and Austria are the world's biggest users. Of course, they use it in cakes and bread. It is used in cheese and with sauerkraut, and also goes into fresh cabbage dishes and salads. It is used in meat dishes (sprinkled over roast pork) and in goulash. While, to my mind, it is the ruination of the fine flavour of paprika, it undoubtedly gives that special taste to the crude alpine goulash one will eat hungrily on skiing holidays, even as far afield as the mountain huts in Czechoslovakia.

Caraway was sometimes coated with sugar to make 'sugar plums', a digestive. It is also, with cumin (and there is often confusion) the flavouring of the liqueur, kümmel, and some kinds of schnapps. Commercially, a caraway flavouring is made in the form of the essential oil obtained by steam distillation of the dry ripe seed. This oil is used in bakery, sweets, candy and other preparations. The most important constituent in this oil is carvone, which makes up over half of the total.

As a final word, a warning: many books on Eastern cookery give caraway as an ingredient in curry. This is nearly always a mistranslation and the ingredient should be cumin (q.v.), which tends to be used more than caraway in the East and tastes quite different.

Cardamom

FR: Cardamome
GER: Kardamome
IT: Cardamomo
SP: Cardamomo
BOT: Elettaria
  cardamomum
FAM: Zingibaraceae
Plate 1, Nos. 6, 6a, 7 and
  Ill. 18, No. 7, page 244

Cardamom is an eastern spice which came into Europe over the caravan routes, even in ancient Greek and Roman times, although it was then used mainly in perfume. It is said to have been grown in the royal gardens of Babylon over seven hundred years before Christ, but, if this is really true, it was well outside its natural climate and habitat. The plant is a perennial of the ginger family and forms a bush with large lance-shaped leaves, somewhat like palm fronds (though absolutely no relative) to about eight feet. It grows wild in the wet hill jungles of South India, often on the sides of ravines and under lofty tropical trees – the sort of place in which one keeps a sharp eye out for snakes. The

Ill. 4   Flavourings: 1 Orris, 2 Screwpine Seed, 2a Screwpine, 3 Maidenhair Fern (Capillaire), 4 Sassafras, 5 Vanilla, 6 Calamus, 7 Khas Khas.

stalks bearing the little seed pods (the part used) sprawl flat on the ground as they grow out from the base of the plant in a rather unusual way.

Today there are cardamom plantations in many tropical countries, including Central America. Usually the site is in partially-cleared forest, with trees left standing to provide some shade. The seed pods appear over a long period and do not all ripen at the same time, so they are gathered every few weeks. They are dried in the sun or over heat, and sometimes bleached white, though their natural colour is pale green or brown.

It is the dried seed pods which are bought in grocers' shops as cardamom. Though they vary in colour and length, they all have a roughly triangular section. As cardamom is an expensive spice, it is best to judge the quality before purchase. This can be done by pulling open a pod and examining the seeds inside. They should be slightly sticky, brown-black and with a strong aromatic smell and taste. Cardamom should never be bought ground as it rapidly loses its essential oils.

Cardamom seed is warm, comforting and vaguely like eucalyptus. It is an ingredient of many liqueurs and is used also in cakes and pastries in northern Europe – Scandinavia, northern Germany and Russia. Sweden, in fact, takes a quarter of the Indian production. It is also a spice greatly liked by the Arabs (Saudi Arabia is India's second customer), its use having been greatly spread about by Arab dhows trading from the Indian west coast ports, in the hinterland of which the cardamom originated. It is responsible for the peculiar and exotic flavour of Bedouin coffee. The long, beak-like spouts of their brass coffee pots are usually stuffed with a few opened cardamom pods. This imparts just sufficient flavour as the coffee pours past, and nothing is more characteristic of the infuriating frontier posts and police stations of the Near East than the taste of cardamom-scented coffee.

Cardamom is a vital spice in curries and pilaus, especially those from northern India and Pakistan. It is also used in discreet amounts as part of the spices in European meat dishes; for instance, in some recipes for German *Sauerbraten*. It is also useful in pickle and in the spices for pickled herring.

Cardamom is an excellent addition to punches and hot spiced wine. It can be used as a flavouring for custard if the bruised spice is steeped for a time in the hot milk.

There are several varieties of true cardamom (Malabar, Mysore, Ceylon etc.) and, within limits, their flavour and appearance are similar. But there are some fifty other species of plant closely related to the cardamom, and the seeds of some of these are sold as 'cardamom', although they may have quite a different appearance and a flavour often rather strongly of camphor. They are inferior, but are likely to be met with because real cardamom is expensive and many of these substitutes have become popular in the last twenty years. How recent is illustrated by the following:

When I was last in Bombay, an Indian friend of mine told me how, when dining out, he had discovered what he took to be a cockroach in his curry. He fished it out and called the waiter. The waiter called the manager who, in turn, called the cook. At this point, according to the classic Italian story, the cook should have eaten the cockroach, smacking his lips and exclaiming, 'You do not like zis *wonderful* little fish?' But the Indian cook respectfully pointed out that the cockroach was, in fact, a large hairy 'cardamom' seed. Whether it was or not I do not know, but such large, hairy brown 'cardamoms', though previously unfamiliar, are now becoming common. But, like cockroaches, they are best avoided.

Carrot

FR: Carotte
GER: Karotte (young spring), Möhre, Mohrrübe
IT: Carota
SP: Safranories (Catalan), Zanahoria
BOT: Daucus carota
FAM: Umbelliferae

Carrots grow wild in Europe, and the wild carrot is common in the hedgerows of Britain. The wild carrot is woody and somewhat poisonous. We owe it to French and German breeders in the sixteenth century who got rid of the poison and turned the rather unpromising root into the cultivated carrot.

Today one will find carrots in markets all over the world. There are many varieties and, in the best breeding, the fibrous central core has been completely eliminated. Most carrots are orange in colour but, in foreign markets, one finds white, deep purple and red varieties. The flavour is the same.

Carrots in small quantity are often used as a flavouring in

soups and stews and are an important part of marinades for fish. As the flavour of carrots is mostly in the skin or just under it, carrots should never be scraped or peeled. This is most important. The difference between peeled and unpeeled carrots is enormous. Very old carrots and some carrots sold in polythene bags develop a dead and slushy covering which must be scraped, so always buy fresh unwashed carrots where possible.

Carrots impart a certain sweetness as well as a certain aromatic quality to dishes in which they are included because they do, in fact, contain a large amount of sugar. In France, they were once tried as a commercial source of sugar.

Cassava
Bitter Cassava, Cassareep, Cassaripe

FR: Cassave, Manioc
GER: Maniok, Brotwurzle
IT: Manioca
SP: Canabe
BOT: Manihot esculenta (Manihot utilissima)
FAM: Euphorbiaceae
Ill. 2, Nos. 4; 4a, page 45

The cassava or tapioca plant (manioc, mandioc, yuca, yucca or jucca in Peru) is a native of South America and a vital food plant in most tropical and sub-tropical countries, though particularly so in South America and West Africa. The plants are perennials, growing a good nine feet high, and have the appearance of small trees. The roots end in very large tubers, and it is those tubers that are used as food. We know the prepared form as tapioca. Between a hundred and two hundred varieties of cassava are known, but there are two main types – sweet and bitter. The root of all cassavas is liable to contain prussic acid (cyanide), the poisonous principle in bitter almonds. Fortunately, prussic acid is volatile and is driven off in cooking.

The tuberous roots of the sweeter and less poisonous cassavas (sweet cassavas) can be eaten boiled, but these and the more poisonous bitter cassavas are often first grated and have their juice squeezed out. The solid part is then baked into cakes called cassava bread, but the poisonous milky juice can be reduced by boiling to an edible treacly substance, flavoured with spices and used in some West Indian dishes, particularly the West Indian pepper pot.

Cassia. *See* Cinnamon.

Catmint
Catnep, Catnip

Catmint is natural to calcareous soils in many parts of Europe and Asia and rather uncommon in southern

FR: Cataire, Herbe aux chats
GER: Echte Katzenminze
IT: Erba dei gatti
SP: Calaminta
BOT: Nepeta cataria
FAM: Labiatae

Britain. It is a common garden escape in North America. A perennial, it grows two feet high, or more, and the leaves and stem are covered with a whitish down: flowers, white with red dots, grow in dense whorls at the top of the stem. Catmint is easy to grow either from seed or by dividing plants.

Catmint has a rather odd minty taste and cats like to romp in it. Catmint tea was famous in Europe from Roman times and was once popular in North America. In the Middle Ages the leaves were used for flavouring meat, and young shoots were used in salads. Catmint is still said to be sometimes used for seasoning in France, though I have never consciously come across it.

Celery

FR: Céleri
GER: Sellerie
IT: Sedano
SP: Apio
BOT: Apium graveolens
FAM: Umbelliferae
Plate II, No. 8

Garden celery was developed mainly by the Italians during the seventeenth century from smallage, the wild celery of European salt marshes which was a very popular herb with the Romans. Celery began to come into general use in England and America only during the nineteenth century. Celery flavour before that was provided by smallage – which is poisonous when raw – or by lovage and alexanders which have slight flavour similarities. Smallage, even when blanched, is exceedingly bitter, and it was the breeding out of this bitterness that was the great contribution of the Italians. Today there are many horticultural varieties of celery, some of which are naturally white and usually called 'self-blanching', others being green but without bitterness. There are also summer and winter varieties as well as varieties grown for the root such as celeriac, Fr: *celeri rave*.

As a flavouring, celery is particularly important in soups and stews. In northern countries, the large salad types of celery are usual, but in hot countries, including Italy, one also finds in the markets the smaller, leafy, green and bitter types of celery used exclusively for flavouring. Celery leaves may be dried and are, in fact, used as a source of the essential oil of celery.

Celery seed is a useful flavouring, but is rather bitter. Celery salt is salt flavoured with celery and, in these days, it is a common commercial condiment.

Cheese

Cheese is one of the most ancient foods known to man. In the frozen Altai mountains of Siberia, a tomb was opened which contained still edible (though well-ripened) cheese made at the time of Christ. Cheese is used not only as an ingredient but also as a flavouring in many dishes. These range from a dressing for a green salad made with strong Roquefort to delicate Mornay sauce. In Italy, grated cheese can be regarded as a table condiment.

Italian cooking, in particular, includes small quantities of grated Parmesan cheese in a great many recipes, so much so that it sometimes seems as if they never leave it out. This gives a characteristic flavour to dishes of meat, fish, rice eggs and vegetables in which the cheese is kept below the level of recognition, as well as, of course, the dishes in which cheese is a dominant flavour.

But the number of different cheeses in the world must run into four figures, and it is exceedingly important to use the right cheese in the right dish. Serious cooks must possess one of the many excellent books devoted to cheeses. For instance, the correct flavouring for Mornay sauce is a mixture of Parmesan (It: *Parmigiano* or *Grana*) and Gruyère (*not* Emmenthal). Both these cheeses are sweet, and to use a pungent or acid cheese instead would produce a quite different result. Stronger cheeses of the same hard type as Parmesan and known as Pecorino are used much in southern Italy. One of this type – Sardo – is made in Sardinia, and is particularly popular in Genoa for making *pesto* (*see* Basil). In the Sardinian mountains one can sit beside the fireside on a cold November night, long after the tourists have gone and, over a glass of Oleana wine, crack walnuts, eat hunks of this Sardo cheese, *Carta di musica* (the paper-thin bread with the musical crunch), and watch a shepherd in baggy pants and Garibaldi hat make the Sardo cheese; gathering together the curd with horny, and not very clean, hands.

Chervil, Garden

FR: Cerfeuil
GER: Kerbel
IT: Cerfoglio

Garden chervil (there are several other plants also sometimes called chervil) is a close relative of the common cow parsley which whitens the hedgerows in early summer. Garden chervil's natural home is in southern Russia, the Caucasus and the Middle East. It was probably first brought

SP: Perifollo
BOT: Anthriscus
cerefolium
FAM: Umbelliferae
Ill. 6, No. 3, page 97

Cow Parsley
FR: Cerfeuil sauvage
GER: Gemeiner Kerbel
IT: Cerfoglio selvatico
SP: Perifollo silvestre
BOT: Anthriscus
sylvestris

Bulbous Rooted Chervil
FR: Cerfeuil bulbeux
GER: Knollenwürzliger
Kerbel
IT: Cerfoglio con bulbo
SP: Perifollo buloso
BOT: Chaerophyllum
bulbosum

to Britain by the Romans and can occasionally be found growing wild as an escape.

Garden chervil has lacy leaves and, like parsley, there are also decorative curled varieties for garnishing. It grows to about eighteen inches high and has tiny white flowers in the usual 'umbels' of this family.

This herb can be grown without difficulty in almost any garden or in a window box, but it does not like hot dry conditions. It is an annual which quickly runs to seed. To maintain a supply of leaves one must sow it at intervals during the summer or cut the young plants back to root level when they reach two or three inches, as this encourages the production of leaves. A winter supply can be had only by growing it in boxes in a warm glasshouse.

Garden chervil is little grown in the United States or Britain, or indeed in any country other than France, but there it is important. Therefore, those who are interested in French cooking must grow it for themselves as it is not available in markets. Its flavour is delicate and much less robust than parsley, which it slightly resembles, but it has a distinctive aroma of its own – some say reminiscent of anise, others of liquorice. It is a herb which has to be used fresh – either chopped or in the tiny sprigs of leaf that the French call *pluches*. It is not a herb for long cooking but is used raw or added when the dish is almost ready and off the boil – for instance, sprinkled into soup just before serving.

Garden chervil is a usual herb in the *fines herbes* for an omelette. It is also one of the classic herbs in *ravigote* sauces, and in these – whether hot or cold – it never becomes strongly heated. It is frequently used in combination with tarragon but sometimes flavours sauces such as Béchamel or even seasoned fresh cream. Chervil is also used to flavour a white wine vinegar. It has all the usual uses in salads and garnishes.

Some authorities recommend herb yarrow as a substitute or, at least, as a garnish (*see* Milfoil).

One must not confuse garden chervil with the 'bulbous-rooted chervil', which is a vegetable and of a different genus of the parsley family. The root of garden chervil is said to be poisonous.

Chicory, Endive (U.S.A.)
Chiccory, Succory, Succery

FR: Chicorée
GER: Chicorie, Indivia, Hindlauf, Wegeleuchte, Wegwarte
IT: Cicoria, Radicchio
SP: Achicoria
BOT: Chicorium intybus
FAM: Compositae

Endive
FR: Chicorée endive
GER: Endivie
IT: Indivia or Endivia
SP: Endibia
BOT: Chicorium endivia
FAM: Compositae

Chicory is native to Europe, including Britain, and is commonly naturalized as a weed in North America. It has sky-blue flowers and is common on calcareous soils. The wild and unblanched plant is exceedingly bitter, but its use is ancient in Europe. Today there are many interesting horticultural varieties, the best known being the tight 'peg' of white leaves forced in the dark and known as *witloof* or *endive de Bruxelles*. But there are other varieties with a completely different appearance, for instance, the decorative pink and red salad plants known as *cicoria di Treviso* (*chicorée de Trevise*), popular in Italy and Switzerland.

Chicory leaves give to salads that touch of bitterness which many people like. The large tap root of some varieties is grown to flavour coffee (Fr: *chicorée à café*). The origin of the use of chicory in coffee is variously given as Sicily in 1769 and Holland *circa* 1800. It seems that it was first used as an adulterant. In 1832 it was forbidden by law in England but, as some liked the flavour, in 1840 it was once more allowed – provided it was properly labelled – which is as it should be.

For coffee, the tap roots are dug, washed, cut into pieces and dried in gentle heat. They are then broken into nibs and roasted. Naturally, there is variation in quality. The best is not very bitter. Such chicory has a caramel taste derived from the sugar in the roots and a characteristic flavour.

Endive is popularly called 'chicory' in the United States and *chicorée* in France, but endives in England. It is a very close relation to chicory and has been a popular salad plant in Europe for many centuries. In many countries the names are thoroughly confused.

Chilli (*see* Pepper, red).

Chinese Five Spices
Five Fragrances, Five Spice Powder

CANTONESE: Heung new fun, Hung-liu, Ngung heung
FR: Cinq épices chinoises, Cinq parfums
GER: Fünf Gewürze

This is a subtle Chinese spice mixture which may be bought in shops specializing in Chinese or Vietnamese foods. It consists of equal parts of finely ground anise pepper, star anise, cassia, cloves and fennel seed. It will be necessary in recipes from the Far East (e.g. *porc laqué*), but is also an excellent mixed spice particularly for pork dishes and is really worth keeping in the kitchen. I often use it for flavouring pigs' liver pâté. Spice mixtures – *see* p. 241.

Chive

FR: Ciboulette
GER: Schnittlauch
IT: Erba cipollina
SP: Cebolleta
BOT: Allium
   schoenoprasum
FAM: Alliaceae (Liliaceae
   or Amaryllidaceae)
Ill. 1, No. 7, page 40

Chives are a well-known member of the onion genus, native to the cooler parts of Europe, including Britain, where they can occasionally be found wild in dry rocky places. They also grow wild in Canada and the northern United States. Though used since antiquity, they were probably not cultivated until the Middle Ages. Chives have hollow, thin, grass-like stems, virtually no bulb and grow in clumps. The flowers are purple and make a decorative edging. They are perennial, easy to cultivate and will grow in any garden soil. They can be raised from seed, but are usually propagated by dividing the clumps. There is a large-leaved form known as the giant chive. Bunches of chives can be bought at most market stalls in Germany, Austria, Switzerland and Scandinavia, though less commonly south of the Alps.

The flavour of chopped chive is delicately of onion, and its bright green colour makes it an ideal garnish. Chives are used in sauces such as *remoulade* and *ravigote*, combined with eggs or cream cheese and sprinkled into soups, potato and other salads and buttered beetroots.

Chives cannot be dried by normal kitchen means, but can be quick-frozen satisfactorily and will keep for a little time in a polythene bag in an icebox or cool larder.

The larger and more strongly flavoured *cuchay* or Chinese chive belongs to another species (*see* Onion).

Chocolate

FR: Chocolat
GER: Schokolade
IT: Cacao (cocoa),
   Cioccolata, Cioccolata
   amara (bitter)
SP: Chocolate
BOT: Theobroma cacao
FAM: Sterculiaceae
Ill. 2, Nos. 2, 2a, page 45

The word chocolate comes from the Aztec *chocolatl* and *theobroma* means 'food of the gods'. Chocolate was used by this people long before the Spaniards reached Mexico.

Chocolate is made from the seeds or 'beans' of a tree native to the lowlands of tropical Central and South America. It has been cultivated for so long that there are probably no wild trees living today. In natural conditions this tree grows to some forty feet high but, as cultivated, it is usually only fifteen to twenty-five feet. It has dark green, shiny, leathery leaves, often a foot long, and the flowers and pod-like fruits hang on short stalks directly on the trunk and large branches. The fruits are something like ribbed and pointed melons, changing from green to yellow-orange or purple-red when ripe, and at this time it looks as if the trees were decorated for Christmas. Inside the fruit is a pinkish pulp, and in this are embedded the pale purple-pink 'beans' arranged in a column around the central core. Today there are many hybrids and varieties and thus considerable variation on this general description.

Chocolate was unknown in Europe or Asia until the sixteenth century. It was first noticed in 1502 when Columbus on his fourth voyage found it in the cargo of an Indian trading boat in the Gulf of Honduras, and it was brought to Spain by Cortes in 1520. At this time it was important as a drink amongst the Aztecs. According to Prescott, the Emperor Montezuma, required fifty jars a day.

To begin with, the Spaniards tried to keep chocolate a secret, but its use gradually spread over Europe as a luxury drink for the rich. The first chocolate house was opened in London in 1657, but high customs duty kept it outside the poor man's reach until 1825.

Today, cocoa beans are produced in many countries having a moist tropical climate, but notably Ghana and tropical America. Flavour depends not only on variety but also on the skill in preparation. After the ripe pods are cut from the tree, they are opened and the beans and juicy pulp scooped out. The beans are then fermented, an important process as the flavour of the bean develops through this fermentation (compare with Vanilla) as does the 'keeping quality'. Unfermented beans cannot be made into chocolate. Next, the beans are dried by being spread out in the sun and frequently turned over. It is during drying that the beans turn from purple to chocolate brown.

In this condition, the beans are shipped to the factory. There they are sorted and classed, then roasted. After roasting, they are broken into nibs, or small bits, and the brittle shell of the bean is winnowed away. The beans are then ready for grinding. This is a very long process, and the skill and thoroughness with which it is done is vital to the excellence of the finished chocolate.

The natural cocoa bean contains too much fat (cocoa butter) for a drink but too little for forming block chocolate. In 1828, a Dutchman, van Houten, discovered how to press out part of the fat. This process improved the drinking chocolate and on the other hand made it possible to make block eating chocolate, which is chocolate with sugar and some extra cocoa butter added. The indefatigable van Houten then treated his drinking chocolate with an alkali and thus developed cocoa. This darkened the chocolate and destroyed part of the flavour, but neutralized the acidity and formed traces of soap. The soap made the cocoa blend more easily with liquid. Later, in 1876, milk chocolate was invented in Switzerland by M. Peter.

So, drinking chocolate is light in colour, has a better flavour than cocoa, is somewhat fatty and usually contains a large amount of sugar. Cocoa is darker, less sweet and fatty, easier to mix, but lacking the fine flavour of chocolate. As for block chocolates, they contain a high percentage of fat and some sugar, but bitter cooking chocolate has less than eating chocolate. It is important for the cook to understand these distinctions.

Chocolate is used mostly as a flavour in sweet dishes (cakes, confections and sauces) and as a drink. The latter includes not only drinking chocolate and cocoa, but also a liqueur, *crème de cacao*, made by infusing ground cocoa beans and vanilla, cloves and mace, then distilling and adding sugar. It is usually unbearably sweet.

In Spain and Italy, chocolate is used as a flavouring with onion, garlic, tomato, oil and spices in meat dishes and even with fish and octopus. The flavour of the bitter chocolate blends well with savoury dishes, the result is interesting and a slight sweetness is both correct and necessary. In Mexico it is added to chilli powder.

Cocoa should not be confused with the coconut or with the coca (*Erythroxylon coca*) of South America, the leaves of which are chewed by the natives and contain cocaine.

Cinnamon and Cassia

Cinnamon

FR: Cannelle de Ceylan, Cinnamome
GER: Kaneel, Zimt
IT: Cannella
SP: Canela
BOT: Cinnamomum zelyanicum

Cinnamon and cassia, together with half a dozen other plants of the same family (Annam or Saigon cassia, massoia bark, Indian cassia, etc.), all provide products more or less of the same cinnamon flavour. In many countries these will be confused and treated as one article; in others (e.g. England), only the true cinnamon is allowed to be sold as such by law.

Cassia (known in many countries as Chinese cinnamon, *canelle de Chine*) is one of the oldest of all spices. It is recorded in China in 2500 B.C. and in Egypt in 1600 B.C.,

FAM: Lauraceae
Plate I, No. 11 and
   Ill. 19, No. 2, page 253

Cassia
FR: Casse, Canéfice
GER: Kassie
IT: Cássia
SP: Casia
BOT: Cinnamomum
   cassia
Plate I, Nos. 4, 10

and came into Europe over the spice routes from the East. Even today most cassia and cinnamon comes from the East.

True cinnamon is a more recent introduction. While cassia came originally from Burma, the true cinnamon is native to Ceylon and was known only to the natives there until it was 'discovered' by the Dutch.

Both cinnamon and cassia come from small evergreen trees or bushes, with something of the appearance of a laurel. The spice consists of the bark peeled from thin branches, and dried in the sun to form curled-up 'quills'. In cassia these quills are usually thick with the corky outside bark left on. In true Ceylon cinnamon the corky layers are planed away and the quills are packed one inside the other. The finest quality is pale in colour and looks like a roll of dried paper.

The flavour of cinnamon is more delicate than that of cassia and is not so pungent. It is also more expensive. It is better to use this in sweet dishes and cakes. Cassia nips the tongue and is more suited to spiced meats, pilaus and curries. The tree differs also from cinnamon in that the leaves, buds and even roots have much the same flavour as the bark. In true cinnamon, this is not the case. Dried cassia leaves (and the leaves of related spices) are much used in India (*tej pat*: often mistranslated 'bay'), especially in Bengali cooking (in expatriate shops confused with bay leaves), while cassia buds, in appearance vaguely like cloves, are available in Western shops. They are convenient when a little cinnamon flavour is required in meat dishes.

For use in sweet dishes, cakes and biscuits, it is usual to buy cinnamon finely ground as it is difficult to grind at home. It should be bought frequently and kept in closely stoppered bottles. (The tin of stale cinnamon on kitchen shelves is all too frequent.) To flavour syrups or to spice wines or creams, it is better to use fine quality sticks, which can be removed when their work is completed.

The use of cinnamon or cassia with meat dishes is not well-known in European or American cooking, but anyone who has been in Arab countries will recognize the effect of putting a small stick in a mutton stew: the flavour combina-

---

Ill. 5 Flavourings: 1 Hop, 2 Quassia, 3 Wood Avens, 4 Sweet Woodruff, 5 Gentian, 6 Sarsaparilla.

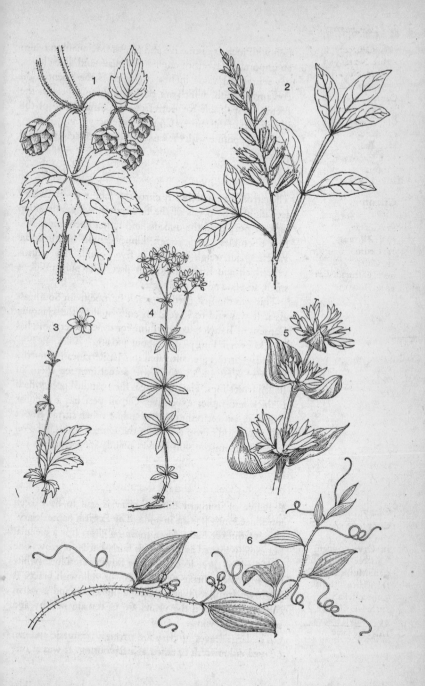

tion with meat is distinctive and pleasant. Cinnamon is also an important flavour of curries and pilaus and, like cloves, has a practical value in hot countries as the essential oil contains phenols, which are powerful discouragers of the bacteria responsible for putrefaction. Cassia is one of the ingredients of the famous Chinese five spices (q.v.).

Do not confuse with the cassia of the pharmacist which is senna pods!

Citron

FR: Cédrat
GER: Zitronat
IT: Cedro
SP: Cidra
BOT: Citrus medica
FAM: Rutaceae

The citron is a small thorny citrus tree (about ten to twenty feet high). The petals of the flowers are white and often pink or purple on the outside, and rather decorative. The fruit resembles a large rough skinned lemon and, in some varieties, can weigh as much as five pounds. The skin is very thick and is the important part. The pulp inside is small, acid and not of much interest.

This was the first citrus to reach Europe from Southeast Asia. It was said to have been cultivated in the Hanging Gardens of Babylon as a perfume for toilet waters, and has been known in Europe since about 300 B.C.

Today citrons are cultivated in Mediterranean countries and the West Indies. One will sometimes see them in Italian fruit shops. The main use is for a candied peel, which is thick and rather expensive. Citron peel has a peculiar aromatic, almost resinous taste unlike other citrus. About half the world's crop is used in the United States. The oil extracted from the skin is used mainly in perfumery but also in liqueurs.

Clary
Clary Sage

FR: Orvale, Sauge
  sclarée, Toute-bonne
GER: Muskatellersalbei
IT: Selarea or Erba
  moscatella
SP: Salvia silvestre
BOT: Salvia sclarea
FAM: Labiatae

A native of southern Europe, clary is said to have been introduced into Britain in 1562. The English name 'clary' comes from the Latin *clarus*, meaning clear. It is a biennial but usually treated as an annual: fairly hardy, it grows one and a half to three feet high. The flowers are bluish-white to white with purple-white, bluish or yellowish bracts. It is grown from seed and needs a light soil and a warm corner, especially if the plants are to remain healthy and survive a cold winter.

The large leaves of clary are strongly aromatic and can be used either fresh or dried as a flavouring. It was at one time used in combination with elder flowers to give wine the flavour of muscatel. Hence the German name meaning 'muscatel' sage. The essential oil distilled from this plant is used in perfumery and smells something like ambergris. The taste of the fresh leaves is aromatic and rather bitter.

Clary is not greatly used these days, but because, if looked after, it is available in the winter, it is a useful plant to have in the garden. 'When tender is not to be rejected in omelets; made up with cream, fried in sweet batter and eaten with sugar and juice of orange or lemon' (1699).

Clove

FR: Clou de girofle
GER: Gewürznelke, Nelke
HINDI: Laoong
IT: Chiòdo di garofano
SP: Clavo
BOT: Eugenia aromatica
FAM: Myrtaceae
Plate I, No. 5 and
Ill. 19, No. 6, page 253

Cloves are one of the best known of all the spices. Their native place is the islands of Southeast Asia, but they were used in China several hundred years before Christ, and were a caravan import well-known to the Romans. This is one of the spices of the Spice Islands and was at one time a monopoly of the Portuguese and Dutch. In the eighteenth century, cultivation was taken to other tropical countries, notably Zanzibar, Madagascar and the West Indies. Cloves flourish only near the sea, and today Zanzibar is the most famous clove-growing island. On a hot muggy evening when the light breezes filter through the trees, if one approaches the island from downwind one can smell cloves even before the land comes in sight.

Clove trees grow some thirty feet high – rather neat evergreens with clusters of crimson flowers. In practice one sees few flowers because, although all parts of the clove tree are aromatic, the buds are particularly so and are picked before they open. The fresh buds are pink. Dried carefully on palm leaf mats or over gentle heat, they turn red-brown and are then the cloves with which we are familiar.

Cloves vary considerably in size, appearance and pungency – depending on their age and where they come from. They should be well formed, oily and plump, and not shrivelled and dusty. However, cloves have such a strong flavour that it is really not necessary to shop around for them as one should for some other spices.

The characteristic flavour of cloves is due to an essential oil familiar, unfortunately, to most people from the dentist. It is a powerful, penetrating antiseptic, a fact that makes cloves doubly useful in pickles, broths and curries.

Cloves should be bought whole, not ground. If a little is needed in powder form, the central 'bobble' can be easily crushed. Cloves are often used stuck into an onion and common uses range from the stock pot to bread sauce and from *coq au vin* to ham with cloves and brown sugar. Another use is with apples, although this is frequently overdone. In the East, they go into many types of curry – often associated with cardamom and cinnamon – and into all sorts of pickle. Finally, they go into most recipes for spiced wine and many liqueurs.

Cloves are in a way a difficult spice to use because their flavour easily gets out of hand and becomes crude and over-powering. However, it is a spice that it would be difficult to do without, and a single clove in a beef stew or *pot-au-feu* – a common addition in France and Italy – is a typical case of good usage. One cannot taste the clove, but the beef is much less aromatic without it. On the other hand, the use of cloves with vinegar – either in pickles or in the spices for 'soused' fish, gives a rather 'tired' flavour. It may be a personal whim, but I often omit cloves from pickle.

Clove Pink

Clove Carnation, Clove
  Gillyflower,
  Gillyflower,
  Grenadine, Picotee

FR: Oeillet-giroflée
GER: Gartennelke
IT: Garofano
SP: Alhelí, Clavel
BOT: Dianthus
  carophyllus
FAM: Caryophyllaceae
Plate VII, No. 2

Modern carnations as often as not have had the scent bred out; but the old-fashioned pink has a beautiful, aromatic scent, rather like cloves.

Clove pinks are probably a native of the Mediterranean area but are now distributed from Normandy to the Punjab. In the past, as long ago as the Romans but also particularly in the seventeenth and eighteenth centuries, they were used as a flavouring and were floated in wine (an old custom was to float the petals in the glasses of engaged couples), and one variety was known as 'sops-in-wine'. They can be used in liqueurs (chartreuse they say, but the formula is secret) and cordials, to flavour vinegar, in salads (mainly as a decoration) and even in soups and sauces.

The flavour can be captured by pouring boiling syrup over the petals, leaving for some hours and then straining.

Clover, Sweet. *See* Melilot.

Coconut

FR: Noix de coco
GER: Kokosnuß
IT: Cocco
SP: Coco (fruto)
BOT: Cocos nucifera
FAM: Palmacea

The coconut palm is a native of Malaysia, although it now grows on tropical coasts all over the world, sometimes being cultivated quite a distance inland. The use of coconut and coconut oil gives a distinctive local taste to cooking. In the West, coconut is mainly used desiccated and is confined to sweet dishes and candy, but in much of the tropics, particularly in the East, it goes into fish and meat dishes as well as being a basis for some Indian chutneys. Very often coconut milk is used, and by this we do not mean the sweetish liquid in the middle of the coconut, but a milk or cream made by finely shredding the flesh, macerating for a short time in hot water, and then squeezing out the cream. This is similar in appearance to cows' milk but has a delicate taste of coconut. It may be obtained with less delicacy from desiccated coconut and some expatriate Indians nowadays use fine coconut butter. When fine coconut milk is called for in curries, it must somehow be provided, as cows' milk will not produce the same effect. If coconut cream is substituted for cream in making a custard, the result is delicious.

Coffee

FR: Café
GER: Kaffee
IT: Caffe
SP: Café
BOT: Coffea arabica,
Coffea robusta and
others
FAM: Rubiaceae
Ill. 2, No. 1, page 45

There are some twenty-five species of coffee of which a number are grown commercially, although *arabica* is the original and still the most important. The flavour of the others is inferior, but they have better qualities of disease resistance or heavy yield.

It is not certain whether coffee (*arabica*) originally came from Ethiopia or the Yemen. They are both mountainous countries and on opposite sides of the Red Sea. The usual story is that the plant was brought from Ethiopia to the Yemen. Dates given vary from A.D. 575 to A.D. 850, which makes it quite unknown in ancient Egypt, Greece or Rome. To begin with, its use must have been very local, for it took almost a thousand years to reach Cairo, at least in noticeable amounts, and the first coffee shop was not opened there until 1550. In 1600, Bacon noted it as something used in Turkey. The first coffee houses began to appear in London and Paris from 1650 onwards, and it then rapidly became popular (Lloyd's 1688). By the end of the century, plantations had been established in Ceylon and the East Indies and, early in the eighteenth century, the French took it to the

West Indies, from whence it reached Brazil in 1727. Today it is grown in almost every country with a suitable tropical climate.

Coffee is a small tree, but it is usually grown as a bush. It is a jungle plant and likes partial shade. The bushes are laurel-like in general appearance and bear beautiful white flowers like gardenias and with a sweet scent of jasmine. The berries are red when ripe, and about the size of a cherry. They grow in clusters. Each cherry contains two 'beans' – flat sides together, enclosed in a parchment envelope. Surrounding this is the pulp of the fruit which is sweet and much liked by monkeys, who will raid coffee plantations if given the chance. A small percentage of fruits contain a single rounded bean, instead of the two flat-sided beans and this is called peaberry coffee.

The sweet fleshy covering and the parchment envelope must be removed. In some of the finest coffees, this is done by first drying the whole berry in the sun (cherry coffee) but more usually the cherries are allowed to ferment slightly, and the then squashy covering washed off before the beans are dried in 'parchment'. In either case the beans are eventually separated, cleaned and graded to size. Peaberries are also separated from the normal flatsided beans.

Raw unroasted coffee beans are greenish or yellowish and have no coffee flavour. At this stage, up to a point, they improve by keeping. There are vast numbers of different types which, after roasting, will develop various degrees of aroma, body, acidity and colour. This is a field for the expert taster, and coffee is usually blended; the varieties with strong aroma and poor body may, for instance, be mixed with those of strong body and poor aroma. If coffee is for flavouring, however, it is preferable to ignore blends and to select entirely for aroma – for instance, the best *mocca*.

Many people say it is a pity that coffee does not taste as superb as it smells when it is being roasted. Unfortunately, this beautiful aroma is due to the most volatile of the essential oils, and these are greatly lost in roasting. To obtain the best coffee, the beans should be quickly and evenly roasted (eight to twelve minutes at 390°F., 200°C.). (Peaberry is superior because it is round and roasts more evenly.) If coffee is under-roasted, flavour is not developed.

If over-roasted, as is commonly done with inferior coffee it becomes bitter and the finer aroma is lost. As long as the coffee remains hot it will continue to deteriorate, so the moment roasting is finished it must be cooled rapidly. But even when cooled, essential oils will evaporate slowly, so the sooner it is used the better. Coffee is often roasted with a little sugar which helps to seal the outside of the bean.

On grinding, the essential oils begin to be lost at an even greater rate, and the oxygen in the air also begins to destroy the flavour. Even half an hour between grinding and using is sufficient to give an easily noticeable loss; so any home that values its coffee must be equipped with a grinder. This is not a fad, it makes the world of difference, and small electric grinders are both cheap and efficient.

Coffee should, ideally, be made with water which is not quite boiling – again this conserves aroma. It is significant that the countries that go in for percolators and espresso coffee – e.g. France and Italy – buy the worst coffee. The best goes to America, Germany and Scandinavia.

Fine grinding allows the goodness to emerge more easily and is more economical, but it does make the coffee difficult to clear. The best coffee is made in earthen pots with filtration. This is certainly the method of choice when strong coffee has to be made for flavouring. Even the best pre-ground vacuum packed or gas preserved coffees (as well as soluble 'instant' coffees and coffee extracts) are obviously not in the running.

For the most exquisite result, if expense is no object, very coarsely ground or cracked freshly roasted coffee is put directly into cream which is at room temperature, a process that extracts only the delicate, volatile part of the flavouring. Such cream has the fragrance of freshly roasting coffee without bitterness.

Not only the coffee beans, but also the leaves and bark contain alkaloid stimulants (such as caffeine) and, in some places, these are chewed or made into 'teas'.

Cola

Colah, Kola, Kolla
FR: Cola, Kola

Cola nuts are much used for chewing. They contain large amounts of two stimulating alkaloids, caffeine and theobromine.

The tree has a straight trunk and grows to a height of

GER: Kola
IT: Cola
SP: Cola
BOT: Cola nitida
(Cola acuminata)
FAM: Sterculiaceae

fifty or sixty feet. Although native to the forests of tropical West Africa, it is today cultivated in the West Indies, Brazil and tropical Asia.

It has large oval leaves, and the flowers are yellow outside, streaked inside with red. Clusters of pods are borne, each pod containing a number of nuts. These are either red or yellow and, when chewed, stain the lips.

The taste of cola nuts is at first bitter and then sweet. A simple drink can be made from them by powdering them and then boiling some of the powder for a few minutes in water. Cola is, of course, used in many soft drinks and is also used for colouring and flavouring some wines. Essence of cola nuts can be obtained for use in drinks or for flavouring creams.

Comfrey. *See* Borage.

Coriander
Chinese Parsley,
Japanese Parsley

ARAB: Kizbara and
many variations
FR: Coriandre
GER: Koriander,
Krapfenkörner,
Schwindelkraut
INDIA: Dhania, Kotimli
IT: Coriandolo
SINGAPORE: Ketumbar
SP: Coriandro, Cilantro
BOT: Coriandrum
sativum
FAM: Umbelliferae
Plate II, No. 7 and
Ill. 11, No. 1, page 144

A hardy annual, coriander grows up to two feet high with white, pink or pale mauve flowers. For seed it must be sown in spring and harvested immediately it ripens (August to September) or the seed will drop. But it is easier to buy it. For leaf, sow in succession during the summer. It is not too fussy about soil, can easily be grown in a box, and everyone who likes curries should grow it.

Coriander is native to southern Europe and the Middle East, though now grown all over the world. It is one of the most ancient herbs ('And the house of Israel called the name thereof manna and it was like coriander seed, white; and the taste of it was like wafers made with honey.' *Exodus*, XVI, 31). The use of coriander – both in cooking and medicine – goes back many thousand years, not only in Europe but also in India and China.

In talking about coriander, we must distinguish sharply between the green leaf and the ripe seed. The taste is absolutely different. (The root is a unique Thai contribution to South East Asian food. It is used crushed with garlic to flavour meat and it also makes something specifically local out of curries introduced from India and soups derived from Chinese recipes. *See* S.E. Asian Food – Rosemary Brissenden. Penguin.)

The word coriander comes from the Greek *koris*, a bug,

because of a fancied likeness between the smell of the leaves and bed bugs. Most readers will not have experienced the joys of bed bugs, but if they have travelled rough in the East, they may be in a position to judge. There is really little similarity.

Green coriander is not much used in Europe, and in England it is usual to dismiss it as 'unpleasant' or 'not a kitchen herb'. This is nonsense. In fact, it is probably the most commonly-used flavouring herb of any in the world, being found in almost every market from Beirut through India to China and Japan and loved, not only in the whole of southern Asia, but also in the Americas in Mexico and South America.

Due to immigrants from Pakistan and the West Indies, green coriander is now to be had once more in Britain, but it was first introduced a long time ago by the Romans and was used in English cooking up to Elizabethan times. Then, like many other herbs, it fell out of fashion. Those people who have lived in India will immediately recognize green coriander as the essential flavour missing from expatriate curries. It adds a great deal to many types of curry and, ground with coconut, green chilli, salt and a squeeze of lemon or sour curd, is the basis for a most delicious and very common Indian chutney. Indeed, the flavour of green coriander marries particularly well with green chilli, and there is no better breakfast in the world than chapatties spread with coriander chutney and honey syrup and eaten in the early sunshine to the call of doves and barbets.

Bunches of green coriander can be recognized in markets, not only from the smell, but because the lower leaves are fanlike, the upper feathery. It is not a herb to dry but may be quick frozen or preserved with salt in oil.

The coriander has a spherical seed, is easily split in two, and varies when ripe from pale green to cream or brown. It can be bought from all good grocers, either whole or ground, for, being cheap, it is unlikely to be adulterated. But it should not be stale as, after grinding, it rapidly loses its best flavour.

The taste is sweet, aromatic and vaguely like orange peel. The way that this is related to the 'bug-like' taste of the green plant is clear only if you taste the ripening seeds over a period. In India, coriander seed is usually roasted gently before grinding, and this brings out a more curry-like flavour. However, there is a tremendous variation in coriander from sample to sample. Seed is extensively grown in Russia and Hungary, North Africa, India and South America, often for the production of the essential oil by steam distillation. Both the seeds and the oil are used commercially in bakery, liqueurs, vermouths and as condiments in food manufacturing.

In English or North American kitchens, coriander seed is mainly a pickling spice although old recipes included it in meat dishes such as steak, kidney and oyster pie. Probably its appearance is familiar to people who do not know it by name. In France it is seldom used, and only locally in Italy. But in cooking which has been influenced by the Arabs, coriander becomes most important. This would include the Middle and Near East, North Africa, the Balkans, Spain and Portugal – thence Mexico and South America.

In classical cooking, coriander seed is almost always used in dishes which are *à la greque*. It is used in the spicing of some sausages and goes well with fish. Roughly powdered, it is a flavouring for roast pork, lamb, the stuffing for kid or spicy meat dishes of many kinds from North Africa or the Levant.

By the time one comes to Indian, Malay or Indonesian cooking, coriander seed is used in large quantities and, if there is such a thing as a basic spice for curry, this is it. Because it is a mild spice, it has to be used by the tablespoon to balance other spices used by the teaspoon or less.

Coriander is also used in sweet dishes. In the Balkans, it is used in bread. It is used in the spice for some kinds of cake. The seeds are crystallized in sugar as 'sugar plums'.

Coriander seed should be on every cook's spice shelf, being one of the most interesting and neglected of spices; and green coriander is essential for those who like curry.

Costmary
Alecost (Britain),
    Bibleleaf (U.S.A.)

FR: Balsamite

This perennial is hardy, grows to a height of three feet and has yellow button-like flowers. It differs from tansy (*Tanacetum vulgare*) in not having feathery leaves, and has a pleasanter scent. In Britain it does not seed, so propagation is by division of creeping roots; in the United States it does

GER: Balsamkraut,
Frauenblatt,
Marienblatt,
Pfefferblatt
IT: Balsamite
SP: Balsamita
BOT: Chrysanthemum
balsamita (Tanacetum
balsamita)
FAM: Compositae

seed. It grows easily in most soils, but dries satisfactorily and can be bought from herbalists.

Costmary came from the East and was known to the Egyptians, Greeks and Romans (who probably brought it to Britain). Culpeper, the sixteenth-century herbalist, calls it 'common'. The colonists took it to America, where it now grows wild as a roadside plant in eastern and mid-western states.

It gets its name bibleleaf because the long leaves were used as bible markers by early American colonists, and alecost from ale (beer) and costis, a spicy herb. It was used for flavouring home-brewed ale. Costmary, therefore, means 'Mary's spicy herb' and can be used in soups, game, poultry and veal, forcemeats, salads and even in cakes.

Cottonseed Oil

BOT: Gossypium
FAM: Malvaceae

Cottonseed oil is expressed from the seeds which are a by-product of the cotton industry. The United States is the world's largest producer, and the refined and deodorized oil is used in making margarine and as a cooking and salad oil. In the East, and particularly in Egypt, a less refined cottonseed oil is one of the most common of all local cooking oils and creates regional flavours. A high-protein flour is made from the seed as well.

Cowslip

FR: Fleur de coucou,
Primevère commune
GER: Primel,
Schlüsselblume
IT: Primula
SP: Primula, Vellorita
BOT: Primula veris
FAM: Primulaceae
Plate VII, No. 5

The flowers of the common cowslip have a delicate, sweet scent and were once much used for making cowslip wine and a tea, supposed to be a soporific. The flowers were candied and used fresh in salads or as decoration. Until recently, cowslip flowers were sold in season in some country markets in the English midlands. Now, however, the cowslip is becoming scarcer in Britain due to modern agricultural methods and the destruction of natural meadows, so it is no longer easy to gather the quantities necessary for making wine.

The primrose (*Primula vulgaris*) has similar uses, and the young leaves are good in early spring salads, although, if one is sensitive to them, they may cause dermatitis.

Cress

There are several plants that come under the general name of cress or cresses. Most belong to the cabbage family and

FR: Cresson
GER: Kresse
IT: Crescione
SP: Lepidio
FAM: mainly Cruciferae

Watercress
FR: Cresson de fontaine
GER. Brunnenkresse
IT: Crescione d'acqua
SP: Berro de agua,
   Crenchas
BOT: Rorippa
   nasturtium-
   aquaticum
   (Nasturtium officinale)
FAM: Cruciferae
Ill. 16, No. 1, page 216

Garden Cress
FR: Cresson alénois,
   Passerage cultivée
GER: Gartenkresse
IT: Agretto
SP: Lepidio
BOT: Lepidium sativum
FAM: Cruciferae
Ill. 16, Nos. 2, 2a,
   page 216

American Cress
FR: Barbarée
   Roquette des jardins
GER: Barbarakraut
IT: Barbarea, Erba
   Sauta Barbara
SP: Oruga del jardín
BOT: Barbarea verna
   (Barbera praecox)
   and Barbarea vulgaris
FAM: Cruciferae
Ill. 16, No. 3, page 216

Brazil Cress
IT: Spilante
BOT: Spilanthes oleracea
FAM: Compositae

Indian Cress
IT: Tropeolo or
   Cappucina
BOT: Tropaeolum majus
FAM: Tropaeloacea

they all taste hot and peppery – more or less like water-cress. These are important plants for adding piquancy to many salads, for garnishing and in some chopped herb mixtures and sauces. More rarely they are cooked or used as flavouring in cooked dishes.

WATERCRESS is a native of Europe naturalized all over North America. It grows wild in streams, but because of the danger of infection from contaminated water (it was a frequent cause of typhoid in the past), it is today usually grown in specially prepared beds and tanks fed from pure springs or boreholes. Although watercress grows wild in southern Europe, it is far more popular in the north, probably because there is less choice of outdoor salads in winter.

The best watercress is dark green, bronzed or almost black, crisp looking and stems not overgrown with root-lets. It cannot, however, be judged only on appearance, and often the less fleshy looking cress has the better flavour. It should not be stored in the refrigerator, but put in cold water with the leaves just showing and kept in a cool larder. When needed, it should be washed quickly and not soaked for hours simply because it grows in water.

Watercress is used as a garnish in salads, with cheese and in sandwiches, but it can also be used to flavour soup, boiled to add flavour to 'greens', as a sauce for freshwater fish (made like parsley sauce) and in various chopped herb mixtures, e.g. with potatoes and in herb butters.

GARDEN CRESS (Land Cress, Peppercress, Peppergrass). This is the 'cress' of 'mustard and cress', an annual native to Persia but now established in Britain and North America. It grows twelve to eighteen inches high and has white flowers of typical cruciferous type.

This is a pungent salad plant. Besides its use as a very young plant in 'mustard and cress', there are also many horticultural varieties including the so-called Australian cress which has golden leaves.

Other species of wild *Lepidium* are also used at times and are commonly called 'peppergrass' or 'pepperwort'.

AMERICAN CRESS, Belle Isle Cress, Land Cress, Mustard Greens, Scurvy Grass, Spring Cress, Treacle Mustard, Treacle Wormseed, Upland Cress, Winter Cress, Worm-seed, Yellow Rocket. This cress is a close relative of the yellow rocket (*Barbarea vulgaris*) and has many popular names. It is a hardy perennial or biennial, a native of continental Europe but naturalized in Britain and the United States. It is rather similar in appearance to watercress, but the leaves are smaller and it has not such a delicate flavour. A very useful winter salad plant and substitute for watercress, it is both cultivated and gathered wild in spring, both in Europe and by Italian families in the United States.

Other cresses are the so-called Brazil and Para cresses, cultivated in warmer countries for salads. They are pungent. Indian cress, originating in Peru, is sometimes used as a name for the common garden flower, nasturtium (q.v.).

Cumin

FR: Cumin, Cumin de Maroc
GER: Kreuzkümmel, Stachelkümmel
INDIA: Jeera, Zira
IT: Cumino
SP: Comino
BOT: Cuminum cyminum
FAM: Umbelliferae
Plate II, No. 1, and
  Ill. 11, No. 4, page 144

This annual is delicate, as it is a hot country plant. It stands a foot high, but sprawls due to weak stems. The flowers are mauve and white. It can be grown from seed in warm situations in good sandy soil, but since it is the seed and not the leaf that is used, there is little point.

Commercially, cumin is grown particularly on the North African coast, Malta, Sicily, the Middle East and India. It is also grown in America. The dried seed is available whole or ground. If bought ground, it should be fresh, since as with most spices, grinding allows the aromatic oils to escape with a quicker loss of aroma.

Cumin came originally from the East, but it was being grown in the Mediterranean region many years before Christ and was used by the Romans as a substitute for pepper, even being ground to a paste to spread on bread. Because the seeds are somewhat similar to look at, there is great confusion between cumin and caraway in European languages, although the flavours are so very different. Indeed, in many places true cumin is known only to people who make *couscous* or Eastern or Mexican dishes.

Cumin was always used in cooking, but it also had medicinal uses. One of the strangest of these was to encourage a pale skin and, according to Pliny, the oil expressed from the seed was used by scholars who wanted to fool their teachers into thinking that they were working harder than they were.

The seed has a unique, pungent, aromatic flavour and is a very popular culinary spice both in the East and in Mexico and North Africa. It is very common in curries, but Indian cooks always say that it is not greatly liked by Europeans. Perhaps it is an acquired taste, although many Americans use it in spicy dishes such as *chili con carne* (Mexican). Cumin is also a distinctive and powerful spice (unlike caraway, whose flavour tends to blend into meat dishes, as one sees in Austrian cooking) and tends to dominate any dish in which it is included. It is absolutely essential on the shelf if one enjoys curries or Oriental, Mexican and other spicy dishes. In European cooking it is sometimes used in pickling (e.g., pickled cabbage), but never in sweet dishes, though it may enter into the liqueur, kümmel.

Great confusion is caused in many books because of the mistranslation of the Indian word *jeera* or *zira*. This usually means cumin and may have *safed* (white) or *kala* (black) added to distinguish different types of cumin. However, *jeera* is also used for caraway (not greatly used in India), for nigella (*Nigella sativa*. Indian: also *kala jeera* or more correctly *kalonji*) and for a plantain seed (*Plantago pumila*). Unless there is good reason to believe to the contrary, in curry recipes one should always assume that *jeera* means cumin and that caraway is a mistranslation and ought also to read cumin. One could never substitute one spice for the other without completely changing the dish.

Curry Leaf

HINDI: Katnim, Mitha neem
TAMIL: Karuvepila
BOT: Chalcas koenigii (Murraya koenigii)
FAM: Rutaceae
Ill. 19, No. 1, page 253

The peculiar smell of Madras curry powder is due largely to the leaves of the curry plant. In South India there is scarcely a garden without this plant, although in North India it is rarely used.

The plant is a native of southwest Asia and grows profusely at lower elevations in the forests of the Himalayan foothills. Anyone who visits the Corbett National Park in Kumaon will notice the strong appetizing smell of curry as their elephants bursts through the thickets and bruises the leaves of this plant, which in places forms quite a proportion of the undergrowth.

Ill. 6   Flavourings: 1 Fennel Stalk, 1a Fennel Bulb, 2 Dill, 3 Chervil, 4 Curled Parsley, 4a Plain-Leaved Parsley, 5 Sweet Cicely, 6 Alexanders, 7 Lovage.

Curry leaves may be bought dried or fresh from shops specializing in Indian spices, although the dried leaves have usually lost their flavour. They are only essential for those who make South Indian vegetarian dishes, but the flavour is interesting.

The word *chalcas* comes from the Greek for copper, and the wood of the curry bush has a copper-coloured grain. (There are many other species of *Chalcas*, including *Chalcas exotica*, the orange jasmin). Interesting facts about this tree are that lemons can be budded on to it and that it belongs to the same family as rue and lemons.

Curry Powder

FR: Poudre de cari
   (de curry)
GER: Currypulver
IT: 'Curry'
SP: Polvo de curry

The word 'curry' probably came from the Tamil (South Indian) word *kari* (a sauce). It has become the group name for almost any hot spicy dish originating in the East. As there are hundreds of quite distinct types of curry in India alone, it is as meaningful as an Indian calling everything European, from *coq au vin* to goulash, 'stew'. India has a highly refined culinary tradition, with the unique distinction that it has managed to solve the problem of making vegetarian food interesting and tasty.

In India, curry powder is rarely used. It is not just a question of freshly ground spices being more aromatic, but also that, as different proportions of spices go into different dishes, the uses of a pre-mixed powder are limited. The nearest the average Indian household gets to curry powder is in the *garam masala* which means literally 'hot mixture'.

Garam masala is in no way intended to be the entire spicing for a dish. It is only a basis. It is made at home – or bought in the bazaar – at frequent intervals and is a convenience because not only is grinding spices hard work but also the various ingredients have in many cases to be separately roasted before being ground. So it saves time to make a quantity. A *garam masala* might consist of half a pound of gently roasted coriander seed, half a pound of gently roasted chilli and an ounce of black pepper. This would be ground fine and stored in a tin with a closely fitting lid. There are many gradations of complexity from this to curry powder. Even in India, powders are sometimes made up for specific types of dish – an example would be *sambar* or *kolumbu* powder. Such powders, and also certain pastes ground with vinegar – such as *vindaloo* paste – can be obtained ready-made from Indian shops.

But what we call curry powder was invented for Europeans. It was no doubt first made for ships and East India Company servants returning to their homeland. (How few memsahibs learned Indian cookery when there were so many servants.) Curry powder is intended to be a complete spicing for a 'curry', but as curry recipes vary depending on what part of India they come from, so also do the recipes for curry powder. It is not a standard substance. This does not matter so long as it is intended only for making curry. Curry powder has, however, been adopted by English and Continental cooking, and it is used in dishes that have nothing to do with curries, so the lack of a standard recipe is a cause of confusion. It makes a world of difference to a dish calling for a little curry powder whether the powder selected was, say, the famous Vencatachellum's Madras Curry Powder or a continental powder tasting of little more than raw turmeric. This is something to which all cooks must be alert.

Readers interested in Eastern food should be prepared to roast and grind their own spices. Good results can be obtained with nothing more elaborate than an old iron frying pan, an electric coffee mill used for spices only and a fine sieve.

All the common and some uncommon ingredients used in the curries of India and Southeast Asia have been dealt with individually in this book, but it will be useful to give a short analysis of curries and curry powder in terms of the most common ingredients and their commonest Indian names.

BLACK PEPPER (*kali mirchi*) is a common ingredient of curry powder and curries. In some places long pepper, *pipel*, is also used. The hotness is different from that of red chilli, and it is aromatic. White pepper (*safed mirchi*) is rarely, if ever, used in curry.

CHILLI. The most important ingredient is the dried red chilli (*lal mirchi*), which is ground to a fine powder and controls the 'hotness' of the curry. Green chillies (*hari mirchi*) are also used; besides being hot they have a very distinctive taste. The seeds are particularly pungent and are sometimes omitted. Naturally, green chilli cannot go into a curry powder, but it may be included in a paste.

CLOVES (*laung*), CINNAMON (*dalchini*) and CARDAMOM (*elaichi*). Although these have different flavours, they blend together in curries and can be considered as a group. Only if one or the other is very dominant does it change the character of the curry, but together they produce a rich and aromatic quality.

CORIANDER (*dhania*). Coriander seeds are one of the most important of all curry spices. They are lightly roasted before grinding. The flavour is mild and rather sweet, and nearly every curry powder will contain large quantities. Indeed, this is usually the spice to be first considered in relation to the quantity of meat being cooked. It controls the basic flavour, just as chilli controls the hotness.

CUMIN is the Indian *jeera*, often wrongly translated 'caraway' in recipes, and there are several types (white and black) of varying strengths. The flavour is powerful and more in evidence than other flavours in the curry.

CURRY LEAVES (*karipatta*). These give the distinctive taste to Madras curry powder. They will quite change the taste of the curry if the leaves are fresh, but in my experience the dried leaves sold in shops have usually lost most of their flavour.

FENUGREEK (*methi*). Fenugreek seed, roasted and ground, is an ingredient of many curry powders but if over-roasted is very bitter. It is the dominant taste in many bought powders.

GINGER. Dried ginger (*sonth*) may or may not be used in some curry powders. Fresh ginger (*adrak*), which is less pungent, is available all over Southeast Asia and is a more usual ingredient in local curries or in curry paste. Ginger, naturally, makes a curry hot, and many people who can stand dishes hot with chilli cannot stand them hot with ginger. In India, ginger is often added as a digestive.

MACE (*tavitri*), NUTMEG (*taiphal*), ALLSPICE (*kabab cheene*). These and other spices may sometimes be used in curry, but they are less usual, and one would hardly regard them as everyday curry spices, though allspice is used in pilau and mace in curries from Malaysia.

MUSTARD SEED (*rai*). Brown mustard seed goes into many curry powders, but not for its hotness. When roasted dry, it acquires a strange nutty flavour, and it is much used after 'popping' in hot butter or *ghee* as a finishing for Indian dishes. Mixed powdered mustard in which pungency has been allowed to develop is rarely used in Indian preparations.

POPPY SEED (*khus-khus*) and LENTILS (*gram*). These give some flavour, but are usually added more to improve texture.

TURMERIC (*haldi*) gives colour to curries, and this is often its main function. Curry powders with too much turmeric taste raw and may have an earthy flavour, redolent of an abandoned spice cupboard. In many areas turmeric is dominant in fish curries.

Curries in Asia vary, but often contain onion, garlic, salt and usually a souring agent such as tamarind, lime, unripe mango or other sour fruit as well as other flavours derived from mustard oil, coconut, candlenut, lemon grass, galangal, dried prawns, asafoetida, crude sugar and so on. An idea of the enormous variation in recipes for curry powder can be seen in the following analyses. Each letter represents a different combination.

	A	B	C	D	E	F	G	H	I	J	K	L	M
Black pepper	1	1	4	1	1	1½	2	2	½	1	1¼	8	4
Chilli	1	2	-	1	8	1	3	2	6	8	4	-	-
Cloves	1	1	4	-	-	-	-	-	-	½	2	2	
Cinnamon	-	2	1	-	-	-	-	-	1	½	2	2	
Cardamom	1	1	1	-	-	1	-	-	1	½	2	4	
Coriander	8	6	-	8	6	8	8	8	8	8	8	8	8
Cumin	-	2	4	2	1	-	1	1	1½	4	2	6	4
Curry leaves	-	-	½	-	½	-	-	-	-	-	-	-	-
Fenugreek	-	½	-	2	1	-	1	-	1½	-	1	-	-
Ginger	1	-	-	1	-	2	-	1	-	-	-	-	-
Mace, Nutmeg, Allspice	-	1	1	-	-	-	-	-	-	-	-	-	-
Mustard Seed	-	-	-	½	1	-	-	2	-	-	-	-	-
Poppy seed, Lentils	-	-	-	1	-	-	-	-	-	-	-	-	-
Turmeric	10	-	-	5	-	10	4	2	2	3	2½	-	-

Numbers indicate parts by weight.

Daikon

This is a large white type of radish commonly grown in Japan. It is eaten cooked or raw, but also is grated and the expressed juice used as a flavouring in bean curd stew etc. Japan probably uses more white radish than any other country in the world.

Dandelion

FR: Dent de lion
   Pissenlit
GER: Hundeblume,
   Löwenzahn,
   Milchdistel,
   Mönchkopf,
   Röhrlkraut
IT: Dente di leone,
   Soffione
SP: Amargón,
   Diente de león
BOT: Taraxacum
   officinale
FAM: Compositae
Plate VII, No. 1

In its natural wild form, it is rather tough and very bitter, but there are improved cultivated varieties.

Dandelions as a salad plant are particularly valuable in winter and may also be cooked like spinach, preferably mixed with sorrel. They have a strong action on the kidneys, hence some popular names in France and Germany. Other names come from the jagged shape of the leaves, supposed to resemble lions' teeth.

Dandelion wine is made from the petals of the flowers. The leaves and the root are used to give bitterness to herb beers (dandelion and nettle, dandelion and burdock and so on). Dandelion root roasted, dried and ground is used as a coffee substitute, like chicory. It contains no caffeine, is considered to be a sedative and is often sold in health food shops.

Dill

FR: Aneth odorant,
   Fenouil bâtard
GER: Dill, Till, Tille
IT: Aneto
SP: Eneldo
BOT: Anethum
   graveolens
FAM: Umbelliferae
Plate II, No. 5 and
   Ill. 6, No. 2, page 97

Dill is a herb important for both its seeds and its leaves. Its origin is variously given as southern Europe and western Asia, but in either case it has been used for a long time in Europe: certainly it was used by the ancient Greeks and Romans and spread north into central Europe in medieval times, if not before. It is a typical plant of the parsley family, with yellow flowers in umbels and feathery thread-like leaves, very similar to fennel, but much smaller, growing only to about three feet high.

The flavour of the leaves is also quite different from fennel, distinctive, perhaps a little towards parsley but not like anise. The flavour of the seed is quite unlike the green leaf, being bitter and rather like caraway, due to the presence of the same essential oil (carvone).

Dill is an annual, easily grown from seed sown in spring and thriving in almost any soil. It is hardy, but prefers a

---

Ill. 7   Flavourings: 1 Tamarind, 1a Tamarind Pod, 2 Sumac, 3 Nigella, 4 Wood Sorrel, 5 Common Sorrel, 6 Sheep Sorrel, 7 Round-Leaved Sorrel.

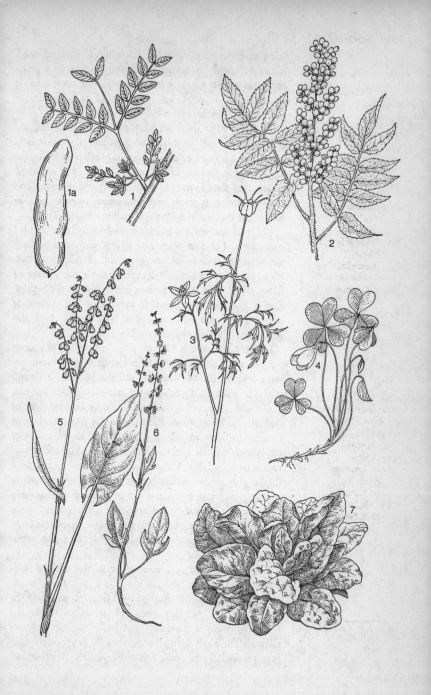

warm position out of the wind. If left, it will often self-seed. It can be bought in some continental markets as a green herb, but usually if one wants green dill one must grow it oneself. It can be dried, but loses most of its flavour in the process. It can be satisfactorily quick frozen.

In southern Europe from Spain and Portugal to Bulgaria and Rumania, dill may be found growing as a cornfield weed, but it is not a common herb in Mediterranean cooking, except in Greece. Dill is more popular in Scandinavia (where they tend to overdo it), Germany and in central and eastern Europe. It is, for instance, a very popular herb in Russia, the Balkans and Rumania, also in Iran and Turkey.

The best known use of dill is undoubtedly in pickled cucumbers. These are soured by a lactic fermentation (as is sauerkraut or sour milk), and green dill, usually the whole plant together with the half ripe seeds, is the dominant flavour. In North America these are known as dill pickles. Dill is also used sometimes in sauerkraut and, indeed, it seems to go especially well with sour dishes. It is also macerated in vinegar to make dill vinegar.

In parts of northern Europe, dill is often used as a sauce for fish as an alternative to fennel sauce (e.g. in Germany with eels). In Russia, Rumania and the Balkans, it figures with cucumber and with yogurt and sour cream – sometimes with all three together. It would be an ingredient in stuffed vine leaves from Rumania, if not from Turkey or Greece. In these regions it is also often added to dishes containing spinach, and to casseroles of chicken and mushrooms or baby lamb. Occasionally it is chopped and added to the dish at the outset, but dill loses its aroma during cooking, so more often it is put in just before removing from the fire. In both Scandinavia and southeastern Europe and Turkey, the flavour of dill is strongly characteristic of the cooking in the places where it is used. Dill is also popular in parts of Russia.

Dill seed is used as a condiment in the same way as caraway. However, its main use is as a source of dill oil. Essential oils are steam distilled both from the seed and the 'weed' of dill. Another species of dill called Indian dill (*Anethum sowa*) is also used and has a slightly different flavour. These oils are used commercially as a food flavouring, particularly in commercial dill pickles. Another use, well known to most of us, is in dill water or syrup, optimistically given to crying babies as a digestive and soothing medicine.

This is a useful herb, well worth growing, and, if used with discretion, it can bring a range of new flavours to our cooking.

Elder
European Elder

FR: Sureau noir (tree)
Baie de sureau (berry)
GER: Holunder (tree)
Holunderbeere (berry)
IT: Sambuco (tree)
Bacca di sambuco
(berry)
SP: Saúco (tree)
Baya de saúco (berry)
BOT: Sambucus nigra
(European elder),
Sambucus canadensis
(American Elder)
FAM: Caprifoliaceae
Plate VII, No. 7 and
Ill. 8, No. 2, page 114

Elders are common small wayside trees of Europe, West Asia and North America, and there are many species. The common elders of North America and Europe have large clusters of white flowers and, later, masses of tiny purple-black berries. The trees when bruised or broken have a decidedly unpleasant smell, but some people advocate an imitation bamboo pickle made out of the young shoots.

Elder flowers, either fresh or dried, are the basis for many old-fashioned tisanes, which are supposed to be both healthy and to promote sleep, but elder flowers are also a useful flavouring. They give off a sickly aroma, which some say is like muscatel grapes; at any rate they were once used in Europe to flavour up inferior Moselle wines. Angelica was also used for this purpose, and, like angelica, elder flowers are used to flavour stewed fruit, jellies and jam. The taste goes particularly well with gooseberry jelly, the jelly being stirred with a spray of elder flowers until it has picked up as much of the flavour as is needed. The flowers can also be fried in batter.

The best known use of the berries is for elderberry wine. They were at one time used on the continent to give colour to grape wines and particularly to port. The flavour of elderberries is quite strong, not all that pleasant and rather bitter, although the unpleasant taste disappears if the berries are dried. In small quantities they can be used with apples or other stewed fruit and to add colour to crab-apple jelly. In some countries of northern Europe (such as Denmark), elderberries make a fruit soup served with cooked apple and dumplings or fried bread. Elderberries also form the basis of a ketchup (*poulac*).

Elecampane

Elecampane is a plant with yellow daisy-like flowers, growing three to four feet high – sometimes taller. It is a

FR: Aunée, Hélène, Inule
GER: Echter Alant
IT: Enula (campana)
SP: Enula campana
BOT: Inula helenium
FAM: Compositae
Plate V, No. 8

native of Europe and northern Asia and has been naturalized in America. In the past it was much grown in England, mainly as a country medicine, but the root was candied and, certainly until well into this century, various sweets were flavoured with it.

Elecampane can easily be grown in the garden in a moist situation with some shade. The roots should be dug in the autumn. The whole plant is aromatic and may be used as a flavouring. It should not be confused with the golden samphire (*Inula crithmoides*). Its other close relative is the ploughman's spikenard (*Inula conyza*), a fairly common plant on chalky soil in England and Wales.

Endive. *See* Chicory.

Essences

Essences are essential flavours extracted by maceration or distillation and bottled, usually in an alcoholic solution. Unfortunately, during extraction, we lose some of the finest overtones of flavour. At worst, commercial essences contain synthetics or cheap substitutes. It is best not to use any essences unless they are made and guaranteed by a first-class manufacturer, in which case they may be expensive.

Common essences used by the trade are: allspice, almond, anchovy, basil, caraway, cardamom, cassia, cayenne, celery seed, cinnamon, cloves, coriander seed, fennel, garlic, ginger, lemon, mace, marjoram, nutmeg, orange, peppermint, pineapple, raspberry, ratafia, spearmint, strawberry, vanilla, and 'peardrops'(jargonelle or amyl acetate).

At home, one should probably limit essences to: finest peppermint oil (if you make your own peppermint creams); rose-water, *kewra* and orange flower water; and perhaps a good coffee essence for creams, mousses and ices (although it is far better to start with freshly roasted beans). (*See* Spirits and Liqueurs; Oils, essential.)

Fennel

Fennel is a hardy perennial often grown as an annual. It is a large plant, standing up to six feet high, with yellow flower

FR: Anet doux, Fenouil
GER: Fenchel
IT: Finocchio
SP: Hinojo
BOT: Foeniculum
vulgare, var. dulce,
sativum etc.
FAM: Umbelliferae
Plate II, No. 6 and
Ill. 6, No. 1, page 97

heads and bright green feathery leaves. It can be grown very easily in any ordinary soil from seed sown in April and will stand for several years, especially if it is not allowed to flower.

Fennel is used both as a herb and for its aromatic seed. There are also varieties grown for the bulbous stalk bases (Florence fennel) and for the stalks (*carosella*). These are popular vegetables, particularly in Italy, but they require careful cultivation in a suitable climate to be of much value.

Fennel is native to southern Europe, where it has been used since time immemorial. The Romans used it a great deal and, no doubt, were responsible for introducing it into Britain. It was later taken to America and today in California it is one of the most common naturalized weeds. Commercially, fennel is grown for seed in many countries, particularly in France, Germany and Italy, but also in India, Japan and America. Indeed, there is scarcely a country outside the humid tropics where one will not find fennel being grown for seed. The leaf can be dried by modern methods or quick frozen, although it does not keep very well in the refrigerator. It is best to arrange a fresh supply, and one plant will suffice the average family.

The flavour of fennel varies greatly according to the type. Wild fennel is slightly bitter and has no anise flavour. Sweet (or Roman) fennel, on the other hand, lacks the bitter principle and tastes strongly of anise. In fact, it contains large quantities of the essential oil, anethole, which makes up ninety per cent of the essential oil in anise itself. Bitter fennel is the type most cultivated in central Europe and Russia, whilst the sweet fennel is the type usually grown in Italy, France and Greece. It makes quite a difference which type is used for flavouring.

In English cookery, fennel was well established before the Norman Conquest and was traditional all over Europe in its use with both fresh and salted fish. Indeed, so firmly did fennel become linked with fish that very poor people on fast days are said to have eaten fennel alone, whilst the rich ate the fennel with the fish. Fennel is still used with fish, in the court bouillon for fish, as fennel sauce, finely chopped in mayonnaise and in stuffing. Perhaps the most curious use of fennel is in the well-known Provençal *grillade au fenouil*, in which *loup de mer* (sea bass), red mullet, or sometimes trout is grilled and then flamed in brandy on a bed of dried fennel which burns and imparts a unique flavour.

Fennel is particularly good with pork (Italy), with sucking pig and in marinades for wild boar. Finely chopped, it can be used with veal and in soups, vinaigrette sauces and salads. Italian cooking in particular contains recipes in which the flavour of fennel is an important part. The green seed of wild fennel is especially nice and is often included in the bouquet used for cooking snails.

The seed of fennel is a useful spice with a flavour something like anise but not so sweet. It had a great reputation in medicine long before the green plant was used as a culinary herb and, with dill, is still a common ingredient of the gripe water given to babies. It is, in fact, a good digestive and, according to some authorities, also an aid in slimming; but its uses in cooking are not many. In Florence, there is a kind of salami called *finocchiona* flavoured with fennel seed. In India, it is sometimes used in curries, but even more frequently as a digestive breath sweetener to be chewed after meals. The vegetable variety of fennel, known as Florence fennel or *finocchio*, is a kind of 'bulb' formed by the swollen bases of the stalks. The flavour of this vegetable when raw is very delicately of anise and it is liked in salads by almost everybody. Less well known is the variety of fennel known as *carosella* or *cartucci*, which makes a feature of the peeled stems and is popular in southern Italy. Fennel is used in the preparation of various alcoholic drinks and the liqueur, *fenouillette*, depends on it. Fennel root was one of the flavourings of sack, a drink based on mead and popular at the time of Shakespeare.

Fenugreek

FR: Fenugrec Sénegré, Trigonelle
GER: Bockshornklee or Griechisches Heu
INDIA: Methi
IT: Fieno greco
SP: Alholva, Fenogreco
BOT: Trigonella foenum-graecum
FAM: Leguminosae

Fenugreek is from the Latin *fenum graecum*, 'Greek hay'. A native of western Asia, it has been grown, as its name suggests, in Mediterranean countries since ancient times and is now naturalized there. It is occasionally cultivated further north as part of seed mixtures for forage. In general appearance it is something like a clover with a tiny pea-like flower. The seeds are bitter with a faint but characteristic smell and they contain a yellow colouring. They are used as a spice in the countries bordering the eastern Mediterranean, such as Greece and Egypt, but fenugreek will most

(Papitionaceae)
Plate II, No. 10 and
Ill. 10, No. 6, page 136

often be met with as an ingredient of Indian curries. For this purpose it is usually lightly roasted before grinding so that it just changes colour; if over-roasted it turns red and is then very bitter indeed. To begin with the flavour and scent of fenugreek seed is not strong – though it is very variable in both size and flavour – but after roasting and grinding if it is kept for some days the characteristic smell of cheap curry powder (or poultry spice) develops. Many people do not like this, others do not like a curry without. Fenugreek contains coumarin and is a usual ingredient of bought curry powders. It has a reputation for preventing wind, a reputation it certainly does not share with other members of the pea-bean family.

Fenugreek is also important for its green leaf, especially in India where it is curried as a vegetable. I have experimented with it cooked as a spinach in the Western manner, but it is exceedingly bitter and rather unpleasant when prepared in this way. Curried as in Indian recipes, where bitter plants are often used, it is excellent and, as it is very easy to grow in the garden (viable unroasted seed can be bought as a spice in Indian shops), I can recommend growing it to those people who enjoy Indian food. Other species of *Trigonella* are also eaten in India, and there are both wild and selected garden varieties, so there can be considerable variation depending on where the seed has come from.

If fenugreek seed is sown in boxes and grown to the two-leaf (cotyledon) stage like mustard and cress, it makes a five-star salad when dressed with oil and vinegar. The taste is refreshing, new and unusual. I learned this from an American family living near Bombay. They had found that it was doubly useful where market green salads were risky. Home grown fenugreek provided a fresh clean salad which even the young children could eat safely.

Fines Herbes

FR: Fines herbes
GER: Küchenkräuter
IT: Verdure Tritate
SP: Hortalizas

This is a fixed combination of three or more delicate herbs, used to flavour certain dishes. The herbs, as used in French cookery, are usually parsley, tarragon, chervil and chives. Other herbs may be called for in particular recipes.

The most common use of fines herbes is in omelettes, but they may be called for in many other dishes. In older books, fines herbes may also mean a mixture of chopped mushrooms and shallots, also called *duxelles*.

Fishy Flavours

Many fish or shellfish have virtually no fishy flavour at all if cooked and eaten when completely fresh: the fish as an organism is dead but the cells are still living.

We know fish of this sort only in restaurants where they are kept alive in tanks or when we buy fish still kicking on the slab. Raw 'live' fish as eaten, for instance, in some parts of Holland or in the East, have no fishy taste. The flavour is marine, tasting of the sea, until it has been kept for a few hours. Caviar eaten on the shores of the Caspian has also no fishy flavour whatever.

If the ideal is fresh fish, then most people do not like the taste of fish which is slightly stale. But man has always liked the frank taste of carrion and fish that has really 'gone off' or been changed by fermentation stands high on the list. Some of these products are almost unbelievable. While writing this book I brought home from Sweden a tin of *surströmming*. My recipe: send the family away for the day and then open the tin at the bottom of the garden, standing upwind and holding a spade. After relishing the horror of it, bury it quickly and pretend you have tasted it.

There are many more reasonable preparations of fermented, dried or salted fish to be found throughout the world. An example would be anchovies, stockfish (dried unsalted) or salt cod (Fr: *morue*) which forms the basis of many famous dishes such as the *brandade de morue* of Provence, *bacalao* and typically Mediterranean Friday dishes in which salted fish (after soaking) is cooked with potatoes and black olives. All of these dishes taste strongly of fermented fish and would be quite different and less interesting if made with fresh fish.

In the East a great deal of sun dried fish, shrimp, shellfish, squid and octopus is eaten. For instance, 'Bombay duck' is the dried body of a small gelatinous fish (*Harpodon negerus*). The beaches of the fishing villages near Bombay are planted with huge racks of this and other fish hung up to dry in the tropical sun. The smell of these villages is rather like a fish glue factory. Bombay duck and other dried fish delicacies, such as Japanese dried squid, have recently come into vogue as sophisticated 'cocktail snacks'. Dried octopus is another world-wide commodity, and the beaches in some places (for instance, Mauritius) are at some seasons festooned with these cephalopods drying in the sun. *Beche-de-mer*, or *trepang*, which the Chinese use to make a soup and which commonly enters Malaysian recipes, consists of sun dried sea cucumbers (wrongly called sea slugs) which are primitive animals shaped like a cucumber but related to the starfish and sea urchin. Balachan (Balachong, Blachan etc) or Malacca Cheese and Trasi come from the coasts from India to Vietnam and have many variations. They are essentially pastes of high dried prawns and are very important flavourings in South East Asian cooking. Anchovy is no substitute.

There are a number of important sauces and condiments derived from fish by processes of fermentation: *garon* (old Greek), *garum* and *liquamen* (Latin). *Garon* was used in ancient Greece six or seven hundred years before Christ, and similar products were used in cooking and as a sauce at table by the Romans ('the best strained *liquamen* ex-factory of Umbricus Agathopus. Pompeii'). Small fish, entrails and all, were fermented in brine for two or three months, and the liquid strained off. Apart from leaving in the entrails and valuing the liquid more than the fish, this process is remarkably like the present day method of curing anchovies. It is probably a direct descendant that Italians to this day use the liquid from anchovies, or even salted herrings, as a flavouring; whilst in Egypt and the Sudan a powerful sauce called *faseekh* is made by fermenting small fish with salt in old petrol drums.

Similar processes are used to produce the Nam Pla of Thailand, the Ngapi of Burma and Ngnoc-nam the national condiment of Vietnam. Vietnam is rich in fish, not only from the sea but also from the tributaries and delta of the Mekong River and the flooded paddy fields. *Nguoc-nam* varies considerably in flavour and quality, the best being made from fish fillets, and is called *phu-quoc* after the island it comes from. It is said that there is no Vietnamese meal without *nguoc-nam*. It may be poured over rice or served in a small dish beside each plate into which are dipped the morsels of fish or meat. The sauce is usually adjusted with lemon juice, sugar, garlic and red pepper. The flavour, to me at least, is reminiscent of fish glue, but these sauces are full of amino acids, nutritious and wholesome. In Vietnam a few drops of *nguoc-nam* are put into babies' feeding bottles. Because of the historic connection, one can buy Vietnamese foodstuffs in France or eat them in restaurants.

Another example of a flavouring sauce from southeast Asia is *prahoc*. The heads are cut off small fish and they are put in baskets, well-trampled and then washed by repeated dunking in water. This gets rid of the scales and entrails. The water is then pressed out between banana leaves under heavy stones and the fish mixed with salt (one part salt to ten of fish), dried for a day in the strong sun, pounded and packed in earthenware jars to ferment. Every day over a period of about a month, the juice that comes to the top is taken off. This is *prahoc sauce*. (*See also* Ketchup and Anchovy).

Fruits
Ill. 8, page 114

The acidity of fruit is due to various organic acids, and the sweetness to sugars, mainly fructose and glucose. (*See* Sugars.) Unripe fruit contains quite a lot of starch which changes to sugar as the fruit ripens. The relationship between sweetness (q.v.) and sourness (q.v.) is critical in determining a well-flavoured fruit.

Fruits of many kinds – unripe, ripe or dried – are used all over the world as both souring agents and sweetening agents in sweet and savoury dishes.

Fruits have also their own, often strongly individual, flavour. Flavour as well as acidity may differ sharply between the ripe and unripe fruit (e.g. in mangoes), or between the rind, pulp and seeds, (e.g. lemons and peaches). It may also change completely on cooking or drying (e.g. blackcurrants and figs). Fruits vary greatly in the way they change with canning, deep freezing, storage and transportation. Sometimes essential oils or synthetic flavours are added to commercial fruit products to bolster or imitate flavours lost in preparation. In the kitchen a liqueur or *eau-de-vie* may be used for a similar purpose, or small quantities of other fruit, such as quince or lemon, added to improve flavour.

Fruit flavours with meat and vegetables, while common in parts of the Middle and Far East, are less so in English cooking though, in a limited way, popular in America Often the fruit is served as an accompaniment to be eaten with the meat or fish at table, but it is difficult to draw the line between garnish, sauce and flavouring. Some examples follow:

APPLES: with goose and pork (many European countries), but in the Middle East baked apples stuffed with chicken; with sauerkraut or red cabbage (Germany and Poland); with fish mixed with horseradish or cooked in a pie with herrings (Yorkshire).

APRICOTS: with pork and in sauces (Europe, the East and South Africa).

CHERRIES: with duck; and crystallized cherries with chicken (Middle East).

CRANBERRIES: as a sauce with turkey.

RED CURRANT: jelly with mutton, hare, oxtail soup.

GOOSEBERRIES: for sour sauces; and with mutton (Middle East).

GRAPES: with sole and partridge.

ORANGE: with duck.

PEARS: braised with meat (South Africa).

PINEAPPLE: with pork, ham and veal (Danish).

PLUMS: sour and sweet with meat (Middle East).

POMEGRANATE: juice with meat (Middle East).

PRUNES: with pork and bacon (Europe); and in mutton stews (Arab).

QUINCES: with pork and goose or with other meat (Persia).

There are also a number of wild fruits – often very astringent – such as sloes, rowan berries and crab apples, which have their uses. As the use of fruit with meat, fowl and fish can create very interesting combinations and, as this aspect of flavouring is often neglected, I commend it to your attention and creative genius.

Galangal

FR: Souchet long, Souchet odorant
GER: Galangawurzel, Galgantwurzel

There are two galangals – greater and lesser. They are closely related, although the lesser is the more important. Greater galangal is of the ginger family and is native to Indonesia. The spicy roots, larger than those of the lesser, are covered with knobs and, though both are red-brown outside, the greater is pale yellow or white inside. The

IT: Galanga
SP: Galang
BOT: Greater galangal:
Alpinia or Kempferia
galanga; Lesser
galangal: Alpinia
officinarum
FAM: Zingiberaceae
Ill. 18, Nos. 2, 2a,
page 244

flavour is rather like ginger, and it is used in regional curries.

Lesser galangal is the rhizome of a plant native to southern China and used there since antiquity. It is also mentioned in ancient Indian writings. The plant is perennial with racemes of showy flowers. The roots are small. redbrown on the outside and pale red inside. The flavour is something between pepper and ginger. This was once an important spice in Europe and is still used in liqueurs and bitters. In Southeast Asia (Indonesia and Malaya particularly) it is an important ingredient in many dishes and one of the spices that distinguishes the cooking from that of India. It is locally known as *laos*, *leuqkuas* or *kah*.

Galangal should not be confused with 'Galingale', an old word for both galangal and the roots of the sedge – e.g. chufa nuts.

Garlic

FR: Ail
GER: Knoblauch
IT: Aglio
SP: Ajo
BOT: Allium sativum
FAM: Liliaceae
(Amaryllidaceae,
Alliaceae)
Ill. 1, No. 8, page 40

From the Anglo-Saxon *Gar* (a lance) and *Leac* (a pot herb).

Garlic is probably native to Asia but has been cultivated near the Mediterranean since the days of the ancient Egyptians. Today it is grown in warm climates all over the world. There are many varieties: some with bulbs of white skin, others with pink or mauve skin. The bulbs vary greatly in size, as do the size and number of cloves they contain. Some cloves are very small but there are also giant forms. The flavour varies with both variety and climate. Some garlic is mild, sweet and almost nutty, other is strong. The best garlic comes from warm countries. Garlic grown in cold or damp areas is liable to be rank and ill-flavoured.

Garlic prefers fairly rich, light, well-drained soil. Given this and sufficient sun it is easy to grow. The bulbs are broken up into individual cloves and planted about two inches deep and six inches apart in the row. In warm countries planting is in autumn, but further north this must be delayed until early spring. When in summer, the bulbs are mature and the tops begin to turn colour, the plants are pulled and dried off for storage.

Good garlic is hard, the cloves are not shrunk away from

Ill. 8 Fruit Flavourings: 1 Crab Apple, 2 Elder, 3 Rowan, 4 Cranberry, 5 Sloe, 6 Quince.

the paperlike sheath, and there are no discoloured spots. In certain seasons it is difficult to find garlic in such perfect condition and, if one is forced to use faded cloves, all discoloured spots must be carefully cut out. Discoloured garlic has a bad taste and will spoil any dish. In countries which rely on home-grown supplies, it is nearly always going off at the end of the storage season, and before the new crop has come in. On the other hand, in early summer, the new garlic in the markets has often been harvested too soon, and this also is inclined to have a rank flavour.

In Britain, garlic was undoubtedly used more in the past than it is today when, in spite of some revival, many people still will not use it – for social reasons. It is the same in North America. This is not a factor in countries where everybody uses it, although the early morning train of workmen who have been wolfing raw garlic for breakfast can be a little overpowering. However, the more modest aroma of cooked garlic is scarcely noticed and drinking red wine is said to give further improvement. Provençal girls can be safely kissed.

Garlic is exceedingly healthy. It contains antiseptic substances which tone up the digestive system; it reduces blood pressure and clears bronchitis. In the past it was known as 'poorman's' or 'churl's treacle' (treacle originally meant an antidote for poisons, stings and bites). The Roman soldiers ate garlic as a stimulant before going into battle and it was also given to cocks before a fight. 'Mariners would almost as lief go to sea without a compass as without a plentiful supply of garlic in the stores.' Yes. I never set out on an expedition without a few knobs of garlic in my pocket. Garlic is a very concentrated flavouring and it improves a vast number of dishes. There are panic-stricken exhortations in Anglo-Saxon cookery books 'to use a very little', but many wonderful dishes contain a great deal of garlic and, if one is going to be hung, why not enjoy being a wolf.

If a very little flavouring of garlic is required, the standard method is to rub the bowl with a clove, or rub it over the joint, and so on. Slightly larger quantities are most easily prepared by rubbing the clove on a plate against the slightly upturned points of a fork. For still larger quantities, the cloves may be put through a garlic press or finely chopped.

A quick Spanish trick is to put the clove under the kitchen knife and squash it with a sharp blow before chopping. Cloves of garlic are often rather difficult to peel. Another trick I learned from my Spanish maid was to hold the point of the clove concave side downwards against a plate and gently squash down with the thumb. The flesh snaps loose from the paper-like casing. In her rough peasant cooking, the whole crushed clove, skin and all, was then thrown into the pot – not a bad idea as one can fish it out intact before serving, although she did not. The flavour of raw garlic can also conveniently be introduced into dishes as garlic butter (to be added at table by those who like it), as garlic-flavoured oil (in which a roughly broken clove of garlic has been shaken) or as pieces of toast or stale bread that have been rubbed with garlic. There is also garlic vinegar (which is vinegar in which garlic has been macerated) and garlic salt (which may be bought as a commercial product or made at home by pounding garlic with salt).

The flavour of garlic is pungent and cannot be described in terms of onion. Some authors attempting to classify flavours (an impossible task when the scientific basis of the sense is not understood) have listed 'garlicky odours' as fundamental. Garlic has both flavour and pungency when eaten raw, as in the very strong raw garlic sauces (such as the *aïoli* of the South of France and Spain, and the *skordalia* of Greece). In lesser quantities, it has flavour only, without pungency, and the quantity is very critical. Indeed, garlic demonstrates clearly the principle of the adjustment of flavouring described on pages 29–30.

The flavour of cooked garlic is rather different from that of fresh garlic and interesting taste results are obtained by combining raw and cooked garlic. For this reason a fish soup already containing garlic may be served with croütons rubbed with fresh garlic and a *rouille* containing raw pounded garlic. In Catalan sauce recipes half the garlic may be pre-roasted and half used raw.

Garlic is used in the everyday cooking of the whole of southern Europe, the Middle and Far East, Africa, the West Indies, Mexico and South America. It blends with all meat, game, fish, shellfish and most vegetables and herbs. It is often married with parsley and mushrooms and seems to bring out the flavour of the latter. It would probably be an easier task to list the dishes in which garlic is not used, than those thousands in which it is. Garlic is probably the greatest flavouring discovery man has made – after perhaps the onion – and it is significant that it plays an important part in all the countries which have the best food – ranging from France to China.

Garlic Mustard

Alliaria, Donkey's Foot,
Jack-by-the-Hedge,
Onion Nettle,
Sauce Alone

FR: Alliaire
GER: Lauchhederich,
Lauchkraut
IT: Alliaria
or Aglliaria
SP: Erisimo
BOT: Alliaria petiolata
(Sisymbrium alliaria)
FAM: Cruciferae
Ill. 16, No. 6, page 216

A common hedgerow plant, it is native to all temperate Europe and Asia, and has been naturalized in eastern Canada and the United States. It is perennial or biennial, has white flowers and grows two to three feet high. The coarsely-toothed nettle-like leaves have a strong smell of garlic when crushed.

Garlic mustard was once commonly used as a flavouring and salad herb. It was eaten with bread and butter, boiled as a pot-herb, fried with herrings and bacon and, in Germany, was used as a salad with salt meat. It acquired the name 'sauce-alone'. Some authorities say that this was for the reason it suggests, but more probably the word 'alone' is derived from some Latin-rooted word for garlic – *allium*. This plant may crop up in the old country recipes. It tends to lose its flavour in cooking, but is excellent raw in sandwiches with cheese or meat. The clusters of flowers make a pretty garnish.

The related hedge mustard (*Sisymbrium officinale*) has yellow flowers and is common in English hedgebanks. Known in the eighteenth century as 'yellow julienne' it is also a wholesome though very pungent plant and is used occasionally in France. (*See* Rocket.)

Gentian

FR: Gentiane
GER: Enzian
IT: Genziana
SP: Genciana
BOT: Gentiana lutea
FAM: Gentianaceae
Ill. 5, No. 5, page 83

We usually think of gentians as plants with beautiful blue flowers, but the species mostly used as a source of bitters, *Gentiana lutea*, has yellow flowers. It grows in the Alps, Carpathians, Balkan Mountains and further eastwards in other suitable mountain areas. The root of this gentian tastes sweetish at first, and then horribly bitter. It is used in apéritifs, especially those originating in the Alpine regions. Examples are *suze* (France), or *enzian* (Austria). Some people get to like the flavoured bitterness of gentian root, but it is surely a taste with which we are not born.

Geranium
Pelargonium,
  Rose Geranium

FR: Bec de grue,
  Géranium rosat,
  Pélargonium
GER: Geranie, Pelargonie
IT: Pelargonio or
  Geranio odoroso
SP: Geranio
BOT: Pelargonium
  capitatum
  (Pelargonium
  graveolens) and also
  Pelargonium
  ororatissimum
FAM: Geraniaceae
Ill. 9, No. 4, page 123

Pelargoniums, native to South Africa, were introduced to Europe in 1690, and began to be cultivated by the French perfumery industry for 'rose geranium oil' in 1847. Pelargoniums are now grown commercially in many warm parts of the world – southern France, Spain and North Africa. Particularly famous is the oil from the island of Réunion.

Good rose geranium oil, almost indistinguishable from oil of roses, shows much variation in aroma (caused by soil and climate), even in plants grown from cuttings from the same parent. There are also a number of varieties; lemon geranium, orange geranium, apple geranium, nutmeg geranium and so on.

The plant is not frost hardy, but can be easily struck from cuttings and then planted out after all danger of frost is past, in a sunny, well-drained position allowing about three feet between plants; cut it back and bring indoors or place under glass for the winter.

All the green parts of the rose geranium are aromatic, particularly the leaves, yet the flowers are odourless. The plants are at their most fragrant just before they flower and when the leaves begin to yellow. At this time the lemon-like perfume characteristic of young leaves has changed to become more like roses.

In cooking, the leaves give an exotic scented flavour, something like rosewater. They are used for scenting fruits, sweets and jellies. Elizabeth David, in *Summer Cooking*, recommends two or three leaves per pound of blackberries as giving a wonderful flavour to blackberry jelly with which it has an 'extraordinary affinity'. She also recommends it with lemon water ice, for which she gives the recipe. The essential oils of the rose geranium are *geraniol* and *citronellol*, which are also the main constituents of attar of roses (not to be confused with European species of *Geranium* – e.g. Herb Robert or cranesbills.)

Ginger

FR: Gingembre
GER: Ingwer
IT: Zenzero

Ginger is one of the best known of all spices. The plant has long leaves and fat creeping rhizomes and at first sight vaguely resembles an iris, but a second glance shows that it belongs to quite a different family. It grows to about three feet high and the flowers are mainly yellow with a purple

sp: Jengibre
BOT: Zingiber officinale
FAM: Zingiberaceae
Plate I, No. 16 and
   Ill. 18, No. 6, page 244

lip, spotted and decorative. The 'root' – which is the spice – is known as a 'hand' and does look rather like a swollen hand with flat deformed fingers.

Though originally a denizen of the moist tropical jungles in Southeast Asia, ginger is commonly grown in gardens where there is some shade and a tropical climate. It has been used in Asia, from India to China, since the dim ages, and dried ginger had reached the Middle East and southern Europe even before Roman times. Indeed, it was one of the first spices to reach Europe from Asia. It was then thought to be an Arabian product. Because the fresh rhizomes keep alive for a considerable time, the Spaniards had no difficulty in transplanting them in their sailing ships to the West Indies. Ginger was quick to establish itself and, as early as 1547, it was being shipped to Spain from Jamaica. Today it is grown commercially all over the tropics from southern China and Japan to the Caribbean, Queensland, West Africa, India, Indonesia and even Florida.

Ginger was important in Europe during the Middle Ages, not only as a flavouring but also as a medicine. It was used against plague during the Black Death, and was perhaps of some help since it certainly promotes sweating (although the only person of my acquaintance who had bubonic plague and recovered, before the days of antibiotics, claimed that he owed his life to Scotch whisky). When your guests mop their brows after eating one of your special hot curries, it is usually because there is plenty of ginger in it.

FRESH GINGER. The fresh rhizome is commonly sold in the markets of countries where ginger grows. Nowadays, due to the influx of immigrants from India and the West Indies, one can also buy it in Britain. The hands should be plump, not shrivelled, the flesh firm and only slightly fibrous. The taste is milder and subtly different from that of dried ginger – it is difficult to describe except perhaps to say that it is less 'spicy'. Fresh ginger, peeled and ground to a pulp, is used in many types of curries. In tropical countries it is preferred to the dried spice for most purposes. It may be pickled in slightly salted vinegar. In Delhi there is a shop that sells a twenty-year-old pickle called *gillori* ginger. It consists of large wafer-thin slices of fresh ginger rolled into little triangular parcels around a stuffing of spices and pinned with a clove. It is immensely pungent and aromatic and, like *fernet branca*, will ostensibly cure any known ailment.

Fresh ginger, after scraping, may be preserved in strong spirit or sherry. It is also canned, crystallized in sugar or preserved in syrup. The finest preserved ginger is known as 'stem' ginger and contains very little fibre, being made from the youngest rhizome shoots. Ginger preserved in sugar is, of course, originally Chinese and is eaten as a sweetmeat, but it or the syrup is also used to flavour cakes and creams.

DRIED GINGER. The rhizomes may simply have been washed and dried with the skin on – in which case the product is usually dark, scaly and known as green or black ginger – or have been parboiled, skinned and bleached white. Often this second type has a fine powdering of lime preservative on the outside. It is reputed to be best. The classic way to use dried ginger is 'bruised' – this means hitting it with a rolling-pin or hammer to open the fibres and allow the hot aromatic flavour to escape.

POWDER GINGER. Ground ginger suffers from all the defects of ground spices. Poor quality ginger may have been used; it may have been adulterated; and ginger contains not only a pungent non-volatile resin but also a volatile essential oil which is responsible for that special ginger flavour but is easily lost in the air. The dedicated cook will use whole dried ginger: bruise it well to break it and then pound or grind it in an electric coffee mill kept specially for spices. The fibrous matter can easily be sieved out, and the powder used immediately will contain all the fresh aromatic ginger aroma.

In European cooking, ginger is mainly used in sweet preparations. Almost every country has its ginger-spiced breads, biscuits and cakes. Parkin; Ashbourne biscuits; Flemish, Dutch, German and Swiss gingerbreads; ginger toast and ginger snaps – the books abound also with ginger-flavoured puddings, creams and sweet sauces, not to mention ginger beer, ginger wine and cordials, 'dry ginger' and punches. As a table condiment it is used to sprinkle on fruits, particularly melons and peaches.

Ginger is one of the common spices for pickles, bottled sauces and chutneys, but it is unusual in Europe and North

America to find it used in meat and fish dishes. Items such as 'American ginger snap sauce' to go with meat or fish and ham cooked in ginger beer are sufficiently unusual to cause remark. In Asiatic cooking on the other hand, ginger is very much used with meat, fish and shellfish. Some books say that ginger should not be used with fish, but if the Chinese are any judge, this advice is incorrect. Indeed, ginger seems to have the power of neutralizing the more unpleasant fishy smells and, with the aid of ginger, a little sherry and grated turnip, one can make an excellent soup from a cod's head that would otherwise be presented to the cat. In the whole of the Far East, particularly in Korea, China and Japan, one will find many recipes for fish and meat that contain a little ginger, essential in their flavouring formula.

Ginkgo Nut
Maidenhair Tree

BOT: Gingko biloba
FAM: Ginkgoaceae
Ill. 17, No. 5, page 229

The maidenhair tree, a sort of living fossil originating in China and Japan, bears – on the female tree – small, foul-smelling, yellow plum-like fruits. The kernel, extracted after the fruit has been rotted off, is the ginkgo nut. This has an individual taste and is used as a flavouring in Chinese and Japanese cooking, as well as being eaten roasted as a nut. It can be obtained from specialist shops.

Grains of Paradise
Guinea Grains,
  Melegueta Pepper

FR: Graines de paradis,
  Malaguette,
  Poivre de Guinée
GER: Malagettapfeffer,
  Paradieskörner
IT: Grani di Meleguetta,
  Grani di paradiso,
  Mani guetta
SP: Malagueta
BOT: Aframomum or

These come from a plant related to cardamom, and are indigenous to the coast and islands of tropical West Africa along the Gulf of Guinea from the Congo to Sierra Leone. Part of this coast was once known as the Melegueta or Pepper Coast. Although it is grown in other tropical areas, most of this spice still comes from Ghana.

The plant grows to about eight feet high, has long leaves and showy yellow orchid-like flowers in dense spikes. The brown seeds are the spice and are formed in the pulp of a sour pear-shaped orange fruit.

Grains of paradise are hot and peppery and were formerly much used in cookery as a pepper substitute and

Ill. 9   Herb Flavourings: 1 Tarragon, 2 Pyrethrum, 3 Southernwood, 4 Geranium, 5 Vervain, 6 Lemon Verbena, 7 Comfrey.

Amomum melegueta,
Amomum granum
paradisii
FAM: Zingiberaceae

spice. They were also used with ginger and cinnamon to flavour the spiced wine known as hippocras. Even today grains of paradise find their greatest use in doctoring wine. (*See* Cardamom.)

Although grains of paradise are not commonly stocked by grocers, they can be found with some searching from druggists and may be needed by those who enjoy trying very old recipes.

Ground Ivy
Alehoof

FR: Herbe de Saint-Jean,
  Lierre terrestre
GER: Gundelrebe
IT: Edera terrestre
SP: Hiedra terrestre
BOT: Glechoma
  hederacea
FAM: Labiateae
Ill. 13, No. 2, page 168

A small creeping plant very common in Britain, growing in hedges and waste land. It has purple-blue flowers and is no relation to ivy. When bruised, it has a crude minty smell. Ground ivy was once used to flavour beer and was one of the 'Cries of London' in times past. Being so common and easily recognized, it is suitable for beginners to experiment with.

If the plant is dried in the shade at the time of flowering, the dried blossoms and leaves can be made into a tisane. Infuse 1 teaspoon of dried ground ivy in a cup of boiling water for 20 minutes then sweeten it with honey. This is said to be good treatment for coughs and colds. It was once used in beer, before hops, as a preservative and clarifier.

Harvey's Sauce

One of the old English sauces which may be called for in devilled dishes. In 1870, the Courts decided there was no exclusive commercial right to the name 'Harvey's Sauce', as there are recipes for it dating back to at least the seventeenth century.

Though there are many formulae, it is, in general, based on walnut and mushroom ketchup – flavoured with anchovy, garlic, and often soy sauce and vinegar. It has the appearance of Worcestershire sauce, but is not hot although it does contain some chilli.

Honey

FR: Miel
GER: Honig
IT: Miele
SP: Miel

Honey is the most ancient sweetening substance, and it is only in the last two hundred years that refined sugar has become sufficiently cheap to come into general use. Methods of getting honey vary from the highly organized commercial operations of today to the gathering of wild honey in the forests of the Sunderbans or by the pigmies in the Congo. In primitive societies, bees are often kept in hollowed-out tree trunks, and in some places, such as the forests of northern Persia, the hives must be hung high in trees out of the reach of bears.

An average honey would contain thirty-eight per cent fruit sugar, thirty-one per cent glucose, and seven per cent malt sugar as well as others. But percentages vary, and the higher the glucose the more easily it will granulate. However, honey almost always granulates with age – sugar crystals form – and the process can be accelerated by stirring. On the other hand, granulated honey, if kept for half an hour at a temperature just too hot to touch, will become runny and will not easily granulate again. So one can produce commercially the sort of honey the market prefers. Cane sugar, by the way, is not found in honey because although it is in the nectar of flowers, enzymes in the bees' saliva change it to glucose and fruit sugar.

Honey also contains gummy and fragrant ethereal substances, as well as organic acids and usually pollen grains, and there is enormous variation depending on the flowers it came from. The colour can be anything from white or cream to brown, red, purple, black or even sea-green. Even when fresh, it can be thick or very thin, as is often the case with wild or tropical honeys. But it is the flavour with which we are mainly concerned here, since this varies enormously. There are between two and three hundred sorts of honey in the United States alone. The most common honey comes from fields of clover and its relatives; from white clover and sweet clover, lucerne, alsike and so on. Clover honeys are mild and are the best for all-round cooking purposes; but there are specially flavoured honeys from orange blossom, grapefruit, sage, eucalyptus, raspberry, fireweed. Rosemary honey comes from Mediterranean hillsides, resinous honeys from pine forests, perfumed flower honeys from Grasse and the Italian Riviera, or from Alpine flowers. One can also get buckwheat, acacia, gooseberry, sycamore and, I have read, exotic green honey in red combs from Africa and black honey from Brazil. If you ever use such delicacies in cooking they should not be heated, as this drives off the aromatics.

Honey from some flowers, such as oleander, is poisonous

and some narcotic. Heather honey, from the Ling (*Calluna vulgaris*) is different from other honeys as it is gelatinous, the best full of air bubbles. It does not flow when the comb is cut. Honeys from other heathers are red and fragrant, but flow normally.

When honeys are heated in cooking, not only is the delicate aroma driven off, but the sugars caramelize. In dishes containing honey which are not cooked, the selection of the honey is critical, and there is plenty of scope for individual enterprise.

Hop

FR: Houblon
GER: Hopfen
IT: Luppolo
SP: Lupulo
BOT: Humulus lupulus
FAM: Cannabaceae
Ill. 5, No. 1, page 83

This well-known twining climber can be found growing wild in northern temperate regions (including England and North America) and in similar climates further south in mountains (e.g. southern Europe). Hops were cultivated by the Romans, but not in England until the sixteenth century.

The female flowers are small, green, fir-cone-shaped catkins. They contain resins and bitter aromatic substances (some of which, incidentally, are narcotic, which perhaps is one reason why beer makes people feel sleepy). These catkins are picked in late summer and dried in a gentle heat for use in brewing. Dried hops can be bought by those who wish to make their own beer or used as a source of bitterness, which is extracted simply by boiling the hops in water (*See* Beer). In commercial brewing, other bitter substances such as quassia are often used, but hops have also a preservative function.

Hops are easily grown and make a decorative screen for the garden (they twine in the opposite direction to runner beans). The male flowers and young shoots (*jets d'houblon*) are eaten in most hop-growing areas as a vegetable and are prepared with butter and cream as a garnish (*à l'anversoise*). Parboiled and dressed with oil and lemon juice, they are an excellent salad.

Horehound
Hoarhound

FR: Marrube
GER: Weißer Andorn

There are two distinct kinds of horehound, white and black. Black horehound (*Ballota nigra*) is not used as a flavouring. The plants are easily distinguished: white horehound has white flowers, while black horehound has pale

IT: Marrobio, Marrubio
SP: Marrubio
BOT: Marrubium vulgare
(white horehound)
FAM: Labiatae
Ill. 13, No. 5, page 168

purple flowers and is, moreover, covered with a white down on stems and leaves.

White horehound is native to Central Asia and Europe, and has been naturalized in North America. It is common on chalky soil in Britain. The flavour is aromatic and, to some, not very pleasant. It is used for flavouring candy (horehound candy) and horehound ale. Some recommend it for sauces, stews, salads and even cakes. Horehound tea is a remedy for colds and coughs, a cure that was known in the days of Gerard.

Horseradish

FR: Cran, Cranson de
Bretagne, Raifort
GER: Kren (South
Germany, Austria),
Meerrettich
IT: Kren, Rafano
SP: Rábano picante,
Rábano rústico, most
usually 'horse radich'
BOT: Armoracia
rusticana
FAM: Cruciferae
Ill. 10, No. 4, page 136

The horseradish seems to have gone through a large number of different scientific names. Books will give it as *Aromoracia lapathifolia* and *Cochloearia armoracia* (which would put it among the scurvy-grasses) or *Radicula armoracia* and *Rorippa armoracia* (which would put it among the cresses). To add still further to the confusion, some authorities claim horseradish was used by the Greeks one thousand or more years before Christ and in England before the arrival of the Romans, but De Candolle (1806–1893), in *L'Origine des Plantes Cultiveés*, lists horseradish amongst the species probably cultivated for less than two thousand years. My copy of the second edition of Gerard's *Herbal* (1633) implies that although horseradish was then known in Britain as a condiment, it was 'used in Germany'. The English preferred mustard.

Horseradish is native to eastern Europe and is commonly cultivated in northern countries, especially in northeast Europe. Being a tough plant which, once established, is difficult to eradicate, it has gone wild in parts of England and North America. On the other hand, it is little known in southern Europe. For instance, it is used in Italy from Turin to Venice, but rarely further south.

Although horseradish will grow anywhere except in badly-drained clay, in order to get good roots it is necessary to grow it properly on well-manured, not too heavy and well-drained land. It also prefers sun. Propagation is by planting sections of root, with or without bud. It is best to lift the roots in autumn, store them in damp sand or ashes and reserve sufficient for planting out the following spring.

Horseradish produces large docklike green leaves and

although the young leaves are good in salad, usually only the thick white roots are eaten. Roots have to be scrubbed clean of soil, and discoloured skin removed. Most of the pungency is found in the outer part of the root and not in the core. It may be prepared by fine grating or fine scraping with a sharp knife. This is tedious if the roots are thin and not well grown.

The flavour of horseradish is exceedingly pungent and apt to 'run up the nose'. This is due to volatile essential oils similar to those in mustard and formed by the same enzyme mechanism (*see* Mustard). If horseradish is cooked, pungency is not formed, and it is not of much use putting grated horseradish into hot dishes, as the volatile oils will be driven off. In any case, it rapidly loses its pungency after grating.

Horseradish is used either alone or with grated apple as a garnish for fish; as a flavouring for mayonnaise for use with fish or in salads of chicken, tomato or eggs; and in other more elaborate preparations. Horseradish sauces possibly have their origin in Germany, but have been in the repertoire of Scandinavia, Britain and northeastern France for long enough to be considered indigenous. Recipes usually but not always, contain vinegar and cream. Sometimes they are based on brown gravy, egg yolk and oil and hard-boiled egg yolk, also on white sauce. Occasionally these sauces are gently cooked or warmed, but more often they are uncooked. In France, they are usually more delicate, based on cream and lemon juice. In America there are recipes for iced horseradish sauces and dips.

In England today, horseradish sauce is popularly served only with roast beef, but it had a much wider use in the past. Horseradish goes well with fish, particularly fresh-water fish and smoked fish, with chicken and boiled fowl and with hard-boiled eggs.

Horseradish is also used to produce horseradish vinegar – by maceration – and there are old English recipes for horseradish pickle in which pieces of the root are preserved in vinegar. Horseradish may also be cut in slices and dried in a very gentle oven. It can then be pounded and bottled. Good commercial dried horseradish, particularly from Sweden and the United States, is available. It retains its pungency and is much better than the revolting bottled horseradish sauces or half-preserved grated horseradish as sold in some markets.

Horseradish Tree
Ben Tree, Drumstick

IT: Moringa
BOT: Moringa oleifera
(Moringa
pterygosperma)
FAM: Moringaceae
Ill. 3, No. 5, page 54

This is a small tree with scented white flowers which grows wild in the forests of the western Himalayas. It is commonly cultivated in India and southeast Asia and also, to some extent, in the southern part of the United States. It has run wild in the West Indies. The chief commercial use for this tree is the production of ben nuts, and ben nut oil is used in commerce.

The tree gets its name of 'drumstick' from its long pods. These have nine ribs and are up to eighteen inches long. Although rather fibrous, when cooked they have a meaty taste and are very distinctive in Indian vegetable curries. The small leaves are also used in curries or are pounded with green mango and onion as a flavouring for chutney. The name of 'horseradish tree' comes from the fact that the root is pungent like horseradish and is sometimes used as a flavouring.

Hyssop

FR: Hysope
GER: Eisop, Joseph,
Kirchenseppl, Ysop
IT: Issopo
SP: Hisopo
BOT: Hyssopus
officinalis
FAM: Labiatae
Ill. 13, No. 3, page 168

This pretty herb comes from southern Europe, the Near East and southern Russia. It is a common garden escape in parts of the United States, but is not wild in Britain. It is a shrubby plant, about eighteen inches to two feet high, with dark green leaves and royal blue flowers (there are also white or pink varieties). Hyssop is perennial, fairly hardy and prefers a sandy light calcareous soil. Propagation is from seeds, cuttings or division. It needs to be renewed every three or four years but is easy to grow.

Hyssop has been used around the Mediterranean since before Christ, though more in medicine than in cooking. Both the flowers and leaves are used, fresh or dried. The flavour is bitter and slightly minty with a dash of rue. It is much used in liqueurs. Some herb enthusiasts advocate it in soups, ragoûts or salads, and being decorative, fragrant and long lasting, it is a nice herb to have in the garden.

Juniper

There are many species of Juniper. They range from the dwarf juniper (*Juniperus Nana*) which grows high in the

FR: Genièvre
GER: Wacholder
IT: Ginepro
SP: Enebro, Junípero, Nebrina
BOT: Juniperus communis and other species
FAM: Cupressaceae
Plate IV, No. 2

Alps to species which grow into large trees and are found in the warmer countries. The species used as a flavouring (*Juniperus communis*) is found over the entire northern hemisphere including Britain. The plant is a bush, usually waist-high, and so exceedingly prickly that if one wishes to pick the berries one must wear strong gloves. The berries take three years to ripen, and, at any time, berries of several stages are to be found on the same bush. Only the ripe berries, which are blue, are used as a flavouring, and these are usually ripe in autumn, depending on altitude and locality. Juniper is usually found in separate male and female bushes, and, naturally, only the female bushes bear the berries. Juniper is easy to grow in most gardens.

Juniper berries vary considerably in strength, and, in general, the further south they grow the more essential oils they contain and the stronger the flavour. Berries from Italian hillsides may be two or three times as strong as those which grow in Sweden or Britain. The flavour of the ripe berries is sweet, aromatic and rather of pine because they contain elements of turpentine.

Juniper berries are used to flavour gins, steinhager and other spirits. The word gin is derived from ginepro or some similar word and not from the town of Geneva. Nowadays, of course, the flavouring in gin is often added in the form of distilled oil of juniper. This oil is also medicinal.

Dishes flavoured with juniper may be found in almost all European countries from arctic Sweden to Spain, but particularly in mountainous or wild areas where the plant grows – in Italy, central France and Provence, the Alps and Germany. It is used in marinades for wild boar, pork and venison; in stuffings for chicken, blackbird, thrushes and the countless other small birds indiscriminately slaughtered for food in southern Europe; and in pâtés. In Germany, juniper berries are a common flavouring for sauerkraut and are made into a conserve (*Latwerge*) for eating with cold meats. In English cooking, juniper was used more in the past than it is today, especially in curing ham, but I have known at least one Cumberland farmer's wife who used juniper in beef stews as a matter of tradition. Juniper berries are usually crushed before use. They go well with most other herbs – parsley, thyme, fennel, marjoram, bay – as well as with garlic, spices, wine, brandy and port when these are used in meat dishes, e.g. *Garenne à l'Alsacienne* (Alsatian wild rabbit with red cabbage, bacon fat, white wine and brandy).

Juniper is rather a neglected flavouring in English and American cooking. The berries may be bought dried although these are often quite useless (or the wrong species) or gathered during October holidays on the Mediterranean hillsides. It is the latter which are so aromatic with some of the best flavourings of European cooking. Other species of juniper with which this might be confused have red berries and are quite harmless, though lacking in flavour.

Ketchup
Catchup, Catsup

Usually ketchup in Britain and catchup in the United States, the word came to Europe from the East Indies in the late seventeenth century. It has many forms in the countries of the Far East – *ketsiap, keotsiap, kitjap, ketjap* and so on. It seems probable that ketchup originally meant the brine in which fish had been pickled or, in other cases, fermented fish extracts. (*See* Fishy Flavours.) Today a ketchup means almost any salty extract of fish, shellfish, fruits, vegetables or mushrooms. In exploring the cookery of an eastern country, one must only use a ketchup made in that country. Otherwise, the dish will probably be incorrectly flavoured.

TOMATO KETCHUP. This is really a sauce, but it is often used as a flavouring in modern English and American cookery.

MUSHROOM KETCHUP. This is the black juice of mushrooms, extracted by salt, then boiled and usually seasoned with pepper, herbs and spices. Although today it is a commercial product, it was once commonly made at home, and many recipes for it are to be found in old cookery books. Before pastures were improved by the application of basic slag and other fertilizers – which kill the mushroom – and when horses were common on every farm, the fields were white with wild mushrooms in summer. Previous generations gathered them by the clothes-basketful, and there were far too many for immediate consumption. As field mushrooms do not dry well, salted mushroom ketchup was a way in which these could be preserved. In continental Europe, where numerous other species of fungus are eaten, the tendency is to either pickle them (the ones that pickle well are the most prized in eastern Europe) or dry them, as is commonly done in Italy.

Today, however, when commercially grown mushrooms are always available and wild mushrooms are scarce, mushroom ketchup is much less commonly used. Nevertheless, it is a useful flavouring to have on the kitchen shelf. (*See* Mushrooms, Toadstools and Fungi.)

Old English cookery books also give recipes for many other ketchups, and these one will scarcely find today. Oyster ketchup, based on oysters with white wine, brandy and/or sherry, shallots, spices and salt. A poor man's version was mussel ketchup, based on mussels and cider. Windermere ketchup was mushroom ketchup with horseradish. Poulac ketchup was based on elderberries. Wolfram ketchup on ale, anchovies and mushrooms. One may also mention Irish walnut ketchup, fish ketchup and Prince of Wales' ketchup. These are mostly English concoctions of the eighteenth and nineteenth centuries, which would no doubt be of interest to anyone who could bother to make them. Recipes for many are given in older cookery books, for instance, in Cassell's *Dictionary of Cooking*, published at the turn of the century.

Turning now to the Far East, ketchup (or *ketjap*) will be found absolutely necessary in preparing Indonesian or Indonesian–Dutch dishes. The genuine articles are difficult to obtain, but must be obtained if a correct result is to follow.

Khas-Khas

Vetiver
IT: Vetiver or Andropagone
BOT: Vetiveria zizanioides, Andropogon muricatus
FAM: Gramineae (Poaceae)
Ill. 4, No. 7, page 70

Visitors who have suffered the hot weather in India will know the wet cooling screens erected over windows and doorways. These screens are often made from the root of the khas-khas grass, a close relative to the other aromatic grasses. (*See* Lemon Grass.)

Khas-khas is grown in India, Java, Réunion, Brazil and other hot climates. The essential oil from the root is used in perfumery and to flavour sherbets and sweetmeats. Khas syrup and khas water may be obtained from shops specializing in Indian products.

Lactic Acid

Though never used in its pure form as a flavouring in the kitchen, the taste of lactic acid is well known to us all in sour milk. In 1857, Pasteur discovered that bacteria were responsible for the souring of milk, and since then an enormous number of bacteria capable of doing this have been isolated. Such bacteria are very common and may be reckoned to be present on almost all unsterilized articles in the kitchen.

Lactic acid bacteria ferment simple sugars in the same way as yeasts, but because one enzyme (carboxylase) present in yeast, is absent in lactic acid bacteria, the end product is not alcohol but lactic acid. Some organisms will convert ninety-five per cent of the fermentable sugars to lactic acid: others form a mixture of lactic and acetic acid or similar volatile organic acids responsible for flavouring.

Sour milk products are of such importance that they have a separate section. Lactic acid fermentation also produces sauerkraut and sour cucumber (dill pickle) and develops flavour in other pickles. I have, for instance, a recipe from North India for spicy fermented turnip pickle.

Sauerkraut (German *sauer*: acid, *Kraut*: cabbage) is made by lactic fermentation of finely shredded cabbage with from two to three per cent of salt. The finely shredded cabbage is packed into tubs in layers sprinkled with the salt and kept down by weights under the surface of the liquid, extracted by osmosis from the cabbage. This provides ideal conditions for the growth of a sequence of bacteria producing lactic acid. The one and a half to two per cent of acid formed acts then as a preservative. In other words, it makes a pickle. In making sour cucumber, the bacteria act in a similar way. The making of such products at home is not as difficult as it sounds, for these are everyday peasant operations in some countries.

In sauerkraut, sugars have been largely if not completely used up, so we have an ideal vegetable for slimming. Lactic acid also has a good effect on the digestion and rapidly kills or immobilizes organisms that might cause tummy upsets or disease.

Lady's Bedstraw
Yellow Bedstraw

FR: Caille-lait, Gaillet

This common European and British wild plant is now a weed in parts of the eastern United States. It sprawls and has tiny yellow flowers. It was once used by people (presumably ladies) to sleep on because of its smell of fragrant

GER: Echtes Labkraut
IT: Caglio or Presvola
SP: Galio
BOT: Galium verum
FAM: Rubiaceae
Plate V, No. 9

hay. Belonging to the same family as the plant from which was extracted the dye, madder, a dye was also extracted from bedstraw, although its chief use is to curdle milk in cheesemaking as the juice acts in the same way as rennet. The name Galium is from *galion*, a plant mentioned by Dioscorides as suitable for curdling milk.

Lady's Smock

Bitter-cress, Cardamine,
Cuckoo Flower

FR: Cardamine des près,
Cresson élégant
GER: Wiesenschaum-
kraut
IT: Billeri, Crescione dei
prati, Cardamine,
Viola da pesci
SP: Cardamina
BOT: Cardamine
pratensis
FAM: Cruciferae
Ill. 16, No. 5, page 216

This common wild plant of moist meadows in Europe and North America is known to almost everyone for its pale pink-mauve or white flowers, the four petals of which are arranged in the typical cross of the family. Its alternative name, bitter-cress, suggests correctly that it is related to watercress and can be used in the same ways, having a somewhat similar flavour. Since it is one of the first plants of spring (it often starts to flower in April), it is useful in early mixed salads. It contains valuable minerals. Older books describe large bunches on sale in continental markets. The word cardamine comes originally from the Greek meaning 'to overpower the heart', which refers to the supposed medicinal qualities of lady's smock.

Leek

FR: Poireau
GER: Breitlauch, Porree
IT: Porro
SP: Puerro
BOT: Allium porrum
FAM: Liliaceae
(Amaryllidaceae,
Alliaceae)
Ill. 1, No. 5, page 40

In England and America, leeks are usually regarded as a vegetable; in continental countries, especially in France, they are regarded also as a flavouring.

The cultivated leek was possibly derived from the wild leek (*Allium ampeloprasum*) which grows from the coasts of South Wales and Cornwall, in Britain, through Europe and as far as Persia in the East. However, the leek is such an ancient vegetable that nobody can be quite sure of its origin. Certainly it was grown in Egypt at the time of the Pharaohs and was later used by the Romans, who, some say, brought it to Britain.

Today many varieties of leek are grown over most of Europe, though they are less popular in America. Types range from the gigantic leeks grown for competitions in the north of England, to the small, tender and delicate varieties favoured on the Continent. Some have a bulbous base, others are straight; some are thin and others thick.

Leeks are biennial. They will stand considerable ill-treatment, but grow best in a rich soil with plenty of phosphate. Some varieties are exceedingly hardy. Local instructions for cultivation will be found in books on vegetable gardening.

If buying leeks in shops, one should look not for size, but for plenty of the blanched white part. It is the white which is used; the green is virtually all discarded. It is also important that leeks should be fresh – stale leeks are acrid. On the Continent, leeks are available over a much more extended season than they are in Britain.

Leeks have a reputation for being hard to clean, and they are, unless the following routine is observed. Take each leek in turn, cut off the roots and the green part of the leaves, strip off the outer sheath, and make two cuts at right angles at the top, enough to open up the part where mud may have collected. Then wash the leek under a running tap, opening each leaf layer and rubbing any mud away with the fingers, and it is vitally important to keep the head downwards so that the mud is washed out of the leek. Never wet the leek with the head upwards or put it straight into a basin of water. Some advocate standing the leeks (still head downwards) in a jar of clean water after washing, but if the operation under the running tap has been done properly, it is sufficient to put the clean leeks into a colander and give them a final rinse when all are done.

The flavour of leeks is rather like onion, though much milder and sweeter, but they are assertive and need to be used with judgement.

The flavour differences between leek, onion and shallot are worth a little consideration, and recipes often contain both onion and leek, and sometimes onion and shallot. Leeks are particularly important in flavouring soups and are much used in France. They are part of the vegetable flavouring of the *pot-au-feu* and also of a number of meat and vegetable soups. They dominate in *potage bonne femme* and, of course, in its American derivative, *crème vichyssoise*. But leeks are also used in fish soups and in stock and court bouillon for lobsters and fish; for instance, in *la bourride* with eels – and so on. They also may be part of a bouquet for cooking pork or lamb.

Leeks are greatly used in the cooking of eastern Europe, as in Rumania, where a well-known hors d'oeuvre is made of leeks with olives in a slightly sweet-sour, oily tomato

sauce. In many dishes like this, the leeks have been lightly browned in oil, and the flavour of leeks, like onions, is much changed when they are browned. Leeks, again like onions, acquire a rank taste if exposed to the air for long between cutting up and cooking. Young tender leeks can be used raw in salads, a use which dates back to the Romans.

Lemon

FR: Citron
GER: Zitrone
IT: Limone
SP: Limón
BOT: Citrus limon
FAM: Rutaceae

The lemon is thought to be a native of Southeast Asia, possibly Malaysia. All citrus fruits probably originated in Southeast Asia inside a triangle drawn from India to southern China and southwards to Indonesia. Of these, fruits, the most westerly in origin seems to have been the citron (q.v.) which probably reached Persia by the sixth century B.C. in the time of Cyrus the Great, and had arrived in Greece and Italy by the end of the third century. The lemon appeared in Europe probably about the middle of the first century A.D., although some authorities put it later. As limes, lemons and citron are confused in ancient writings, it is difficult for anyone to be quite certain.

Today lemons are cultivated all over the world in suitable climates, particularly in the Mediterranean region and California. There are many varieties and some so-called wild lemons, which may be either varieties or quite different species. It is a field in which the experts can still argue and does not greatly concern the cook unless he keeps house in the East.

Lemons grow on small spiny trees which are from ten to twenty feet high and bear white and purple flowers. Of all citrus trees the lemon is the most beautiful, with rather pale green leaves, yellow fruit and a particular delicacy of form.

Lemon juice is the modern souring agent of European cooking. It is often used to replace vinegar in salads, although inferior to good wine vinegar because it has little flavour to match its sourness. This sourness is mainly due to citric acid, of which lemons are a commercial source. Serious cooks will always use freshly squeezed lemon juice except in dire emergency.

Ill. 10   Herb Flavourings: 1 Rocket, 2 Burnet, 3 Nasturtium, 4 Horseradish, 5 Fenugreek, 6 Caper.

The juice of lemon has very little aromatic flavour, and the taste of lemon comes from the rind or zest. This contains the essential 'oil of lemon', which, in the kitchen, is taken with a fine grater, by peeling wafer-thin slivers or by rubbing the skin with a lump of sugar. Commercially, the essential oils of lemon (produced particularly in California, southern Italy and Sicily), are obtained by pressing. The traditional old method, however, by which oils from the skin not only of lemon but also of orange and bergamot were obtained in southern Italy, made use of a sponge. The fruits were cut into halves or quarters, the acid pulp removed and the skin pressed by hand against a sponge which collected the oil. If a piece of lemon peel is bent inside out and, at the same time, viewed against the light, the spray of oil bursting from the cells can be easily seen.

The flavour of lemon peel is one of the most important in European cooking, and small quantities of it make a tremendous contribution to items as different as cake and vinaigrette sauce. The aromatic quality depends on the variety of lemon, its freshness and whether it has been tree ripened or picked green. For instance, if lemon curd (which seems to be unknown around the Mediterranean) is made there from tree-ripened fresh lemons picked straight from the garden, the result is quite fabulous. But variety is also important. The most beautifully aromatic lemons which I, personally, have come across were a very oily, but rough skinned, variety which grew in the garden of an Indian agriculturalist at Almora in the Himalayan foothills. Unfortunately, lemon growers and importers seem to think lemons are only used for the juice, so any lemon that looks good (probably treated outside with preservatives and dyes) will do, they think, provided it is sour. Commercial lemons are often picked green (they deteriorate quickly if allowed to ripen on the tree) and so they can never hope to be as good as those picked ripe in a Mediterranean garden.

Other sources of a lemon flavour, though somewhat deficient, are used (see Lemon Grass and Verbena). Lemon essence should only be used in emergency. The best will be flavoured with essential oils from the skin of fresh lemons but inferior kinds may have essential oils from other sources. There are also lemon-flavoured liqueurs.

Lemon Grass

IT: Cimbopogone
BOT: Cymbopogon
  citratus
  and Cymbopogon
  flexuesus
FAM: Gramineae

Lemon grass is common everywhere in the tropics of Southeast Asia. It is also nowadays cultivated in Africa, South America and, in the States, in Florida. It is a typical grass but has a bulbous base and a strong taste and smell of lemon.

Lemon grass contains a great deal of citral, the essential oil used in artificial lemon flavours and in the synthesis of other artificial flavours. The grass is often used in the cooking of Ceylon and Southeast Asia, but as citral is also the most characteristic flavouring in the yellow outer coat of lemon peel, this may be substituted in recipes calling for lemon grass. It is also available as 'Sereh' powder. Other species of *Cymbopogon* yield citronella, ginger grass and palmorosa oils, which are used commercially for their pleasant smells, but as far as I know, not in cooking.

Lime

FR: Limette, Limon
GER: Limette, Limone
IT: Lima, Limetta
SP: Lima
BOT: Citrus aurantifolia
FAM: Rutaceae

The lime, like the other citrus fruits, came originally from Southeast Asia, but its history is obscure because it was confused with the lemon in older writings. The lime tree is shrubby, untidy and covered with sharp spines. The flowers are rather small and white, and the fruits are usually round, greenish-yellow and only an inch or two in diameter. They have a thin tight skin, which has the characteristic smell of lime and a very sour and slightly bitter juice. The lime prefers a more tropical climate than the lemon, and it often replaces lemon in the cooking of tropical countries.

However, limes vary greatly – according to climate and variety. Some are very rank in skin aroma and smell strongly like insect repellant; others, like commercial lime juice. Where the flavour of lime is called for in cooking, it really cannot be replaced by lemon, which will always give a markedly different result. Unfortunately, limes cannot regularly be found in markets outside the tropics although they are obtainable in many regions of the United States.

The so-called sweet limes (*Citrus limetta*), which look like green oranges, are found in the tropics, India and Palestine. They are probably mutants of the lemon, are always used as a fruit and are not to be rated as a flavouring. In the East, there are a number of other more or less lime- or lemon-like fruits, some of which are semi-wild. These have different aromas in rind and leaves, sometimes suggesting other flavours such as eucalyptus or ginger.

Tropical citrus fruits should not be confused with the lime or linden trees of Europe and North America (*see* below).

Lime, Linden
Basswood (U.S.A.)

FR: Tilleul feuilles, Tilleul de Hollande
GER: Linde
IT: Tiglio
SP: Tilia
BOT: Tilia vulgaris (common lime), Tilia cordata (small-leaved lime), Tilia platyphyllos (large-leaved lime), Tillia americana (linden or basswood)
FAM: Tiliaceae
Plate VII, No. 8

Lime trees are familiar in Europe and North America. The common lime of Europe is a hybrid between the small- and large-leaved lime.

In nearly every continental market which is sufficiently rooted in the country to have a herb stall, one will find the dried flowers of the lime on sale for making into lime tea. Lime flowers are yellowish, hang in clusters and have a powerful and beautiful scent. Although lime tea is drunk mainly as a digestive tonic or for its calming influence just before going to bed, the flowers are also used sometimes to flavour creams and sweets, as well as being a common ingredient of home-made liqueurs. The North American equivalent is basswood from the flowers of which is made the delicate basswood tea.

Liquorice
Spanish Juice, Black Sugar

FR: Réglisse
GER: Lakritze, Süßholz
IT: Liquerizia
SP: Orozuz, Regaliz
BOT: Glycyrrhiza glabra and other species
FAM: Leguminosea (Papilionaceae)

Liquorice comes from the root of a small perennial legume with purple-blue flowers resembling those of a bean. One can find it growing wild in southern Europe and the Middle East, from central Italy through Dalmatia and Hungary to the Ukraine and the Caucasus, and in Asia Minor as far as Afghanistan. The first time it was pointed out to me was on the banks of the River Jordan. Liquorice has been used since ancient times. No doubt Christ chewed the sweet root as a child just as we did.

Liquorice can be bought simply as a dried root or in black, flint-hard sticks made from the juice of the root concentrated by boiling. These black sticks dissolve to some extent in water. The taste is bitter-sweet.

Liquorice is grown in Spain and Italy, also in Turkey and the U.S.S.R. It was once cultivated near Pontefract in Yorkshire (Pontefract cakes) but nowadays, although the industry is still centred there, all the liquorice used is imported.

Liquorice is used in sweets and candy, in drinks and in brewing.

Lovage
Love Parsley

FR: Livèche
GER: Badekraut (Lev. off.), Großer Eppich, Liebstöckel, Mutterwurz (Lig. off.)
IT: Levistico or Sedamo di monte
SP: Ligústico
BOT: Levisticum officinale or Ligusticum officinalis
FAM: Umbelliferae
Ill. 6, No. 6, page 97

The true lovage is a native of southern Europe, although another species (*Ligusticum scoticum*) also known as lovage – sea lovage or Scottish lovage in America – grows wild in the north of Britain and northern Atlantic coasts of America. This was in the past much used in Scotland, cooked or raw, and locally called *shunis*. Black lovage is alexanders.

Lovage is a very large umbelliferous perennial growing up to seven feet high. It has a thick hollow stem and looks something like a vast celery plant with greenish-yellow flowers. Much used by the Greeks and Romans, and formerly in both Britain and America, it is today unknown to most people in these countries though still used in southeastern Europe. All parts of the plant are used – leaves, seeds and roots.

Lovage is easy to grow and prefers a good moist soil and sun. It can be raised from seed or propagated by root division. One plant would be more than sufficient in the garden, unless the roots are to be used as a vegetable.

The flavour of lovage is distinct and difficult to describe. To me it is a pleasantly musky-lemon-scented celery. Claire Loewenfeld in her book *Herb Gardening* says it reminds her of 'yeast and Maggi soup'. This underlines the difficulty of describing things which are essentially based only on a subjective experience.

Lovage is sometimes used (blanched or unblanched) in salads. The stems can be candied like angelica and the seeds used on bread and biscuits, particularly on cheese biscuits. However, the great use for lovage is undoubtedly as a flavouring for soups, to which it gives an unusual taste.

Lovage indeed, is perhaps the most interesting of all the neglected old-fashioned herbs and is well worth experiment. If you grow it you will find uses for it.

Mace

FR: Fleur de Muscade, Macis
GER: Muskatblüte (Gewürz)
IT: Macis
SP: Macia, Macis
BOT: Myristica fragrans

Mace is the dried aril of the nutmeg. When the fruit first burst open, the mace is seen as a bright scarlet cage surrounding the hard black shell of the seed or 'nutmeg'. It is removed, pressed flat, dried, and then becomes the typical 'blades of mace' which look rather like dried yellow-brown seaweed.

The flavour of mace is similar to nutmeg but more refined, and mace is much more expensive. Price is also

FAM: Myristicaceae
Plate 1, No. 13

some indication of quality, but poor mace is usually brittle and has little aroma. Mace may also be obtained ground, which is useful for putting into cakes and sweet dishes, but unless it is kept very tightly corked and frequently bought fresh, like all ground spices, it is apt to lose its aroma. As it is expensive, it is also liable to be adulterated. An essence can be made of mace by macerating it in strong spirit such as vodka.

Mace forms a common part of the spicing in cakes, and many soups and stews also call for a 'blade of mace'. The latter is particularly useful in dishes such as clear soups, sauces and jellies in which grated nutmeg might spoil the appearance. Some curry recipes call for mace, but this is unusual in India since mace would be considered too expensive.

There are some kinds of mace on the market derived from other species of nutmeg. These carry such names as wild mace, Bombay mace and Papua mace. For cooking, they are inferior.

Maidenhair Fern
Capillaire

FR: Adranthe, Capillaire commun, Cheveux de Venus
IT: Capelvenere or Adianto
GER: Kapillarkraut, Venushaar
SP: Culantrillo
BOT: Adiantum capillus-veneris
FAM: Adiantaceae
Ill. 4, No. 3, page 20

This is the common maidenhair fern, which, when boiled with water and sugar, forms the syrup, capillaire. In the nineties, it was said to be 'often preferred to wine by Young Ladies'. M. André Simon in his *Guide to Good Food and Wine*, says that, according to Boswell, Doctor Johnson used to enjoy capillaire in his port. Comment on the Doctor's port is unnecessary.

When boiled, maidenhair fern produces a mucilaginous liquid, even a jelly, with the characteristic taste, but this is often flavoured with other things. In Victorian times, maidenhair was a fashionable part of flower arrangements and was also used to decorate cakes and desserts. The plant can be found growing wild over most of continental Europe and in temperate and tropical America in damp, shady situations, often in the entrances to springs and wells; it is however, rare in Britain.

Malt

FR: Malt

Malt can be prepared from any grain, but is usually made from barley. To make it, the grain is steeped in water until it begins to germinate (the acrospire should be the length of

GER: Malz
IT: Malto
SP: Malta

the grain), and then it is killed by heat. The higher the temperature to which it is heated the darker the malt. During germination an enzyme called diastase, is formed and, if the sprouted dead grain is stirred up in water and kept gently warm, the diastase converts the starch into a mixture of dextrin (office gum) and malt sugar (maltose). In brewing this is known as 'wort'. For kitchen use, one would usually buy malt extract, a brown sticky substance obtained by extracting the soluble part of the malted grain with water, then filtering, and finally evaporating it in a vacuum pan.

Malt extract contains malt sugar, which is less than a third as sweet as ordinary cane sugar, ferments easily, and tends to retain moisture. It is, therefore, not only suitable for making home-made beer (suitably flavoured with hops) but also for making brown bread. It promotes activity in the yeast and causes the bread to keep moist for longer than it otherwise would. Apart from its sweetness, malt has a very definite flavour which it imparts to cakes or bread if used in quantity.

Malt coffee is a coffee substitute made by roasting grain which has undergone the malting process. This is a well-known substitute for coffee in times of scarcity or when natural coffee has been taxed out of the reach of the poorer people. It is also, because of its food value and freedom from stimulants, used as a children's or invalids' drink.

Malt vinegar is vinegar made from fermented malt liquors. (*See* Vinegar).

Mango

FR: Mangue
GER: Mango
IT: Mango
SP: Mango, Manguey
BOT: Mangifera indica
FAM: Anacardiaceae

This is one of the oldest tropical fruits and has been cultivated for six thousand years. It is a native of India (where they still grow the best mangoes) but today is grown in almost all tropical countries. There are many varieties. At worst, this fruit is small and fibrous, with a strong taste of turpentine; at best, it is of beautifully firm but melting texture and has a most exquisite acid-sweet flavour. Many people regard this as the world's finest fruit.

(The mango should not be confused with the mangosteen, a fruit native to Malaysia, and another claimant to the world title. Mangroves are again different. They are trees and bushes of tropical swamps.)

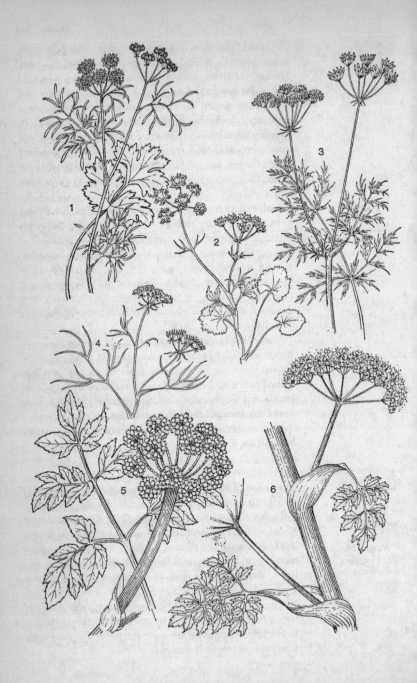

The mango tree is big and spreading, with dark green leaves and copious shade. Mango groves in India are cool and full of birds; in them it is possible to satisfy a taste both for ornithology and mangoes under the same roof. Although the fruits vary greatly according to variety, a typical ripe mango would run at not more than three to the pound, be oval in section, have a smooth but tough thin skin, coloured anything from dark green to yellow or red. Inside would be a pulp varying from yellow to the colour of canned peaches, and, in the middle, a large flat stone from which the flesh will not cleanly separate. Mangoes must be exactly ripe.

In India, ripe mango is used to make sherbets, fools, jam and ice-creams. There are canned mangoes and bottled mango juice but unfortunately neither of these products have much flavour relationship to the fresh fruit. Ripe mango pulp is also available dried in slabs. It has an unusual flavour and is sweet.

Unripe or green mangoes (usually of prolific but unrefined varieties) are an important flavouring ingredient in curries, chutneys and pickles. The taste is sour and astringent with a pine flavour. Dried slices of unripe mango – leathery and white or biscuit coloured – can be bought at Indian spice shops. It is also available as a powder, known as *amchoor* or *amchur* (*am* or *aam* being the usual Hindustani word for a mango). *Amchoor* is particularly used as a souring and flavouring agent in vegetarian curries. Some Eastern dishes also call for the dried seed of the mango: the flowers are eaten in Siam, and the tender leaves in Java.

There are people who dote on sweet mango chutney, a particularly British taste which came into vogue at the end of the last century, but Indians are more likely to relish the dry pickles made from salted green mango. These pickles, whether hotly spiced or mild, are second to none in a country famous for pickles '... from the Andhra *avkhai* with pungency matured over months in subterranean jars to "bud fruit" pickle of the far south, nearer in flavour to olives than to other mangoes'.

Ill. 11 Spicy Flavourings: 1 Coriander, 2 Anise, 3 Caraway, 4 Cumin, 5 Angelica, 6 Asafoetida.

Marigold
Pot Marigold

FR: Souci
GER: Ringelblume
IT: Calendula or
   Florrancio
SP: Calendula
BOT: Calendula
   officinalis
FAM: Compositae
Plate VII, No. 3

A well-known garden flower, with brilliant, golden-orange blooms and pale green leaves, it is native to southern Europe and Asia. The generic name *Calendula* and many of popular names abroad (e.g. *tous les mois*) refer to the long flowering period. It is a hardy annual, and can be grown without difficulty in any garden.

Marigold petals (not the centre), fresh or dried, have been used as a poor man's substitute for saffron right back to Roman times. They have a slight aromatic bitterness, though nothing like true saffron, and are used in fish soups (particularly conger soup), meat soups in Holland, as a colouring in cheese and butter, in cakes (the colour being first extracted in milk) and in salads. Even the leaves are advocated in salads, although they are rough, tough, and bitter to my taste.

Marjoram

FR: Marjolaine, Origan
GER: Maigram, Mairan,
   Majoran, Wurstkraut
IT: Maggiorana
SP: Mejorana, Amáraco
   or Almáraco
BOT: Origanum
   majorana or
   Majorana hortensis
FAM: Labiatae
Plate III, No. 5 and
   Ill. 14, Nos. 4, 5,
   page 189

SWEET or KNOTTED MARJORAM is native to the Mediterranean, and has been cultivated as a flowering herb since ancient times. It is a strongly perfumed herb growing one to two feet high, and characterized by the many tiny 'knots' which it produces. In warm countries it is perennial but in colder countries it has to be treated as a half hardy annual as it will not survive a cold winter. It requires a good but light soil and plenty of sun. Although the seedlings are best raised in a warm glass house, it is possible to broadcast a patch in late spring or to germinate the seeds in a window box filled with good compost and then put the seedlings outside when the weather becomes warmer. There should be about nine inches between plants. Unlike most of the labiate herbs, sweet marjoram (like basil) is sweeter when it is not grown under tough conditions.

Marjoram may be used as a fresh herb, and it dries well. It is also suitable for quick freezing. There is therefore no reason why marjoram should not be available in the kitchen throughout the year.

The flavour of marjoram is related to thyme, with which it is often mixed or replaces, but it is much more sweet and scented. When fresh it can have an almost flower-like perfume. This is one of the most important of all kitchen herbs and has an enormous number of uses. It is used in virtually every country in Europe and the countries with cooking based on European cooking, though not used so greatly in the East.

Marjoram can be added to practically any dish in which one would use thyme, but because of its more delicate perfume, which is easily lost in cooking, it is at its best when added shortly before the end of cooking or used in dishes which are cooked very little, such as an omelette. It may also be used raw. For instance, it is particularly delicious finely chopped and with lemon juice used as a dressing for anchovies.

POT MARJORAM (*Origanum onites*) is frequently grown because sweet marjoram is not hardy, although it has nothing like as sweet a flavour and is even slightly bitter. This is also a Mediterranean plant. It grows about a foot high and the flowers are white. It prefers good light soil and sun but is otherwise easy to grow. Propagation is by seed or by root division and the plant is perennial. Pot marjoram can be used to some extent for the same purposes as sweet marjoram especially in the more strongly flavoured dishes such as with onion, wine and garlic, where the delicate perfume of sweet marjoram would, in any case, be largely lost. It grows wild in Greece and is one of the plants they call *rigani*.

In Greece there are no less than ten different wild species of origanum known commonly under the name of *rigani*. One of these known as winter marjoram (*Origanum heraclesticum*) is sometimes cultivated in gardens. Other species are *Origanum smyrnaicum* and *Origanum paniflorum*. *Rigani* are used with grilled meats and other Greek dishes, but it is almost impossible at present to buy the authentic herbs and reproduce exactly the flavour of such dishes outside that country.

Another long famous species of origanum commonly known as cretan dittany is particularly cultivated on the island of Crete (it is known as *dictamo, ditamo, erontas, stomatochorto* and *malliaro-chorto*), and is used mainly for medicinal purposes though also as a food flavouring.

Wild Marjoram. *See* Oregano

Marmite
Autolysed Yeast,
Yeast Extract

Marmite is the proprietary name of a concentrated yeast extract often used in vegetarian cookery to provide a 'meaty' flavour. The idea of making extracts from yeast was developed in Germany at the end of the nineteenth century, and marmite was first manufactured in England in 1902. Today it can be obtained in most countries. It is made by the autolysis of fresh brewer's yeast with added salt. Autolysis is, of course, the process by which cells are broken down by their own enzymes. The soluble materials are separated from the insoluble cell debris and the resulting liquid evaporated under reduced pressure to give the sticky brown substance we know as marmite. This can be re-dissolved in water, and it contains a high concentration of the B_2 vitamin, niacin and riboflavin. Additional flavouring is provided in the form of an extract of herbs and spices. There are other products of a similar nature, but marmite is the one usually referred to in vegetarian cookery books.

Mastic
Lentisk, Mastich

FR: Mastic
GER: Mastix
IT: Lentischio, Mastice
SP: Almáciga, Lentisco,
   Mástique
BOT: Pistacia species
FAM: Anacardinaceae

Mastic is a resinous substance, usually sold in the form of 'tears'. It is an ingredient of varnish and exudes when various trees of the genus Pistacia are wounded. One of these trees is the lentisk (Pistacia lentiscus), an untidy bush bearing dense clusters of red berries, and one of the most characteristic and abundant plants of Mediterranean hillsides. It is used as a stock for grafting pistachio trees (Pistacia vera). When wounded the lentisk produces the mastic used in eastern Mediterranean countries for chewing. A variety of lentisk (Pistacia lentiscus Chia or Latifolia) grows only on the Greek island of Chios, and from this comes a special mastic used for flavouring bread, pastries, and the Greek liqueur mastiha, which is grape spirit flavoured with Chios mastic. (See Resin).

Meadow-sweet

FR: Reine des prés,
   Ulmaire
GER: Mädesüß
IT: Olmaria, Regina
   dei prati
SP: Barba, de cabra

This is a common flower of damp boggy meadows and bottoms near streams, and its creamy white flowers are known to everyone. The smell of the blossom is something like the smell of hawthorn (of the same family) and most people consider it sickly – even smelling it causes a headache. The plant, however, is quite harmless and is believed to be a good herbal medicine and tonic. As a flavouring, the

Ulmaria
BOT: Filipendula
ulmaria (Spiraea
ulmaria)
FAM: Rosaceae
Plate V, No. 6

flowers used to be added to herb beers and country wines and may be worth trying in jams, jellies and stewed fruits. The roots can be made into a bread, but in what emergency? More practically, the dried flowers may be made into a tea, which is an old-fashioned remedy for kidney disorders and rheumatism.

Meat Extracts
Bouillon Cubes,
Stock Cubes

Meat extracts were first made at the beginning of the nineteenth century, but it was not until after the great German chemist, Liebig, had turned his attention to the process, that the first factory was set up at Fray Bentos in Uruguay. That was in 1847. Then about 1840, Liebig had begun to interest himself in agriculture, to turn away from pure chemistry and towards matters of more obvious benefit to mankind. It was, for instance, due to his suggestion that the first artificial fertilizers were made in 1843. This was also the year of publication of Dickens's *Christmas Carol* when there were still many 'Tiny Tims' to make serious people, like Liebig, consider the scandal of malnutrition.

If raw meat is ground up with cold water, the liquid when filtered off will contain from fifteen to twenty-five per cent of the meat in the solution. If this liquid is boiled, the albumen will be coagulated, and when this is settled, a clear soup can be drawn off: concentrated, by evaporation over gentle heat, it turns into a brown substance with the smell and taste of roasting meat. As it takes thirty-two pounds of red meat to make one pound of such an extract, pure Liebig meat extracts are very expensive.

The cheaper and common stock cubes and meat extracts contain variable amounts of genuine meat extract, mixed with salt, other meat derivatives, and monosodium glutamate to intensify the flavour. There may also be herbs, spices and flavourings, and perhaps autolysed yeast and colouring. The extract formulae and methods used are the secrets of the manufacturing companies, and the only guide for the cook is his own sense of taste, some extracts and cubes being excellent in emergency, others quite useless.

Melilot
Sweet Clover (U.S.A.)

This common plant is tall, rather straggly, with yellow flowers arranged somewhat like a lupin and saw-edged

FR: Mélilot
GER: Honigklee,
Steinklee
IT: Meliloto
SP: Mililoto, Trébol
dulce
BOT: Melilotus
officinalis and
other species
FAM: Leguminosea
Plate V, No. 10

leaves arranged in threes. The plant grows wild in North America and in Europe including Britain where it was probably introduced for making poultices. It is common in fields and waste places, and may be grown as forage.

Melilot, when dried, develops a smell of new mown hay and it was once used in herb beers. Today it is used for stuffing or wrapping the meat of rabbits, or in marinades to impart its sweet haylike flavour to the meat. It may also be used in stews. Unlike most herbs, it is better used dried. This herb has something in common with fenugreek (q.v.) and belongs to the same family.

Another melilot (*Melilotus coerules*) has a blue flower. It is grown in the Swiss district of Glarus, around Lachen at the eastern end of Lake Zurich, and is not permitted to be sold to the public. It was brought to Europe from Asia Minor in the fourteenth century, and has ever since been used to flavour the local Schabzeiger (sap sago, U.S.A.) cheese. The herb is gathered before it flowers, and is combined with other herbs in flavouring the cheese, which is itself often grated as a flavouring.

Milfoil or Yarrow

FR: Achillee, Herbe aux
charpentiers,
Millefeuille
GER: Garbe, Gemeine
Schafgarbe
IT: Millefoglio
SP: Cientoenrama,
Milenrama, Milhojas
BOT: Achillea
millefolium
FAM: Compositae
Plate VI, No. 6

Milfoil is a common plant of hedges and meadows in Britain and other parts of Europe. The name *achillea* refers to the Greek hero, Achilles, who legend says was taught the virtues of the herb by the centaur, Chiron. Milfoil was famous for staunching wounds, and one of the popular French names also refers to this. Presumably French carpenters often cut their thumbs.

Sneezewort (*Achillae ptarmic*) is closely related and has fewer and larger white flowers of the same shape. This is also a common British, Continental and North American plant of wet places and moors. It grows to about two feet high, a little taller than milfoil.

The young leaves of this and other yarrows can be used in salads and can replace chervil as garnish.

Mint

FR: Menthe
GER: Minze

There are many species of mint, mostly native to the temperate regions of the Old World, particularly the Mediterranean area and western Asia.

The classification of the mints is difficult because the

IT: Menta
SP: Hierbabuenas,
    Mentas
BOT: species of Mentha
FAM: Labiatae

Water Mint
FR: Menthe aquatique
GER: Wasserminze
IT: Menta d'acqua
SP: Hierbabuena
    acuática
BOT: Mentha aquatica

Corn or Field Mint
FR: Baume des champs
GER: Ackerminze
IT: Mentastro
SP: Menta arvense
BOT: Mentha arvensis

Horse Mint
BOT: Mentha longifolia

Round-Leaved Mint
FR: Menthe
    rotundifuliée
GER: Rundblättrige
    Minze
IT: Menta selvatica
SP: Matapulgas
BOT: Mentha
    rotundifolia

Spearmint
FR: Baume vert,
    Menthe verte
GER: Grüne Minze
IT: Mentastro verde
SP: Hierbabuena
    punitaguda,
    Menta verde
BOT: Mentha spicata
    (Mentha viridis)
Ill. 15, No. 2, page 201

Peppermint
FR: Menthe anglaise,
    Menthe poivrée
GER: Edelminze,
    Hausminze,

species easily cross and hybridize. This leads to great confusion – even the well-known peppermint is a hybrid and not a distinct species. Mints also vary in flavour according to the soils and climates in which they are grown.

The wild British mints are as follows:

WATER MINT. This is probably the most common wild mint. It likes very wet places. The flavour is too rank for cooking. Crossed with spearmint it gave rise to peppermint, which can also be found wild in many places.

CORN or FIELD MINT. This is also a common mint but grows in dryer conditions, in cornfields and hedges. Crossed with water mint it gives rise to what is called 'whorled' mint. Neither of these is of importance in cooking.

HORSE MINT. This mint is rather local in Britain. It is supposed to be the mint mentioned in the Bible and is cultivated in the East.

ROUND-LEAVED MINT. Wild, this mint is also local in Britain. Well-known cultivated varieties are apple mint, Bowles mint and pineapple mint. These are amongst the best of all culinary mints.

SPEARMINT. Native to the Mediterranean, this is a common escape in Britain. It was probably introduced by the Romans. This is the commonest garden mint and the common commercial mint, but there are many varieties differing in colour of leaf and stem, hairiness, leaf shape and flavour. There are also decorative and curly leaved types.

PEPPERMINT. Although often named as a separate species, peppermint is today thought to be a hybrid between water mint and spearmint. There are cultivated varieties, those usually referred to being black peppermint with dark stems, and white peppermint with green stems. Of these, the white is reputed to have the better flavour. Climate and soil are also important factors.

Peppermint is rarely used in cooking as a herb. It is an exception to the general rule, for it is better to use a fine peppermint oil rather than the fresh herb. Occasionally peppermint flavour is needed in sweet dishes, but its main use is in sweets and candy. Peppermint creams are worth making at home, using the very finest and most expensive peppermint oil obtainable; then the inferiority of commercial candy is very apparent. It is of interest, perhaps,

Krauseminze,
Pfefferminze
IT: Menta pepe, Menta
  piperita
SP: Hierbabuena, Menta,
  Piperita, Yerbabuena
BOT: Mentha piperita
Ill. 15, No. 3, page 201

Eau de Cologne Mint
IT: Menta acqua di
  colonia (menta
  arancio, m. lavanda,
  m. bergamotto)
BOT: Mentha citrata
Ill. 15, No. 1, page 201

that peppermint oil contains menthol, which has an anaesthetic action and causes the sensation of cold in the mouth. There are a number of peppermint-flavoured cordials and liqueurs, of which *crème de menthe* is the best known. Some of these are coloured green and some white. They usually contain other flavourings combined with the peppermint. (*See* Pennyroyal.)

EAU DE COLOGNE MINT (Orange Mint, Lavender Mint, Bergamot Mint). This is yet another species of mint commonly grown in gardens. It has a fragrant odour something like orange flower, though it strikes people differently. It is used sometimes in drinks.

To select the best mint for the garden, one must be guided by trial and the local herb farm. As mints vary widely in their quality, we must look for one or more types suitable for our soil and locality. The mints with the finest flavour are not the commonly grown spearmints but the large woolly-leaved apple mints. Bowles mint is particularly famous. The woolly texture disappears on chopping.

Mints are perennial, but their foliage dies down in winter. They prefer partial shade and plenty of moisture. Pieces of root are planted out in early spring, usually about two inches apart and about two inches deep. In autumn, when the plant begins to fade, it is best to cut the foliage away and mulch with rotted manure. Mints are often attacked by rust, and this applies particularly to the better culinary types of spearmint. The best solution for the cook is to burn the affected plants and start again with healthy cuttings or roots *in another part of the garden*.

Mint can be forced in glass houses during the winter, and such forced mint is occasionally found in shops. Mint can be dried (quickly in a cool oven), or dried mint can be bought, but the flavour is inferior. It is also suitable for quick freezing. If concentrated rather salty mint sauce is made and bottled, it will keep almost indefinitely in cool conditions.

Mint has been used as a flavouring since antiquity. Both spearmint and mint sauce were introduced to Britain by the

Ill. 12   Edible Fungi: 1 Fistulina Hepatica, 2 Pietra Fungaia,
3 Aegerita, 4 Parasol, 5 Shiitake, 6 Jew's Ears, 7 Fairy Ring.

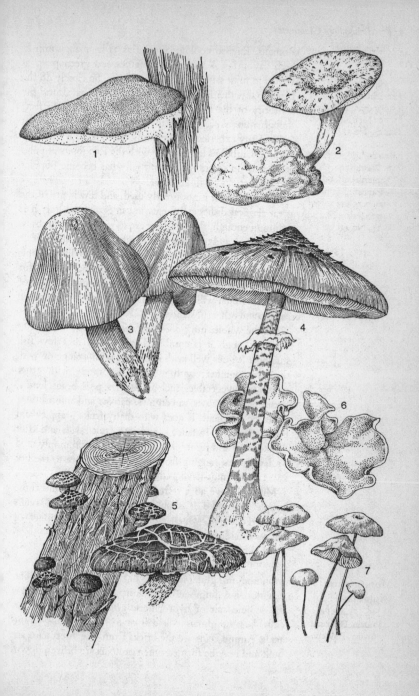

Romans. English cooking uses mint as its main summer herb flavouring – with new potatoes and green peas, as well as in mint sauce for lamb or mutton. So closely do the latter go together in England that their union has almost the authority of the law of the Medes and Persians. In fact, though mint sauce is said to be despised by Frenchmen (who in my experience have rarely tasted it), it is excellent with fat lamb, but less suitable with the lean joints popular at present. In recent years mint jelly has become popular and some cooks use mint butter.

In France, mint is not greatly used, and few if any of the great classical dishes call for it; but in Spain and Italy it is common enough, though there are so many other herbs to choose from, and mint does not combine well with garlic.

In all the countries of the Levant and Middle East, mint is again a common flavouring, as it also is in India. Mint, for instance, is ground with coconut, and forms the basis of chutneys which will also contain onion, green chilli, green mango and other substances.

On the whole, mint does not blend in easily with other herbs although it is combined with them in a few fish stuffings. It goes well with duck and with orange or with the two together; with mutton, but rarely with other meats; with vegetables, such as potatoes, peas, beans, lentils, cucumber, tomatoes, aubergines, carrots and mushrooms, it can be excellent. It goes with many fruits – apples and gooseberries for instance – and into fruit salads and fruit drinks, cups and mint julep. It is also very commonly used to flavour tea, ranging from refreshing iced tea to the hot sweet milky mint-flavoured tea as brewed in India.

Mint is above all a refreshing summer herb, and those people who like it should refer to Elizabeth David's *Summer Cooking*, which contains an unusual number of recipes and ideas for using it.

Monosodium Glutamate

M.S.G., 'Taste Powder', Ve-tsin, Gourmet powder, P'sst etc.

Monosodium glutamate (M.S.G.) is a white crystalline chemical, a sodium salt of glutamic acid, as common salt is the sodium salt of hydrochloric acid. There comparison ends, because glutamic acid is one of the organic amino acids. Amino acids are the bricks from which proteins are built and may be formed when proteins are broken down.

FR: Glutamate de soude
GER: Mononatrium-
glutamat
IT: Glutiminato di soda
JAPAN: Aji no moto
PEKING CHINESE: Mei
Jing
SP: Glutamato de sodio

Some are essential food substances, although glutamic acid itself is not. Glutamic acid is, in fact, a component of gluten (a protein of wheat), the sticky substance that makes flour 'stand up' when baked in bread or cakes.

M.S.G. was originally made from wheat, but chemists are always looking for cheaper sources, and nowadays it is made from glutamic acid recovered from sugar beet molasses or even more cheaply by fermenting with special bacteria, solutions of glucose containing simple nitrogen compounds. Yields as high as twenty-three per cent of the fermented glucose can be obtained by this means.

We mention this in detail because some people like to know what they are eating, especially when the chemical industry is involved. Monosodium glutamate appears to be reasonably harmless, but when used regularly is suspected of causing liver damage and is condemned by some authorities. It is made in almost all industrialized countries throughout Europe, and in America, China and Japan. It is used a great deal in commercial goods, particularly in soups and stock cubes. It also occurs naturally in soy bean sauce.

M.S.G. is available in the shops under various trade names. It has almost no taste of its own but has the unusual property of intensifying the flavours of other things – particularly of meat. It is not traditional in any cookery except as it occurs in natural products of China and the Far East. In Europe and America it is a twentieth-century ingredient. You can add it to anything if you find it improves the flavour.

During the writing of this book I have had correspondence with many countries, and amongst other items received an excellent booklet from the People's Republic of China. This contains a recipe which for sheer splendid economy must surely be quoted.

'A Chinese cook can make a soup fit for the gods merely by adding a handful of fresh greens to 2 cups of boiling water, and pouring the whole over ½ teaspoon of Monosodium glutamate and 2 teaspoons of salt'.

Mouthfeel

This word has been coined by technicians to cover a number of sensations produced by foods which are strictly speaking neither taste nor aroma.

First there is the temperature at which food is eaten; anything from several degrees below freezing to half-way towards boiling (*circa* 106°F., 50°C.). Temperature is an important sensation in itself, and also has a strong influence on the degree with which flavours are tasted. Some are enhanced by heat, others by cold.

Then there is the texture of the food: wetness, dryness, roughness, slipperiness, oiliness, bite and so on. Texture is of enormous importance in food, but it does not directly concern us in this book. Other mouthfeelings, because they are commonly regarded as a part of taste, are of importance to us: pain (strong mustard, red chilli, horseradish, pepper); anaesthesia (cloves and vanilla); coolness (menthol and mint); and astringency or puckering of the mouth membranes (alum and sloes).

Mushrooms, Toadstools and Fungi

Field Mushroom
FR: Champignon des prés
GER: Eßbarer Pilz,
  Wiesenchampignon
IT: Prataiolo
SP: Hongo silvestre
BOT: Agaricus
  campestris
FAM: Agaricineae

Horse Mushroom
FR: Boule de neige,
  Pratelle des jachères
GER: Acker-
  Champignon,
  Heiderling,
  Schaf-Egerling
SP: Fongo commun, Seta
BOT: Agaricus arvensis
FAM: Agaricineae

Oronge or Caesar's
  Amanita
FR: Oronge
GER: Orongenwulstling
IT: Orolo

WILD FUNGI. All countries eat wild fungi, and they grow almost everywhere, including such unpromising places as Mongolia, Tierra del Fuego, the sands of the Sahara and the shores of the Dead Sea. France, Italy, Czechoslovakia and Poland are the great fungus-eating countries of Europe, but other continental countries follow close behind. Eastern countries, particularly China and Japan also eat many kinds of fungi. Britain, on the other hand, by tradition eats only the field mushroom, the horse mushroom and very few others: the situation is generally the same in the United States. There are scarcely any English popular names for fungi as there are in continental languages. The Anglo-Saxon notion is that, apart from mushrooms, all fungi are toadstools and therefore probably poisonous. In fact, most fungi are not poisonous, and the field mushroom in the button stage happens to be one of those most easily confused with the mortally poisonous white *Amanita verna*. For this reason, the field mushroom is avoided in some countries with a better common knowledge of fungi than the British and Americans have.

Wild fungi are important both as food and flavouring, and no serious cook should be without a knowledge of them. European market stalls are full of fungi in late summer and autumn: they are beautiful to look at and excellent to eat. It is comforting to know that in spite of the

SP: Amanita cesárea
BOT: Amanita caesarea
FAM: Agaricineae
Plate VIII, No. 4

Orange Milk-Cap
FR: Lactaire délicieux,
  Rouzillon, Vache
  rouge
GER: Blut Reizker,
  Echtes Reizker,
  Röstling
IT: Fongo dal pin,
  Lapacendro buono,
  Sanguin
SP: Miscalo, Mizcalo,
  Rebollon, Ruvalon
BOT. Lactarius deliciosa
FAM: Russulineae

Chanterelle
FR: Chanterelle, Girolle
GER: Eierschwamm,
  Pfefferling
IT: Cantarello cibario,
  Galletto, Capo gallo,
  Gallinaccio
SP: Canterelo
BOT: Cantharellus
  cibarius
FAM: Cantharellaceae

Fairy Ring Mushroom
FR: Faux Mousseron,
  Marasme montagnard,
  Petit mousseron des
  prés
GER: Feldschwindling
  Suppenpilz
IT: Gambesecche,
  Marasmio oreade
SP: Camasec, Crespilla
  marasmia, Moxerno
BOT: Marasmium
  oreades
FAM: Aqaricineae
Ill. 12, No. 7, page 153

Pepper Cap
FR: Lactaire poivré,
  Poivré Preval, Vache
  blanche

vast tonnage consumed each year in Europe, cases of serious poisonings are rare. Recognition of the common edible and poisonous species is taught in many continental schools: there are usually laws defining exactly what kinds (not easily confused with poisonous ones) may be sold to the public, and there are qualified government fungus inspectors to check the baskets. However, certain excellent fungi are harmful when raw; some are dangerous when they begin to decompose; others require long stewing to make them digestible or special treatment such as pickling and salting. Some need to be peeled; others, such as the field mushroom, are spoiled by peeling, which reduces their flavour. Therefore, when faced with unfamiliar fungi on a market stall, one should never buy without also inquiring as to the use and method of preparation. And one should never use a fungus book written in one country as a bible in another, because this could be misleading.

For gathering wild fungi, there is no rule of thumb way to tell edible from poisonous species; one must learn to recognize the good ones with certainty. The most poisonous fungi of all – the Amanitas – will pass the old-fashioned tests – and put you in the mortuary. For instance, the advice not to eat mushrooms which grow in woods is unreliable because most of the finest edible fungi grow in woods, while the lethal *Amanitas* can occasionally be found in open fields, and as one mycologist aptly put it, 'it takes only one tree to make a wood'.

There is, however, a little general advice. Since all the worst killers (and a morsel is quite enough) belong to the genus *Amanita*, which is easy to recognize, it is best to learn the characteristics and avoid them. Perhaps it would be a pity to miss one of the finest of all edible fungi, the oronge (*Amanita caesarea*), which also belongs to this genus, but even this is sometimes confused with the poisonous Fly Agaric (*Amanita muscaria*) by beginners, so no beginner should eat *Amanitas* until he knows what he is doing. Incidentally, in the Fly Agaric, the volva is so brittle as to be found only in small ridges. Rain can wash the white spots off, but the gills are white. This species is not so poisonous and is supposed to be used in Siberia as a quick way to get drunk.

The classic killer is the death cap (*Amanita phalloides*)

GER: Bitterschwamm,
Pfeffer or Weisser
Milchluig,
Pfefferschwamm
IT: Lattario pepato
SP: Crespilla láctea
piperata, Girgolas,
Hungo pimentero,
Pebraga
BOT: Lactarius piperatus
FAM: Russulineae

The Cultivated
Mushroom
FR: Champignon de
couche, Champignon
de Paris
GER: Kulturpilz
IT: 'Champignon de
Paris', Funghi di
coltura
SP: Hongo plantado
BOT: Agaricus bisporus
(Psalliota hortensis)
FAM: Aqaricineae

Morel
FR: Morille
GER: Speisemorchel
IT: Spugnola rotonda
SP: Cagarria, Colmenilla,
Gallaida, Murgula
BOT: Morchella
deliciosa and many
other species
FAM: Ascomycetes
Plate VIII, No. 9

Plate VIII, No. 1, common in autumn woods of Europe and America, where young specimens glow with a baleful pearly green light (but later turn greyish-buff and look good to eat). This, with its white cousin, *Amanita verna*, which we have already mentioned as having a button very like a field mushroom is a killer almost always fatal. On one occasion over thirty schoolchildren died in a Polish school from a dish in which a few specimens had been cooked. The diagnostic character of the *Amanitas* is the cup, or sheath (*volva*) at the base of the stalk, as shown in the illustration. But this is not obvious in the button, or may have been broken off or eaten by slugs, which is why identification of fungi to eat should never be made on the basis of one specimen. In a group, chance differences can easily be spotted. If a death cap is eaten, it does not show symptoms immediately or cause vomiting for some time (six to twelve hours), by which time the poison is ingested and it is too late. Other harmful fungi cause sickness very soon after eating and are also much less poisonous. My advice is: if you ever feel sick after eating fungi, make yourself sick (by pressing on the back of the tongue); then drink plenty of water and repeat the process. Rough treatment – but on the one occasion when I was given some poisonous mushrooms, in a dish of *pfefferling* (*chanterelles*) at a restaurant in South Germany, I was down next morning with (after my treatment) no more than a slight headache. My companion was in hospital. I give this advice in the hope that no reader will ever have to take it.

Of the many excellent edible fungi, I recommend the whole group usually known as *Boletus*, Plate VIII, Nos. 2 and 3. These, also called 'Squirrel's bread', have a spongy mass of tubes under the cap instead of the more familiar gills. Although a very few (brightly coloured and easily recognized) *Boletus* are mildly poisonous or cause digestive upsets (especially if eaten raw) and a few others are bitter or otherwise unpleasant, it is virtually impossible to sustain any serious damage from them. Some of them turn an alarming Prussian blue when cut, but are nevertheless good edible species. Some books say they are not, but I regularly eat them in England. The famous *cèpe*, so popular on the Continent, is the outstanding edible boletus.

A few of the best edible wild fungi common to Europe

and North America are the field mushroom or horse mushroom, the *chanterelle* (particularly important in the Alps and South Germany), the oronge (superlative cooked or raw, and particularly important in Italy and the South of France: rare in the United States), the orange milk-cap (commonly eaten in the dry, pine areas of southern Europe) and the morel.

There are many species and varieties of morel difficult for even experts to tell apart, and they are famous delicacies not only in Europe, but also in the East. The most recherché, *Morchella deliciosa* (*Morille délicieuse*), has an incomparable perfume and is particularly abundant in the Jura. It is small, dark in colour and often dried. Morels of all kinds are much favoured in France, cooked in butter, stuffed or used as a flavouring.

CULTIVATED FUNGI. With so many good wild mushrooms it may be asked why more species are not cultivated. It is not for want of trying. One of the main difficulties is that many of the best edible species must have a close (mycorrhyzal) association with the roots of trees or other plants with which they associate and cannot survive without them. This is why, to find certain wild fungi, one looks first of all for their favoured trees (one example is the birch boletus, *see* Plate VIII, No. 3). Unfortunately, Boletus and truffles are amongst this group. The best that can be done at present is to introduce species into plantations of their favourite trees. Other fungi are so critical in their cultivation requirements that it is not a commercial proposition, although there are the following exceptions.

THE CULTIVATED MUSHROOM. In the West, this is the most commonly cultivated fungus and a close relative of the field mushroom. It was first cultivated in France around 1700, first as a garden crop and then in caves. Today it is not found growing wild. As a result of research, cultivation is much simplified. No longer is it necessary to use composted horse manure, and mushrooms are now found in shops all the year round, although one will not necessarily find them so frequently on the Continent, especially where people habitually gather quantities of wild fungi.

Cultivated mushrooms vary from white and smooth to brown and scaly. There are variations in flavour, some being almost tasteless and none as good as wild mushrooms. Therefore, it often seems as if in adding mushrooms to the many dishes in which they are part of the flavouring or in preparing *duxelles*, one is spending money in order to 'go through the motions' rather than to achieve the original taste objective. Frankly, dried fungi of other species (mushrooms do not dry well) are often better for flavouring and can be mixed with fresh mushrooms, which provide texture. The flavour of mushroom is brought out by a trace of garlic. Usually the fully grown open caps have more taste than the buttons. Stalks, which are cheaper, are commonly used for flavouring. The dishes in which mushrooms are used as a part of the background flavouring are too numerous to mention. They can go into almost any savoury dish. Canned mushrooms have even less flavour and are useless for flavouring. *See* also Ketchup.

SHIITAKE and MATSUTAKE (Japanese Tree Mushrooms). In Japan and China, various fungi that grow on logs have been cultivated since long before the mushroom was domesticated in Europe. Most famous are the shiitake (*Lentinus edodes;* Peking, *Leong goo*), which grows on hardwoods, particularly oak and Shiia logs (*shiitake* means Shiia-mushroom) and the related *matsutake*, which grows on pine logs. These are excellent fungi when young and fresh and are also available dried, canned and pickled as a Japanese export. The shiitake is always used dried and without the stems in China. Ill. 12, No. 5, page 153.

PADDY STRAW MUSHROOMS. This is the cultivated mushroom of tropical countries, first domesticated in China and later carried by Chinese immigrants into Southeast Asia, Madagascar, West Africa and elsewhere. The paddy straw mushroom (*Volvariella volvacea*) has a cup sheath like the *Amanitas*, but is an excellent fungus despite its very 'toadstooly' appearance. It is available dried and should be kept in an airtight jar as it otherwise acquires a bad smell (although this smell usually disappears on cooking). Plate VIII, No. 6.

MORELS. This is one of the most savoury fungi (*see* Plate VIII No. 9), and several species (*Morchella hortensis, Morchella esculenta, Morchella costata*) have been cultivated. Dried morels are used all over the world: one will see baskets of them in the markets of many Eastern towns. Like all dried

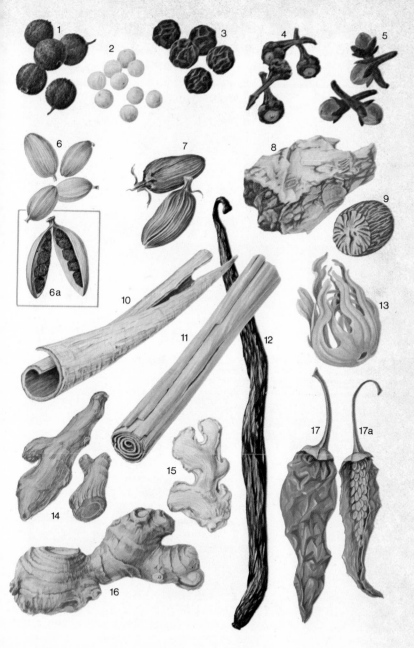

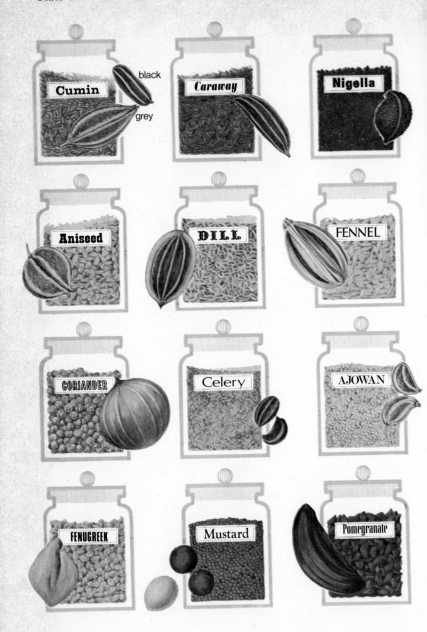

Plate six

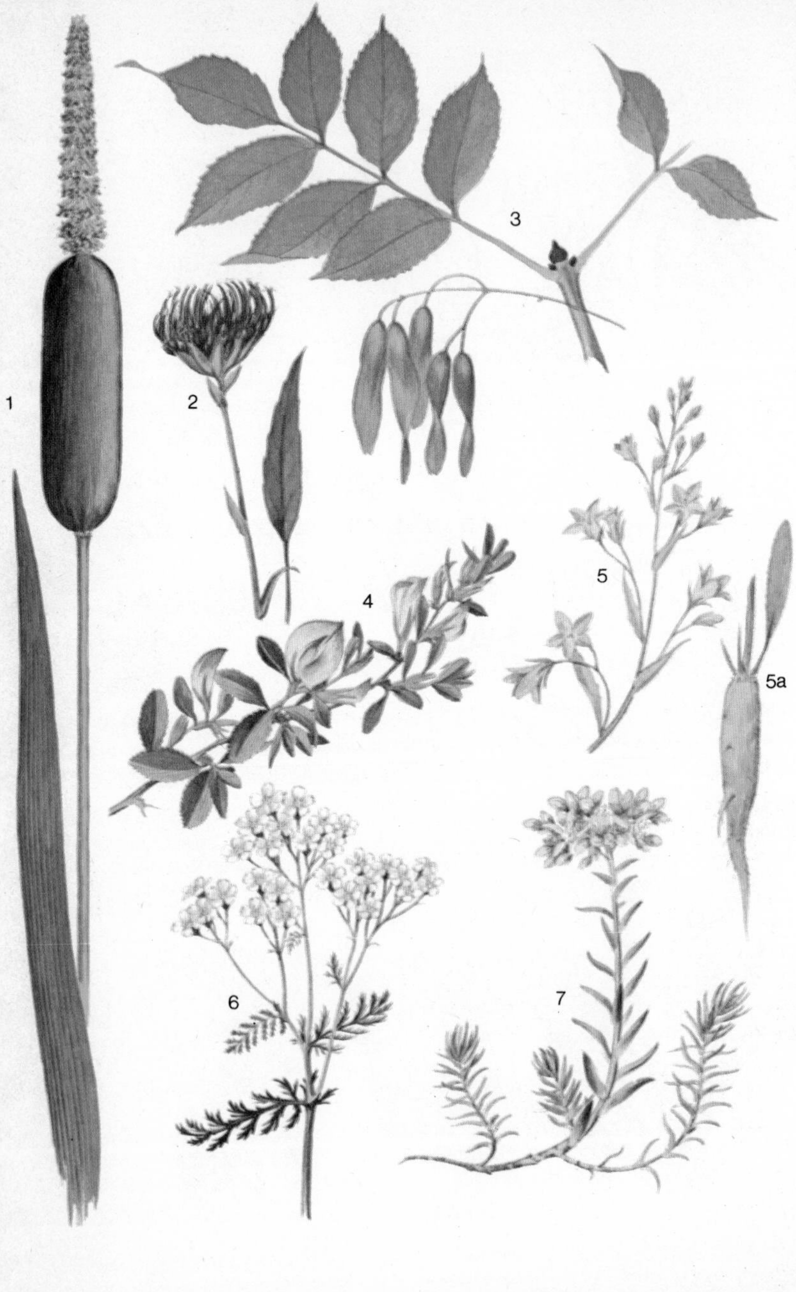

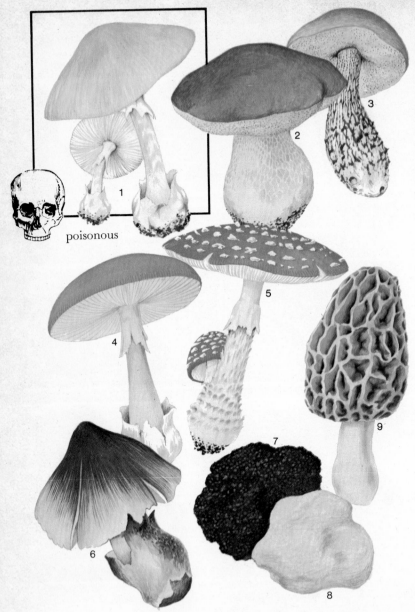

Plate eight

poisonous

1

2

3

4

5

6

7

8

9

fungi they are reconstituted by soaking before being added to the cooking pot.

This does not bring the list of species cultivated to an end by any means. Many other species of true fungi are cultivated particularly in China and eastern U.S.S.R. (e.g. species of *Pleuorotus*). Unless the cook is prepared to study the subject he is really confined to a system of trial and error, based on what he can get. However, the types I have mentioned are probably the commonest, and this section should reassure nervous people that dried fungi hailing from the East are not just a haphazard collection of wild fungi (no doubt containing poisonous species) made by underprivileged children, but fungi that have usually been cultivated by peoples who, in these matters, are probably more expert than we are.

In Europe, there are locally cultivated fungi such as the *Pietra fungaia* (*Polyporus tuberaster*), Ill. 12, No. 2, page 153, which was at one time cultivated in the mountains of southern Italy and is similar to the tuckahoe of Canada; also the *pioppino* (It.), *champignon du peuplier* (Fr.) or *hongo del sauce* (Sp.) which is cultivated locally in Mediterranean areas. This fungus is the *aegerita*, Ill. 12, No. 3, page 153, of the Romans (bot: *Agrocybe aegerita*). It can be used either fresh or dried.

DRIED WILD FUNGI. In Europe, the most commonly dried species is *Boletus*, huge quantities being gathered in some countries (particularly Italy) and then sliced, dried and packaged. Although when old, dark brown, or of inferior quality, this produce has a musty meaty flavour, it is excellent when pale and reasonably fresh. Anyone who has collected *Boletus*, thrown out the maggoty specimens, and then seen how much reduced their bag is by drying, will realize why dried *Boletus* is so expensive.

Another wild fungus which should be mentioned is the JEW'S EAR, Ill. 12, No. 6, page 153, which looks rather like the inside of a dog's ear. Several species are cultivated in China, particularly *Auricalaria polytricha*. These are dried and can be found in shops specializing in Chinese footstuffs.

Readers who wish to dry their own fungi might care to try drying parasol mushrooms (such as *Lepiota procera*), Ill. 12, No. 4, page 153, which are very large, safe, easily found and dried without trouble. Any book on fungi should be consulted. Another excellent wild mushroom which dries easily is the fairy ring mushroom (*Morasmium oreades*), which fortunately cannot be confused with really poisonous kinds.

Although most mushrooms are used to impart (with considerable variations) of the well-known 'fungus' flavour, a few (such as the pepper cap, *Lactarius piperatus*) which is often salted down in eastern Europe and Russia) have peppery or other flavours. The beef-steak fungus has a sour taste. Most notable of all is the truffle, which has a section to itself.

Musk

FR: Musc
GER: Moschus
IT: Musio or Muschio
SP: Almizclena
Ill. 3, No. 6, page 54

Ambrette
FR: Ambrette
GER: Ablemosch
IT: Ambretta
SP: Abelmosco,
    Quimbombo

One may sometimes read of exotic dishes such as this one given by the Persian poet Firdosi: '. . . young calf seasoned with rosewater, old wine, and pure musk'. This sounds like 'recipes for an odalisk', but in fact musk with rose-water was also in common use in English and French kitchens at the time of Shakespeare and used to flavour pâtés, pies and creams. Musk comes from the abdominal scent glands of the male musk deer, a small tusked deer of the Himalayas and other Asian mountains (and sometimes other species of deer). The scent of pure musk is so strong that it causes a headache, and so persistent that the beautiful Hagia Sophia in Istanbul still smells of the musk which was mixed with the mortar when it was built more than a thousand years ago. There are also synthetic musks and musk-scented plants, but these are not the musks of old recipes.

AMBRETTE or abel-musk seeds (*Hibiscus abelmoschus*), a substitute for musk used sometimes in the East for flavour-ing coffee, and which will no doubt be preferred to animal musk by those who wish to use this flavour in cooking. Tastes and smells are often described as 'musky' when they really have little in common with the real musk (octopus and angelica are examples).

Mustard

Mustard, the condiment, is based on the seed of three plants of the cabbage family. Two of them are closely related, have small round dark-coloured seeds and are known as

FR: Moutarde
GER: Senf
IT:* Senape
SP: Mostaza

Nigra or Black Mustard
FR: Moutarde noir,
  Sénevé
GER: Schwarzen Senf
IT: Senape nera
SP: Mostaza negra
BOT: Brassica nigra
FAM: Cruciferae

Juncea or Brown
  Mustard
FR: Moutarde de Chine à
  feuille de chou
GER: Rutensenf,
  Sareptasenf
IT: Senape indiana
SP: Mostaza de Indias
BOT: Brassica juncea

Alba or White Mustard
FR: Moutarde blanche
GER: Echter od. Weißer
  Senf
IT: Senape bianca
SP: Mostaza silvestre
BOT: Sinapis alba
  (Brassica alba or
  Brassica hirta)
Plate II, No. 11

black or brown mustard: the other, known as yellow or white mustard, has rather larger ochre yellow seeds. These three mustards are substantially different in character. Unfortunately, there is confusion of the popular names in American and English usage so it is best to refer to these plants by their Latin names. They are:

NIGRA or BLACK MUSTARD (also called brown mustard in the United Kingdom) probably originated in the Middle East although it is sometimes given as a native of Britain. It is undoubtedly an escape in North America. The seed of this plant was the basis of most mustards until the end of World War II, but because it is a huge plant, often growing eight or more feet high, and because also it drops its seed very easily when ripe, it proved an unsuitable crop for mechanized farming. Today, it is grown in only a few areas where, under a peasant farming economy, hand harvesting by sickle is still possible. Sicily, southern Italy and Ethiopia are some of the areas where it is still produced.

JUNCEA or BROWN MUSTARD (also called Indian mustard and sometimes black mustard).

The seed of this mustard, though usually lighter in colour, would not always be distinguished from that of *Brassica nigra* by anyone other than an expert, but the plant is much smaller (four to five feet high) and it is suitable for mechanical methods of harvesting. It has therefore greatly replaced the old-fashioned '*nigra*' mustard during the last fifteen years. But *juncea* mustard is only about seventy per cent as pungent as *nigra* although otherwise the flavour is almost the same. *Brassica juncea* has three centres of origin: China, India and Europe (Poland). This fact concerns us because seeds from plants of Indian stock have a crude taste authentic in Indian cooking but not preferred in European condiment mustards of the best quality. It is therefore misleading to call *Brassica juncea* 'Indian mustard'.

ALBA or WHITE MUSTARD (U.K.), YELLOW MUSTARD (U.S.A.) is a close relative of the charlock (*Sinapis arvensis*). It has gone wild in both England and America but is probably a native of the Mediterranean region. Correctly,

---

*The Italian word *mostarda* usually refers to a conserve of fruits preserved in syrup flavoured with garlic and mustard, known as *mostarda di frutta*, a speciality of Cremona. Available in Italian shops. Excellent eaten with cold meat and eels.

this is the mustard of 'mustard and cress' (but commercially in these days rape is substituted). *Alba* seed is not so pungent, and lacks 'mustard' flavour. It is much used in American mixed mustards, a little in English mustard, but is forbidden in Dijon mustard.

The pungency of mustard is due to an essential oil which is not present in the living seed or in dry milled powder, but forms when the crushed seed is mixed with water. An enzyme then causes a glucoside (a bitter substance chemically related to sugar) to react with the water, and the hot taste of mustard emerges (compare with bitter almonds). So after mixing with water, time must be given for the reaction to take place if we wish strength to develop. It also means that if we do anything to upset the enzyme, not only will the pungency not develop properly, but also we may be left with unconverted glucoside, which is bitter. And enzymes are very easily upset: they behave almost as if they were living. Some are more sensitive than others but, in general, enzymes are 'killed' by boiling water and inhibited by salt and vinegar.

It is easy to see, therefore, why powdered mustard is mixed with cold water and allowed to stand from ten to fifteen minutes before using. Mixing with boiling water, as some books advocate, kills the enzyme and produces a milder but bitter mustard.

Mustard should not be mixed with vinegar either, which means it should preferably not be put dry into mayonnaise, unless one prefers it both mild and bitter.

Once the essential oils have had time to develop, they will not then be degraded by adding salt and vinegar, or even by heating, although as the oils are volatile they will be easily lost. To preserve mustard's pungency in cooked dishes, add late and cook gently.

White *alba* mustard seed may not be so well flavoured, but the enzymes are strong and not so easily damaged as the enzymes of black mustard. White mustard is also strongly preservative; it discourages moulds and bacteria. This is a reason for its inclusion in pickle. It is also an aid to emulsification and a help in preventing mayonnaise from 'breaking'.

Mustard seed has been used as a spice for thousands of years.

It was used by the ancient Greeks and the Romans, and is mentioned more than once in the Bible. In those days it was simply pulverized and sprinkled on to the food, not, as one can see, an effective way of using it. Later, particularly in France, mustard became the basis for more involved preparations. It was pounded with honey and vinegar or mixed with grape must. Indeed the origin of the word mustard or *moutarde* is usually, though not certainly, considered to come from the Latin *mustum ardens* meaning 'burning must'. Other derivations include *moult ardre* (meaning 'much burning'), but the one I like best comes from Dijon. One of the mottoes of the Dukes of Burgundy is *Moult tarde*, which the Burgundians with typically French wit say means 'Burn everything'. Visitors to Paris may be interested to know that over a thousand years ago the monks of St Germain des Prés were famous for growing mustard. All mustard lovers would no doubt have liked an invitation to a fête given by the Duke of Burgundy in 1336, when the guests saw off *seventy gallons* of mixed mustard in one sitting! It was a Burgundian named Bornibus who discovered a method of pressing mustard into dry tablets. Up to the seventeenth century these tablets were manufactured in Dijon. In 1634, the vinegar and mustard makers of this town were granted the exclusive right to make mustard and, in return, had to wear 'clean and sober clothes' and also to keep only one shop in the town so that there could be no argument about where any bad mustard came from. They also had to put their names on casks and stone jars. Since 1937, Dijon mustard has become an *appellation* controlled by French law. Today, Dijon still makes half of the world's mustard.

In England, the use of mustard was probably introduced by the Romans. At the time when, in France, the Duke of Burgundy was throwing such splendid parties, English mustard was ground in special little querns. (One such is mentioned in an inventory of a house in Cornhill dated 1356 and belonged to a gentleman with the romantic name of Stephen le Northenes.) Later, however, the seed was ground by the millers, sold as dry powder or made up into a paste and sold in parchment-covered earthenware pots. At the time of Shakespeare, Tewkesbury was the famous centre for mustard in England and this was prepared as a paste for: 'His wit is as thick as Tewkesbury mustard' (*Henry IV* pt. 2).

That the English suffered from the same troubles that caused the French to legislate for Dijon is obvious from the following section from Sir Hugh Plat's *Delightes for Ladies* written in the latter half of the seventeenth century. 'It is usual in Venice to sell the meal of mustard in their markets, as we do flour and meal in England: this meal by the addition of vinegar in two or three days becometh exceeding good mustard, but it would be much stronger and finer if the husks were first divided by sieving, which may easily be done, if you dry your seeds against the fire before you grind them. The Dutch iron handmills, or an ordinary pepper mill, may serve for this purpose. I thought it very necessary to publish this manner of making your sauce, because our mustard which we buy from the Chandlers at this day is many times made up with vile and filthy vinegar such as our stomack would abhor if we should see it before the mixing thereof with the seeds.'

From the eighteenth century onwards the common types of mustard used today began to be defined.

ENGLISH MUSTARD. In England mustard developed along the lines of plain powder to be mixed with water at home. At the beginning of the eighteenth century a Mrs Clements of Durham evolved a method of preparing mustard with finer powder and better appearance than had been done before. Her mustard, known as Durham mustard, soon won the approval of the royal family and became famous. The mustard centre shifted from Tewkesbury to Durham.

A hundred years later, at the start of the nineteenth century, a young miller from Norwich, Jeremiah Colman, began to take an interest in mustard and by the middle of the century he had set up a factory devoted entirely to its preparation. Here the seed was pulverized by batteries of thundering pestles and mortars, and the fine powder was separated from the bran by sieving through superfine bolting silk specially woven on the premises. Today the name of Colman is virtually synonymous with English mustard, and it is still ground on the same site in Norwich and grown by the farmers of East Anglia from seed selected by the company.

English mustard of traditional type consists of finely powdered black *nigra* mustard seed (without husk), blended with some yellow *alba*, and a little wheat flour. Wheat flour improves the characteristics of the powder by absorbing some of the oiliness natural to mustard seed. Sometimes a dash of turmeric is included for colour. This mustard is known as Double Superfine. A similar mustard (Warranted Pure) in which yellow *alba* mustard replaced the flour is used in hospitals for patients allergic to wheat flour, and also in America and other countries where food laws prohibit any wheat flour in the formula. Older people who complain that English mustard is 'not as hot as it used to be' should look for the cause not in the wheat flour which is traditional, but to the fact that in these days *nigra* mustard has had to be replaced by the less pungent *juncea*.

English mustard, made correctly with cold water and allowed to develop for ten minutes, is clean and pungent. It has become classic with roast beef and ham in Britain, but in the past was used as frequently with other meats as well. It is also a most useful kitchen spice even for those people who prefer to eat mixed mustards as a relish, because it is free from salt, vinegar, and strong herbs or other spices. It usually goes into Welsh rarebit and toasted cheese, fish sauces and sauces for vegetables, particularly vegetables of its own family, such as cauliflower and cabbage. In mayonnaise and salad dressings, mustard helps to stabilize emulsions as well as adding a nip. Stale mustard loses a great deal of its essential oil and therefore its pungency. As a powder, however, mustard will retain its powers, provided it is not allowed to get damp.

FRENCH MUSTARDS. Powder mustard was made in Dijon up to the end of the seventeenth century, and mixed mustard was made in England in Shakespeare's time, but national preferences have crystallized so that, although today most of the mustard used in Britain is dry, most of the mustard consumed in France and, indeed, in the whole continent of Europe and the United States is mixed. There are, however, some signs that the fashion in England is changing.

The two main types of mustard used in France are the pale Dijon or white mustard, and the darker Bordeaux mustard. Although the Dijon type represents some eighty-

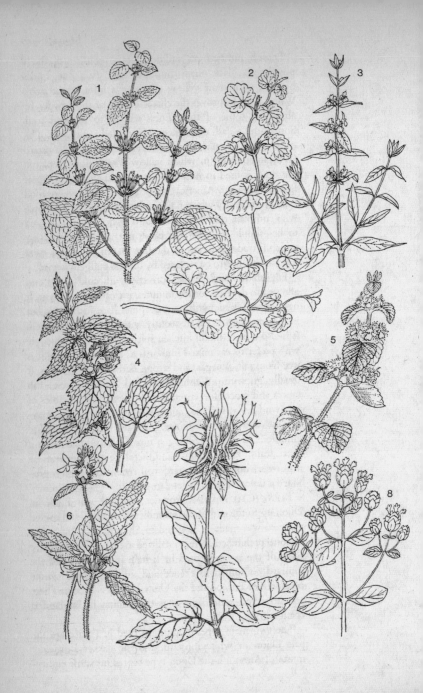

five per cent of the mustard consumed in France, in England 'French mustard' is usually understood to mean the dark Bordeaux type. This is because Bordeaux was the main port from which French wine was exported to England, and consignments were often accompanied by shipments of the dark tarragon-flavoured mustard manufactured in Bordeaux. So as the Burgundians say 'consequently many an Englishman was not only deprived of Burgundy wine, but also Dijon mustard'. Bordeaux mustard is dark (because it contains the seed coat), sour-sweet with vinegar and sugar, and loaded with tarragon, other herbs and spices. It is mild and 'low in the scale', not a clean taste, and quite unsuitable for eating with foods in which it must enhance the taste and not mask it – such as grilled steak. It is more suitable for use with cold meats and sausage. As a flavouring, it is used occasionally in dressings. Dijon mustard is light in colour, sharp and salty, not sweet and with a strong hot taste of mustard (though not usually quite as hot as English mustard). Based on *nigra* (and in these days also *juncea* mustard), it is ground wet with verjuice to a very fine paste and contains no tarragon, although imitations made outside France are likely to do so. It is light in colour because, as in English mustard, the dark seed coat is removed.

Dijon mustards have an exceptionally clean taste and are the kind of French mustard that may be eaten with steak and anything else in which the taste of the dish must not be masked. They are also the mustards to use in French sauces unless there are special instructions to the contrary. In France, they are always used in cooking. The best known brands are Amora (the largest), Grey-Poupon of Dijon (founded 1777) and Bornibus Maille (1747). Olida, made in Yvetot in Normandy, is also well-known, as is Louit for Bordeaux mustard. There are many small companies around Dijon which some local connoisseurs prefer. While writing this book I have had a mustard tasting with nearly thirty different kinds of mustards and the variations are very interesting. Besides the classic Dijon and Bordeaux

Ill. 13 Herbs: 1 Balm, 2 Ground Ivy, 3 Hyssop, 4 White Deadnettle, 5 White Horehound, 6 Betony, 7 Bergamot, 8 Cretan Dittany.

types there are some other important French mustards. One that is light, clean and very mild is the Moutarde Florida based on the wine of Champagne. I would describe it as a ladies' mustard. Other interesting types are Louit's pimento mustard flavoured with red pepper of the Pays Basque and Maille's *Moutarde des trois fruits rouges* which is so red in colour and so mild as scarcely to warrant the name mustard, though sour and aromatic, almost with a taste of anise. These fancy types of mustard are on the increase.

This section would not be complete without mention of German mustard, which goes so well with German sausage. It is of the general type of Bordeaux mustard, dark in colour, sweet-sour and flavoured with herbs and spices. Dusseldorf is the great German mustard centre. Then there is an interesting English mixed mustard, developed at the turn of the century, and known as Savora. Rather mild but aromatic and quite unlike other mustard types, it is today used particularly in South America, but it is also popular on the continent and is manufactured not only in Norwich but also in Dijon. Finally, there is the type of mixed mustard most popular in the United States which is mild, based usually on *alba* and rather like a thick piccalilli sauce. It is the type used with hot dogs. It is important to use the right mustard for the right purpose and far too many restaurants are guilty of crimes in this respect.

MUSTARD SEED. *Alba* mustard seed is commonly used in pickle spice. In the East, black *nigra* and *juncea* seed is much used in curries and pickle. Indian recipes often call for the seed to be put whole into hot *ghee* (clarified butter or vegetable fat) and heated till the seed begins to sputter. This is a garnish for many Indian dishes. Such treatment destroys the enzymes and little or no pungency develops: the taste in fact is pleasantly nutty, rather like poppy seed. It is nevertheless exceedingly important in obtaining the correct flavour in some Indian vegetarian cooking.

Mustard oil is a fatty oil (cooking oil) obtained by pressing the seeds of the field mustard (*Brassica campestris*), rape (*Brassica napus*) and even the turnip (*Brassica rapa*) as well as the other mustards already mentioned. The Indian subcontinent produces about forty per cent of the world's supply of these oils and they are very important in Indian cooking, particularly in that of Bengal, North India and

Pakistan. (Local names: mustard, *rai*; colza or field mustard, *sarson*; rape, *toria*.)

Although this is not an essential oil, the flavour and smell is very distinctive when used as a cooking oil. It is not pungent for, even in the crude state, if it is heated to smoking point any essential mustard oil that it contains will be driven off, but if an Indian recipe calls for mustard oil the flavour will not be the same if other oils are substituted. Mustard oil can be bought in most shops specializing in Indian products.

SALAD and VEGETABLE MUSTARDS. The young plant – in the cotyledon stage – of which mustard (*alba*) is the mustard in mustard and cress. In these days rape is usually substituted. The *nigra* and *juncea* mustards produce a very pungent plant, which is also quite wholesome in salads, if one has a tough palate. The Romans used green mustard as a cooked vegetable. There are a number of other plants of the cabbage family known as mustards (for instance Chinese mustard), but these are vegetables rather than pungent salad plants and do not come within the scope of this book.

Myrtle

FR: Myrtle
GER: Myrte
IT: Mirto or Mortella
SP: Arrayán, Mirto
BOT: Myrtus communis
FAM: Myrtaceae
Plate IV, No. 6

The myrtle should not be confused with the bilberry or whortleberry (*Vaccinium myrtillus*; It: *mirtillo*), which belongs to the heather family and is sometimes called myrtle.

The myrtle we are talking about is a plant with fragrant flowers and leaves, which one finds on the mountains of Spain, Italy, southern France, North Africa and the Middle East. Together with rosemary and arbutus, it perfumes the air of the Mediterranean hillsides, and to many poets it typifies the warmth and blue skies of these places.

Myrtle is an evergreen bush, with straight twigs and stiff foliage, bearing beautiful white flowers and, later in the summer, refreshing aromatic purple-black berries. In ancient times, these berries were dried and used like pepper. The flavour, however, is only mildly resinous anp sweet, a little like juniper.

Myrtle is a flavouring of the dry mountains where it grows and is especially used by the shepherds, who put myrtle branches on the fires over which they roast lamb.

The leaves are also used to flavour roast pork and the small birds which are a delicacy in the Mediterranean countries. The perfume is usually imparted by wrapping or stuffing the meat with myrtle leaves after it has been cooked and whilst it is waiting to be brought to the table.

Nasturtium

FR: Capucine, Cresson
   d'Inde
GER: Kapuzinerkresse
IT: Nasturzio
SP: Capuchina, Nasturcia
BOT: Tropaeolum majus
FAM: Tropeolaceae
Ill. 10, No. 3, page 136

This common garden annual came originally from Peru. It is grown all over the world for its orange or yellow trumpet-like flowers and will thrive in almost any sunny situation. Although commonly known as nasturtium, it is no relative of watercress (formerly Nasturtium officinale), but the leaves have a cress-like flavour and are excellent in sandwiches and salads.

The buds, flowers and seeds of the nasturtium develop the goaty taste of capers when they are pickled. It is best to pick the fruits every few days, still green, and before they get too hard. After washing and drying, put them in a bottle of strongly salted vinegar. They develop their excellent new flavour in about a month and are then regarded as a substitute for capers. In fact, the flavour is not quite the same, nasturtium seeds are more pungent and the buds milder.

Nasturtium vinegar can be made by packing the fully blown flowers in a bottle and covering with vinegar flavoured with a little shallot, garlic, red pepper and salt. The nectar-containing spurs are a delicacy.

Nigella
Devil-in-the-Bush
Fennel Flower,
   Love-in-a-Mist

FR: Cheveux de Vénus,
   Nigelle
GER: Schwarzkümmel
INDIA: Kala Zira,
   Kalonji
IT: Nigella
SP: Neguilla, Pasionara
BOT: Nigella sativa
FAM: Ranunculaceae
Plate II, No. 3 and
   Ill. 7, No. 3, page 103

A small and not decorative type of love-in-a-mist is grown for its black seed, which is used as a spice in Egypt, the Middle East, India and, to a small extent, in Europe. The seeds are peppery, with a rather odd, aromatic flavour. They are used as a substitute for pepper and are sprinkled on bread and cakes. In India they are sometimes called kala jeera (black cumin), being confused with the black variety of true cumin. There is little real resemblance in flavour between the two. In France, nigella is sometimes known as quatre-épices (four spices). It is interesting to experiment with, but is not a very important spice.

Nigella seed is often confused with onion seed, which it resembles. Onion seed has very little taste and I have never been able to decide whether shops which sell onion seed as nigella seed are making a mistake or intentionally selling the former as a substitute.

Noyeau
Noyau

Noyeau comes from the French meaning 'the stone of a fruit', and noyeau or *crème de noyeau* is a liqueur or cordial made from the kernels of fruits, such as cherry, peach, apricot or bitter almond, which develop a bitter almond flavour when macerated in water.

Noyeau is produced in Europe but the very best is said to come from Martinique. The process usually involves the maceration of kernels in strong alcohol, and then re-distilling to get rid of the cyanide. If this is not done, the noyeau will be poisonous and in fact many are poisonous in quantity.

The general effect is of a sweet liqueur tasting strongly of bitter almonds. It is a useful flavouring, superior to almond essence. Victorian cookery books, particularly, contain recipes for home-made noyeau and recipes in which it is used.

Nutmeg

FR: Muscade, Noix de muscade (Banda)
GER: Muskat, Muskatnuß
IT: Noce moscata
SP: Moscada, Nuez moscada
BOT: Myristica fragrans
FAM: Myristicaceae
Plate I, No. 9 and
Ill. 19, No. 7, page 253

The nutmeg tree is a large evergreen, native to some of the Indonesian islands and the Philippines, but now grown in other parts of the tropics including the West Indies. When the fruit is ripe, it looks like a yellow plum. These fruits later dry and then split open. Inside the nutmeg lies in a sort of bright red cage, the aril, and this cage, when dried, we know as mace.

Nutmegs had reached Europe certainly by the twelfth century and were obviously well known to Chaucer.

> 'There springen herbs grate and smalle
> The licoris and the setewole
> And many a clove gilofre
> And note muge to put ale
> Whether it be moist or stale.'

It was not, however, until the Portuguese discovered the Spice Islands in 1512 that the nutmeg came into general use. It was then in great demand and was one of the spices which caused so much trouble and has provided so much material for the history books.

Nutmegs may be dark, or white with the lime used to discourage insects. It is usual to grate nutmeg straight into the dish in which it is required, as once grated it rapidly loses its best flavour. In English cooking today nutmeg is mainly used in cakes and sweet dishes, but it is equally important in savoury and meat dishes. It goes into sausages and other meat products from haggis to mortadella. Nutmeg goes particularly well with spinach, a flavour combination which is especially popular in Italy. The filling for ravioli nearly always contains spinach and with it nutmeg. Since nutmeg also goes well with cheese this is yet another reason why nutmeg is so enormously popular in Italy. Nutmeg is also a common flavouring in the Levant and like cinnamon gives a rather special flavour to mutton. It is also essential in many spiced dishes from the Middle and Far East, although not a common curry spice. It is the making of onion sauce.

Punches and drinks to be taken at night usually contain nutmeg, which has slightly soporific qualities. In fact, nutmeg in large quantities is poisonous, and when put into alcoholic drinks it greatly increases their effect.

Nut

Chestnut
FR: Châtaigne, Marron
GER: Kastanie
IT: Castagno
SP: Castaña
BOT: Castanea sativa
FAM: Fagaceae

Hazel Nut
FR: Aveline
GER: Haselnuß
IT: Nocciola
SP: Avellana
BOT: Corylus avellana
and other Corylus
species
FAM: Betulaceae

If one excepts bitter almonds it is rather difficult to decide whether nuts should be regarded as a flavouring or not. Often they are put into dishes to provide texture; often they are really a basic ingredient. But nuts do also provide an extra flavour so perhaps they ought to be mentioned. Almonds, pine and pistachio nuts, peanuts and, on a whim, the mysterious ginkgo nuts have separate sections.

SWEET CHESTNUTS. The common European (Spanish) chestnut is *Castanea sativa*, but many other species are cultivated from North America to China and Japan. Wild chestnuts extend over a wide area in Europe, but it is in the countries of southern Europe that the large improved varieties are grown. Many do not realize that the number of varieties runs into hundreds. They vary in flavour, sweetness and keeping quality, but the character by which most cooks will judge a variety is whether the brown inner covering will peel off easily or not. The trick is to slit the

Walnut
FR: Cerneau (Green
  Walnut), Noix
GER: Walnuß
IT: Noce
SP: Nuez de Nogal
BOT: Juglans regia
  (European Walnut)
FAM: Juglandaceae

casing and roast them in the oven. The casing will then split and can be broken away. But usually a brown bitter astringent skin still adheres to the nut, especially in much folded varieties. Often this will come away if the nuts are fried in a little hot oil, but no treatment will shift the skin cleanly from a bad variety. This is why, though one tries the tricks one reads about, one is so often disappointed. It would be better if the shops could name the variety as they do with apples.

Chestnuts are the basis of many sweet dishes from the countries of southern Europe, particularly from Italy and are used in sauces for meat dishes, when the sweetness of the chestnut is distinctive. They also make a soup, and are served as a garnish or a vegetable.

HAZEL NUTS, BARCELONAS, COBS, FILBERTS. Nuts of this type grow wild wherever the climate is suitable in Europe, the Middle East, Asia and North America. There are many commercial varieties. Ground hazel nuts are used in confectionery and also in meat dishes. In some countries they are commonly added to liver dishes and are found in Middle Eastern cooking. Roasted they are an important part of the flavour of Romesco sauce.

WALNUTS. The European walnut is one of many species found over the northern hemisphere, often in mountainous country. (The pecan (*Carya pecan*) and other American hickories are related and have somewhat similar flavours. They are used particularly in confectionery.) Walnuts are, however, well established in the traditional cooking of Europe and the Middle East. Green walnuts are pickled in vinegar, preserved in syrup, made into liqueurs (*brou de noix*) or their soft centres are eaten with verjuice or vinegar, salt, pepper and shallot. Walnuts which are barely ripe have a very delicate flavour. In the Middle East, the husked nuts are often sold soaked in iced water so that the skin can be peeled off. They are then even more delicate and delicious. Mature nuts are a common flavouring in cakes, but are also used in stuffings and sauces for chicken (Circassian chicken, for instance) in the Middle East, in *raito*, a traditional dish of salt cod from Provence, and in *pesto*, from Italy. Walnut oil was once much used in France as a cooking and salad oil, but is now rather expensive.

Careful selection of walnuts is important because there

are many varieties of varying excellence: also, stale walnuts become rancid.

Readers interested in the subject of nuts are recommended to consult *Nuts* by Dr F. N. Howes (Faber & Faber, 1948) which deals fully with not only temperate nuts but also with tropical species.

Oil

The word 'oil' is derived from 'olive'. Oils fall into three categories: mineral oils, which are dangerous in the kitchen; fatty oils, the cooking and salad oils; and essential oils, which are vital flavouring substances contained in flowers, herbs, fruits and spices.

FATTY OILS. The fatty oils have very little flavour of their own, but may contain traces of other substances which give them flavour. In the more delicate and traditional oils, such as olive oil, a fine natural flavour is sought after, but commercial oils are deodorized by steam and vacuum stripping. Thus, oils lose their individuality and cease to be easily distinguishable, so they can be mixed or substituted one for another.

However, in places where oils are made by old-fashioned methods or where good cooks abound who neither regard fats as just fat nor mix all sorts together, oils undoubtedly give important flavours to regional cooking. Most people are alerted to the fact that some countries cook mainly with oil and others with lard or butter. This, however, is a crude distinction. Some regional food is dominated by the taste of either goose, pork, bacon or chicken fats; other dishes by butter ... but what butter, since there is a great difference in flavour between a fine Alpine and Normandy butter, and an even vaster difference between these and clarified Indian *ghee* made usually from buffalo milk.

With oils, once again we can enter a world of national flavourings. Olive, sesame, cotton, coconut, palm, poppy, peanut, safflower, sunflower, mustard and almond have been mentioned in their appropriate sections. The nuts of various species of beech (*Fagus*) yield an excellent salad oil used in some parts of France. There are other good, though expensive, nut oils such as walnut, and other lesser known commercially important oil seeds such as niger.

ESSENTIAL OILS. The essential oils, or ethereal oils, are of various chemical composition, and have two things in common besides their oiliness. Firstly they are aromatic; secondly they are volatile and will vaporize when heated (which the fatty oils will not).

Essential oils are the most important of all flavouring substance and can be extracted from the herbs, flowers, or spices that contain them, either by distillation or by dissolving them out with alcohol. Cooks in the past, for instance in Elizabethan times, were often much concerned with their home distillation. A process known as *enfleurage*. in which petals are spread over suitable fatty or waxy substances to absorb the delicate aromatic oils, is also much used in perfumery, and this ought to be of interest to the cook. Butter or cream can easily be flavoured by this method.

In any cooking which involves long fast boiling the most ethereal essential oils are always lost. Therefore, it may be an advantage to add some herbs and spices towards the end of cooking or to avoid as far as possible fast boiling (such as reduction boiling) after they have been added. On the other hand, cooking softens the cell walls and helps to release the volatile oils and distribute their aroma through the dish. As is so often the case there are two conflicting considerations, and one must learn to steer between the two extremes.

As they are oily, the majority of essential oils will not dissolve in water, but some will in fat, cooking oil or alcohol: thus these help to extract the essential oils and, in the case of fats, to fix them. Alcohol, however, is itself volatile and almost all of it evaporates during cooking.

Some of the most important essential oils are not present in the raw material, but are developed when the product is roasted (as in coffee), sweated (as in vanilla), or mixed with water (as in bitter almonds and mustard). (q.v.)

Olive

FR: Olive
GER: Olive
IT: Olive
SP: Aceituna, Oliva
BOT: Olea europea

The olive is a native of the Mediterranean coasts and is one of the oldest known fruits, having been cultivated from prehistoric times. Olives are frequently mentioned in old Greek and Roman writings, as well as in the Bible, and they were used in ancient Egypt four thousand years ago. Today the tree has been introduced to many parts of the world where there is a suitable Mediterranean climate. Olive trees, many of them gnarled with extreme age, grow profusely everywhere around the Mediterranean – except Egypt – and also at the eastern end of the Black Sea. Their beautiful silvery olive-green foliage is the characteristic covering of the hillsides. Olives are evergreen. In springtime they are covered with insignificant flowers which drip gum all over any car incautiously parked beneath. Later in the year the trees form green berries which turn black or very dark purple as they ripen.

There are many varieties of olive differing in size, colour, oil content and flavour. Flavour is also greatly influenced by locality, but the flavour of the olives and of the oil which is expressed from them has no direct connection with size or appearance. The best flavoured olives are often small and unimpressive to look at, and often grow in rough looking locations in remote mountain valleys.

The first man who, having tasted a wild olive, decided he might make something of it must have been a genius. Crude olives are intensely bitter and quite inedible; the bitterness has to be washed out by changes of water and also gradually disappears when olives have been pickled for some months in brine. It does not, however, disappear from all varieties of olive, and some of those grown for oil will never make good eating.

Green olives are gathered unripe: black olives are ripe olives. The olives, tidily packed in bottles, which people are used to in England and America give no indication of the enormous variety sold loose on the stalls in any big Mediterranean market – especially in Spain. Olives may be bought stoned and stuffed with slivers of sweet red pepper, almonds or anchovy; flavoured with thyme, garlic, fennel and other herbs; and crushed, pickled or fermented. When these methods are superimposed on various species, the permutations are endless. In these markets you not only can, but will be expected to taste the wares before you buy them.

Although the habit is occasionally found in other regional cooking (for instance, in Creole cooking), the use of olives in cooked dishes is almost limited to the Mediterranean region. We must regard them as a flavouring, because the addition of a few olives to a dish gives it a particular savour. Sometimes stuffed green olives or various unusual olives –

such as cracked olives or sour olives – are required, but it is the black olive which is most frequently used in hot dishes. These range from salt cod with potatoes to rabbit, chicken, pigeon, thrushes and other small birds and vegetable dishes of tomato or aubergine. Olives are also an ingredient of hors d'oeuvre, salads, sauces and spreads.

Olive Oil

FR: Huile d'olive
GER: Olivenöl
IT: Olio d'oliva
SP: Aceite de oliva

The very word *oil* comes from olive. The finest olive oil is pressed cold from fresh ripe fruits. This is pale yellow or greenish in colour, and has a very delicate flavour. Less good oils are from second pressings made under heat, and the worst oils are made from bad olives, the oil of which is subsequently deodorized. In countries where olive oil is little used, rancid flavours due to long storage may also be a problem. Many people who do not like the taste of olive oil have been put off by medicinal olive oil from the druggists.

When I lived on the Ligurian coast of Italy, the purchase of olive oil was an annual event for those of us who were particular about choosing the best oil. We used to load the car with large wicker-covered carboys and head for certain villages in the mountains which had a reputation for producing the finest oil. According to the experts this depended on the altitude and situation of the olive groves. The quality of the oil, like wine, also varied from year to year. Olive oil was not judged by tasting but a small quantity was put on the palm of the hand, the hands rubbed briskly together and then, with cupped hands, the aroma was sniffed. This technique makes it fairly easy to tell a fine olive oil from a poor one.

Of course in choosing olive oils we all have personal preferences. Some of the oils are light and have a delicate perfume, whilst others are heavy and fruity. There are advocates of both these types of oil for use in salads, but in mayonnaise the fruity oils are always inclined to be too powerful. If you like olive oil, you will probably want both types but for different purposes.

In the countries where olive oil is produced, it is traditional to use it for cooking and frying, either alone or mixed with lard or butter. Olive oil gives a special flavour to foods fried in it. Even in dishes flavoured strongly with garlic and herbs, the flavour of olive oil will always come through. Unfortunately, olive oil is comparatively expensive, and in these days, even in the great olive oil countries of the Mediterranean, other oils (such as soy and peanut) have come to be used for much of the cooking, with olive oil reserved for dressing salads or for export. The selection of good olive oil is a question to which all cooks should give their attention just as much as they would to the selection of a fine-flavoured butter.

Onion

FR: Oignon
GER: Zwiebel
IT: Cipolla
SP: Cebolla
BOT: Allium cepa
FAM: Liliaceae
(Amaryllidaceae,
Alliaceae)
Ill. 1, Nos. 1, 3, 4, 6,
page 40

The garden onion is unknown in the wild state, but its ancestor is almost certainly a native of central Asia. It has been used for over four thousand years and is the most common of all our vegetable flavourings. There are hundreds of cultivated varieties which vary in size, colour, pungency, flavour and keeping quality. It is important to be alert to this when shopping, to learn the type of onion offered and to be selective in choosing them. (A proper tasting carbonnade (*see* Beer) cannot be made without the right type of Belgian onions, very strong.)

Onions have several quite distinct flavours, depending on the degree to which they are cooked. If dishes call for onions to be fried golden or gently sweated in oil or butter, they should not be allowed to brown. Browned onions and, even more so, blackened onions have a different and much ranker flavour.

Onions which have been cut and exposed to the air for a time acquire a stale flavour typical of kebabs and meat which has been mixed with onion overnight. This is a flavour found in bazaar cooking in the Middle East. Chefs who wish to prepare a quantity of chopped onion in advance cook it a while in butter. It can then be kept for a day in the refrigerator.

Although in many peasant communities large chunks of raw onion are happily eaten with bread, the milder spring onions or scallions are more suitable raw in salads. For this purpose, not only varieties of *Allium cepa* but also the narrow-leaved perennial variety which very rarely flowers, sometimes wrongly called the Welsh onion, but properly the Every-ready onion, are used. Like the true Welsh onion the Ever-ready onion never forms a rounded bulb, but always remains like a tightly packed clump of spring onions.

The Welsh onion ('Welsh', in this context, means foreign) or Japanese bunching onion, as it is also called, is the most important onion crop grown in China and Japan. It is unknown in a wild state, but its ancestor is probably a Siberian species. This onion can grow almost anywhere in sun. Less usual is the variety of *Allium cepa*, known as the top onion, tree onion or Egyptian tree onion, a cultivar which forms tiny bulbs with leaves at the top of a hollow stem. The bulbs are exceedingly pungent, but most people consider tree onions hardly worth growing. Another variety of onion, the potato onion, which is grown to some extent in Ireland, has larger bulbs underground than the ever-ready onion, hence its name.

In these days, onion can be obtained dried or as a powder, but however convenient this may be, it cannot really be considered equal to fresh onion. In the East, onion seed is sometimes used as a spice and is sometimes confused with nigella.

There are various schools of thought about the family to which the onion genus should belong. Onions have some traits which would put them amongst the daffodils (*Amaryllidaceae*) and others which would put them with the lilies (*Liliaceae*). Which one chooses would depend on which characteristics one gives the greater importance. It is the sort of problem that gives ulcers to systematic botanists, but, fortunately, not to cooks. The third way out is to give the onions a family of their own, the *Alliaceae*.

There are hundreds of species of the onion genus, *Allium*, and they grow wild in Europe, Asia and North America. No species is poisonous, though some are very unpleasant – rank and pungent. Many wild kinds are made use of locally. They were used by the North American Indians, and onions of some sort have been an important flavouring over the whole of Europe and Asia since there were any records.

Onions have also been in cultivation for a very long time. They were grown in ancient Egypt and, in Roman times, quite a number of varieties were known and used in cooking. As often happens when plants have been cultivated for a long time, the wild ancestors are not known and the botanists get into a frightful muddle which only the most detailed study can clarify. Wild ancestors get lost either because they have become extinct, perhaps due to changes of climate, or because the plants have changed so much under cultivation that one does not recognize them as such.

The onion particularly causes confusion because cultivated species tend to run to certain forms – single bulb, cluster of bulbs, small bulbs with long lasting green tops, bulbils forming instead of flowers, and so on. These differences are of fundamental importance to the cook and gardener, but they do not represent species. In fact, it seems that very few distinct species of onion are cultivated.

There is our European onion, *Allium cepa*, of which shallots are only a variety (though called a species in older books), but with hundreds of other forms and types from scallions to 'keepers', from white to purple, strong to mild, tiny pickling onions to whoppers, potato onions growing underground, tree onions growing in the air etc. But you can always tell if they are varieties of *Allium cepa* by cutting a section through a leaf. If it is hollow and flattened with a concave outside surface and a concave inner surface, then it is a *cepa* variety (cultivar). If not, it must be a variety of one or the other cultivated onion species.

In the Far East – Japan and China – *Allium fistulosum* is the important species, though again the ancestor has died out. *Fistulosum* onions look something like leeks – the true Welsh or Japanese bunching onion is well-known in Europe and belongs to this species – but there are many other cultivars in the East, some with leaves over an inch thick. A section through the leaves of *Fistulosum* onions shows hollow and circular, not flattened as in the *cepa* onions, and by this one can tell the two apart. However, this distinction will probably not last. Onion species rarely hybridize, but using new techniques, cross-breeding can be done. *Fistulosum* onions are immune to some diseases to which *cepa* onions fall ill, so crosses are being tried.

Another Eastern species, *Allium tuberosum* – known by the corruption of the Cantonese as Cuchay or Chinese chives – is commonly used in China, Japan, parts of North India, and wherever there are Chinese imigrants. This onion, for a change, does still grow wild in China and parts of the Himalayas. It is bigger and stronger than western chives and has flat *solid* leaves – not hollow. In warm climates this onion does not flower, but where it does the flowers can be used in salads, combining a taste of onion and honey.

Our own chive, *Allium schoenoprasum*, is the only onion common wild to both the Old and New worlds. It is extremely variable and can be found growing in cool places, even high in the Alps. Its cultivation is recent – probably only since the Middle Ages. It has a grass-thin hollow stem with circular section.

See also Chive, Garlic, Leek, Rocambole, Shallot.

Orange

FR: Orange
GER: Orange
IT: Arancio
SP: Naranja
BOT: Citrus species
FAM: Rutaceae

Sweet Orange
FR: Orange douce
GER: Apfelsine, Süße Orange
IT: Arancio dolce
SP: Naranja china
BOT: Citrus sinensis

Bitter Orange
FR: Bigarde, Orange amère
GER: Pomeranze
IT: Arancio amaro, Arancio forte
SP: Bigarade, Naranja amarga
BOT: Citrus aurantium

Mandarin Orange
FR: Mandarine
GER: Mandarine, Zwergapfelsine
IT: Mandarino
SP: Mandarina
BOT: Citrus reticulata

Kumquat

Probably native to southern China or Vietnam, oranges did not reach Europe until fairly late in history, when they were brought to the Mediterranean by the Arabs (although it is uncertain whether this was in the first or the tenth century A.D.). The earliest oranges to arrive were the sour or bitter species, and the sweet oranges did not arrive until much later. Thirteen hundred is about the earliest possible date, but some experts consider that the sweet oranges which Vasco da Gama brought back with him to Portugal at the end of his voyage round the Cape of Good Hope (1498) were the first to be introduced into Europe. As for the loose-skinned oranges, usually known as mandarins or tangerines, these did not reach Europe until the beginning of the Victorian era. These dates may be of help to anyone trying to decide what kind of citrus is intended in early recipes.

There is considerable argument about the botany of the citrus fruits because they hybridize so easily, but this need not worry the cook, who will be more interested in the enormous number of varieties. The usual classification is as follows:

SWEET ORANGES. These are tight-skinned and are the most usual eating oranges. One can classify them into Spanish, which are large and coarse-grained; Mediterranean, which are fine-grained; blood, which range from mixed red and white to dark red in their pulp; and navel, which have no seeds but a navel at one end.

BITTER, SEVILLE, SOUR OR BIGARADE ORANGES. This orange looks very like the sweet orange. The tree is also similar, having the same dark green leaves and blue spines. The difference between the two lies mainly in the pulp,

FR: Koumquat
GER: Japanische Orange, Kleinfrüchtige Goldorange
IT: Kumquat
SP: Naranja japonesa
BOT: Fortunella japonica and others

which in the bitter orange is too sour and astringent to be eaten raw. Indeed, these oranges are grown mostly for their strongly scented flowers, used for orange flower water and 'oil of neroli', which is used for perfume. The rind of bitter oranges is particularly aromatic and is superior for most flavouring purposes. A variety of bitter orange known as the bergamot orange is grown in the Mediterranean area for its skin, which is the source of 'oil of bergamot', used mainly in perfumery (*see* Bergamot). Although bitter oranges are so valuable in cooking, in flower-producing areas the fruits are usually just dumped in the river. These are the oranges used for marmalade.

MANDARIN ORANGES or TANGERINES. These are both loose-skinned oranges: they peel and quarter very easily. Again, there are many types. The flavour is less acid than that of the sweet orange. The skin is highly aromatic and full of oil, and, unlike other orange skins, has a tangerine flavour.

KUMQUAT. Although kumquats look like tiny oranges growing on tiny orange trees, they are only distantly related. The fruit is no more than an inch in diameter, and most people know them only as preserved oranges. They are, however, occasionally found in shops and are becoming increasingly popular.

The excellence of dishes flavoured with orange depends on the aromatic content of the orange skin. Eating oranges are selected for the flavour of the pulp and the skin is often uninteresting, dyed for marketing purposes, and not considered as a part to be eaten. This is why *canard à l'orange*, Cumberland sauce and, naturally, *sauce bigarade* should be flavoured with the rind of bitter oranges for preference. This is also the best for the dried orange peel so often a part of a bouquet garni in southern France. It may, however, be too bitter for cakes and creams. Though the rind and juice of mandarins and tangerines is less used as a flavouring, for sweet dishes, creams, almond paste and so on, it is excellent and quite as interesting as orange.

The leaves of orange trees are used occasionally as a flavouring, but these are usually available only to people who live where oranges grow and the leaves are easily obtainable. Orange blossoms and orange flower water are also commonly used as a flavouring, particularly in the

Middle East. Fine orange flower water is produced in many places (particularly in the south of France) and also in the Levant, for instance, in Beirut. I have also eaten jam made from orange flowers, which is popular in Persia and the Middle East.

Many liqueurs are flavoured with orange peel. One of these, commonly used as a flavouring for creams and sauces, is *curaçao*, originally a Dutch liqueur based on the aromatic green oranges from Curaçao, an island situated in the Caribbean just north of the coast of Venezuela. There are, however, a large number of other liqueurs predominantly flavoured with orange: *Cointreau, Triple Sec, Grand Marnier, Aurum, Cristal Floquet, Van der Hum* etc. (*See also* Spirits and Liqueurs).

Oregano, Origan
Wild Marjoram

FR: Origan
GER: Oregano
IT: Origano
SP: Oregano
BOT: Origanum vulgare

This is the pungent herb flavouring of the Neapolitan pizza. I hesitate to say pungent because technically it is the same plant which grows wild in Britain on chalk downs and limestone and which is called wild marjoram. The herb as it grows in cold wet climates is not very peppery and has a 'green taste'. The plant as it grows wild in southern Italy is a far more violent herb even than that which grows in northern Italy. Oregano is commonly sold in bundles, often dried, in Italian markets, but wholesalers are unwilling to divulge its place of origin and regard it as their trade secret. There are a number of types, whether varied by soil and climate, variety or species. To add to the difficulties, in some countries (e.g. Mexico) the name oregano is used for similar tasting plants which are quite unrelated botanically.

Oregano is a herb particularly important in Italian cooking, and since it is nearly always used dried, the solution is to buy samples of Italian origin. It is used with tomato, cheese, beans, aubergines, zucchini, fish, shellfish and meat. It is also added to commercial Mexican chilli powders and is a part of the flavouring of chilli beans. Oregano is a useful dried herb for those who like strongly-flavoured dishes.

Orris

The iris species yielding orris are native to the Mediterranean area though now cultivated elsewhere, for instance in

FR: Iris, Racine d'iris
GER: Florentina
  Schwertlilie
IT: Giaggiolo
SP: Raiz de iris florentina,
  Raiz de lirio
BOT: Iris pallida, Iris
  germanica 'florentina'
FAM: Iridaceae
Ill. 4, No. 1, page 70

Persia and North India. The common blue iris of gardens is *Iris germanica*. Irises are particularly cultivated on the hills and mountain slopes around Florence, in sunny clearings or amongst the grape vines. These irises flourish in dry stony soil.

The roots are desiccated and pulverized to make orris powder, which has the sweet scent of violets though a bitter taste. Orris was commonly used in sixteenth- and seventeenth-century kitchens, but the main use today is in perfume, particularly violet perfume, and it is included in the composition of some liqueurs. Orris should not be confused with calamus root or sweet flag, known sometimes as 'wild iris' in the United States.

Palm Oil

BOT: Elaeis guineensis
FAM: Palmaceae

The oil palm bears a great number of nut-like fruits and oil is expressed from both the pulp and the kernel. The oil from the kernel is palm oil, an important source of margarine, and is used in the cooking of many parts of the tropics, particularly the west coast of Africa. Dishes from this part of the world owe their characteristic flavour to it. Palm oil can come from many other species of palm but this one is native to West Africa, though now spread right through the tropics.

Papaya
Papaw

FR: Papayer
GER: Baummelone,
  Papaya
IT: Papaia
SP: Papaya
BOT: Carica papava
FAM: Caricaceae

The papaya came originally from the Caribbean and Mexican area, but nowadays it is one of the most common tropical fruits. The small tree is easily recognized. The fruits look something like a melon and hang under a crown of leaves which top a single scarred stem. It always reminds me of enormous old Brussels sprout plants after the sprouts have been picked off. Originally, there were separate male and female plants, but nowadays horticulturalists have produced hermaphrodite varieties, which is rather inconsiderate.

The ripe fruit has a hollow centre, partly filled with black or grey gelatinous seeds looking something like outsize caviar. The fruit, very important in tropical countries, is excellent and healthy, but with a heavy, rich flavour (which some people do not at first like). The plant, when cut, exudes a milky latex used in chewing gum manufacture and also as a meat tenderizer, as it contains a digestive ferment, *papain*. Many commercial tenderizers contain it. The seeds are mildly pungent, with a taste something like mustard and cress. They are used as a spice where the fruit grows and may be found mentioned in recipes from the tropics. Some people chew them.

This fruit should not be confused with papaw (*Asimina triloba*) or Michigan banana, an edible fruit which grows wild over much of the United States.

Parsley

FR: Persil
GER: Kräutel, Peterlein, Peterling, Petersilie
IT: Prezzemolo
SP: Perejil
BOT: Petroselinum crispum (Petroselinum hortense, Petroselinum sativum)
FAM: Umbelliferae
Ill. 6, Nos. 4, 4a, page 97

Fool's Parsley
FR: Ache des chiens, Aethuse, Persil des fous
GER: Glanzpetersilie, Hundspetersilie
IT: Cicuta aglina
SP: Perejil de perros
BOT: Aethusa cynapium

Neapolitan Parsley
FR: Persil aux feuilles de céleri
GER: Italienische Petersilie
IT: Prezzemolo napoletano
SP: Perejil napolitano

Hamburg Parsley
FR: Persil à grosse racine, Persil aux racines de Navet
GER: Hamburger Petersilie

Parsley is such a common herb and has proved so adaptable to almost all climates that it almost needs no description. There are a large number of different varieties, some plain-leaved, others curly-leaved. In England and America, the curly-leaved varieties are grown almost exclusively, but in other countries the plain-leaved varieties are more usual and the curly-leaved almost unknown. Some people say that plain-leaved parsley has the better flavour, but this probably depends as much on soil and climate as on variety. The plain-leaved parsley is not so pretty as a garnish, but this is no drawback in countries where parsley is added as a flavouring rather than planted like trees in a garden of cold meat. Plain-leaved parsleys are hardier than curled types, not only in the dry conditions of the plants' original Mediterranean home but also, strangely enough in the cold wet climates where curled types predominate. The plain leaves are not so easily damaged by heavy rain or snow. There is, however, one great advantage that curly parsley has: it cannot be confused with the poisonous fool's parsley which is a common garden weed and sometimes roots in parsley beds. Although the leaves of fool's parsley are darker and give out an unpleasant smell when broken, the distinction is not really so obvious, and it is a nuisance to have to examine parsley carefully every time a bunch is gathered. Many people have made themselves ill by gathering fool's parsley in mistake, explaining perhaps, why moss curled parsley is preferred in England.

Although the famous Swedish naturalist, Linnaeus, considered parsley to have come originally from Sardinia, other botanists give its home as the eastern Mediterranean. At any rate, it was already in use in ancient Greece and

IT: Prezzemolo con
radice bulbosa or
di Amburgo
SP: Perejil hamburgo

Rome, though probably more for ceremonial purposes than cooking. Various dates are given for the introduction of parsley into Britain, the mid-sixteenth century being the most favoured, but surely the Romans must have introduced it during their many centuries of colonial rule? Parsley, of course, travelled onwards to America with the early settlers.

Parsley is biennial – that is, if seed is sown in one spring, the plants that grow from it will not seed until the following summer: they then die. A permanent supply can easily be had in temperate climates by making two sowings, one in late spring and the other at the end of summer. Parsley will stand all winter but it is best to protect it under cloches in severe weather. Parsley likes a good soil and a little shade, but in many parts of the world it gets neither. Parsley does, however, require plenty of space: they say that one plant should never be allowed to touch another. Parsley seed is also notoriously slow to germinate. It takes one or two months, and some people soak the seed in lukewarm water before sowing. Another excellent way of encouraging it is to pour a kettle of boiling water along the drill before covering over. If the drill is lined with peat this also helps to promote germination.

For some reason, in many towns fresh parsley is often quite difficult to get. Town dwellers can grow it well in window boxes filled with good compost. It is only necessary to keep the box moist and feed the plants occasionally with liquid manure. In the late autumn, parsley may be potted and brought inside the house. This will provide both fresh parsley for the winter and a pleasant decoration.

Parsley can be preserved by either deep freezing or drying. Home dried parsley is a doubtful proposition, but the latest commercial methods produce a dried parsley which, though nothing like as good as the fresh herb, is useful in an emergency.

As the flavour of parsley is well known to nearly everybody, it would be pointless to describe it in terms of anything else. Most herbivorous animals relish it, but it is said

Ill. 14 Savoury Herbs: 1 Garden Thyme, 2 Sage, 3 Wild Thyme, 4 Wild Marjoram, 5 Pot Marjoram, 5a Pot Marjoram Flower Head, 6 Winter Savory, 7 Summer Savory.

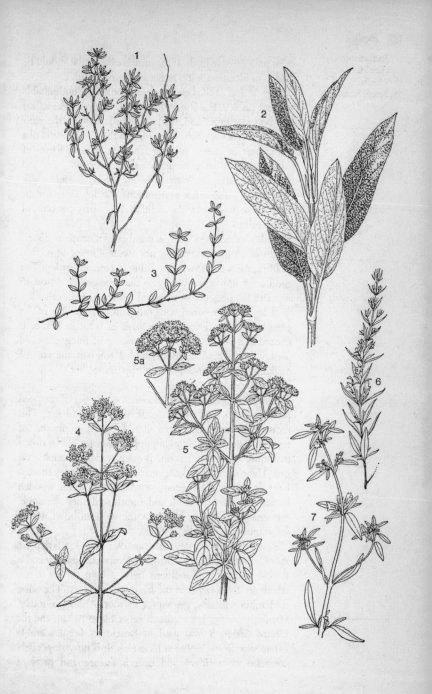

to be poisonous to birds. If the juice is extracted it should be used in moderation as it is rather strong medicine.

A great deal of the best European cooking is unthinkable without parsley. It is always included (often only the stalks) in a bouquet garni, and, finely chopped, it forms the basis of a fines herbes mixture. It enters into the composition of a whole host of sauces, ranging from the various forms of parsley sauce to *sauces tartare*, *vinaigrette*, *ravigote*, *verte* and so on. It is also the basis of *maître d'hôtel* butter, garlic butter, and many other preparations. Parsley sauce can be made more piquant by the addition, up to fifty per cent, of lemon balm.

Parsley enters into a large number of European dishes. Dishes of almost everything not sweet – soup, eggs, fish, shellfish, meat and fowl – are liable to contain parsley. The good cook uses it frequently so that one comes almost to associate the presence of chopped parsley as a sign that the food has been prepared with care and feeling. One of the great uses of parsley is in the form of what in France is known as a *persillade*. This is a mixture of finely chopped parsley (usually with shallot) added towards the end of cooking. It adds not only to the appearance but also to the taste of the dish.

Many continental cooks add small quantities of chopped parsley to the food as instinctively as they add salt. This means of course that there should be the minimum of trouble to get the parsley chopped. Parsley should be rinsed and squeezed dry, unless one is quite certain it contains no grit. There are kitchen gadgets for chopping parsley though I prefer a large sharp French kitchen knife and a wooden board with a folded cloth underneath to deaden the noise. For small quantities a *hachinette*, the wooden bowl with a semi-lunar knife that fits is useful.

Besides the leaf parsley, there are two other kinds that we should mention. One is known as Neapolitan parsley and is a local speciality of southern Italy, grown for its stems, which are eaten rather in the same way as celery. The other is Hamburg parsley, grown for its root. Although, today, Hamburg parsley is an unusual vegetable in Britain and the United States, it was used in Britain to a considerable extent during the eighteenth century. It is nowadays fairly common in northern and eastern Europe and parts of

France. The flavour is something between parsley and celeriac, and it is used as a flavouring vegetable in soups and stews. It frequently forms a part of the flavouring vegetables sold in Germany under the name of *Suppengrün* (soup greens).

Chinese or Japanese parsley is green coriander, and has an entirely different taste. *See* Coriander.

Peanut
Groundnut

FR: Arachide,
   Cacaouette, Pitache
   de terre
GER: Erdnuß
IT: Arachide
SP: Cacahué, Cacahuete,
   Maní (Cuba)
BOT: Arachis hypogaea
FAM: Leguminosae
Ill. 17, No. 6, page 229

An annual legume, native to South America and grown in almost every warm country of the world. The 'shell' is the dried fibrous pod, which is pushed underground during growth.

From peanuts is expressed an important oil: peanut or arachide oil. When purified, this is virtually tasteless and is one of the best commercial cooking oils. It is often used as a substitute for olive oil or to adulterate it, and as a dressing for salads it is better than an inferior olive oil, as is well-known in France.

Roasted peanuts and peanut butter have a characteristic taste and are an important part of the flavour of some spicy sauces from Indonesia. In North America, peanut butter is used extensively in cakes and confectionery.

Pennyroyal

FR: Pouliot
GER: Flohkraut,
   Poleiminze
IT: Puleggio
SP: Poleo
BOT: Mentha pulegium
FAM: Labiatae
Ill. 15, No. 5, page 201

Pennyroyal is a small prostrate species of mint, a native of Europe and locally wild in shady damp places in Britain. The flowers are purple. If cultivated in the garden, this mint requires damp ground and shade. It is usually propagated by roots but may also be grown from seed. Although it will survive for several years, it is liable to be killed by frost.

Pennyroyal has a strong and rather disagreeable minty taste, and the Latin name *pulegium* comes from the fact that the Romans used it to keep away fleas (*pulex*). It is also said to be a cure for whooping cough, asthma and indigestion. However, it is an essential flavouring herb in English north country black puddings which are excellent.

Pepper
Black Pepper

There are two completely different families producing the hot spices which one calls peppers: vine peppers and capsicum or red peppers.

FR: Poivre
GER: Pfeffer
IT: Pepe nero
SP: Pimienta negra
BOT: Piper nigrum
FAM: Piperaceae
Plate I, No. 3 and
   Ill. 19, No. 3, page 253

White Pepper
FR: Poivre blanc
GER: Weißer pfeffer
IT: Pepe bianco
SP: Pimienta blanca
BOT: Piper nigrum
Plate I, No. 2

Long Pepper
BOT: Piper longum
   (India) and Piper
   retrofractum(Java)
IT: Pepe lungo
Ill. 19, No. 4, page 253

Capsicum Peppers
BOT: Capsicum
   frutescens or
   Capsicum annum
FAM: Solanaceae

Chilli Pepper
FR: Piment fort,
   Piment-oiseau (bird
   pepper), Piment rouge
GER: Roter Pfeffer
IT: Diavoletto,
   Peperoncino
SP: Chile (Mexico),
   Guindilla
Plate I, Nos. 17, 17a

Chilli Powder and
   Cayenne Pepper
FR: Cayenne, Poivre de
   Cayenne
GER: Cayennepfeffer
IT: Pepe di Caienna,
   Pepe rosso piccante
SP: Cayena inglesa,
   Pimienta de Cayena,
   Pimienta picante
   (de la guindilla)

VINE PEPPERS. These are tropical and give us the black and white pepper, long pepper and cubeb pepper (rarely used in cooking these days), as well as the 'pan' leaves, which are chewed with betel nut in the East and the *Piper methysticum* and *Piper excelsum*, from which is made that odd South Sea Island drink, kava-kava.

The vine which produces black and white pepper is from the tropical forests of monsoon Asia. It has dark green leaves and hanging strings of berries which are at first green and then, when ripe, bright orange-red. It is nowadays grown in most tropical countries having a suitably warm, wet climate (India, Indonesia, Ceylon, Madagascar and Brazil), usually in partial shade and trained up concrete posts or the shade trees in the coffee plantations.

Pepper has been an important spice, as a caravan import into Europe, certainly since the days of the ancient Greeks and Romans. It has been used for barter, tribute and ransom, as well as flavouring during a long and interesting history. Venice and Genoa grew rich on it. It was a prime cause of the search for a sea route to the East and the chief spice from the Spice Islands. It has become basic to most countries in their cooking, and when one does not find it on the table (as in Iran, where sumac or dried and powdered sour limes may replace it), one is likely to miss it as much as one would miss salt.

Good pepper is still quite expensive, and there is a great deal of poor pepper sold. Since it is so important, it is worthy of the cooks' careful attention. Pepper is best bought unground, partly because ground pepper is very easily adulterated (such things as powdered date stones and inferior spices are used) but mainly because the aroma of pepper is fugitive, and once ground it very rapidly loses part of its flavour. So pepper should be bought in the form of whole peppercorns, and ground fresh in a peppermill. This is not just a fad; the difference is enormous.

There are many distinct varieties of pepper known to the trade. They vary in aroma and pungency, size and colour of corn, and are often called after their place of origin. The easiest way to ensure having good pepper is, as with most things, to demand and pay for the best. However, as some indication, the pepper should be even in size and colour (it has been graded), hard enough not to be crushed between

Sweet or Bell Pepper
FR: Piment doux
GER: Paprika
IT: Peperone
SP: Pimiento dulce,
   Pimiento encarnado,
   Pimiento morrone
BOT: Capsicum annuum

Paprika
FR: Paprika de Hongrie,
   Piment doux
   d'Espagne
GER: Paprika
IT: Paprika
SP: Paprika, Pimentón
BOT: Capsicum
   tetragonum

the finger nails and free from stalk and dust – leave that for people who buy their pepper ready ground. Since peppercorns keep almost indefinitely, once one has discovered a good type it is a good thing to buy a quantity of it and store in a glass jar.

Pepper contains the alkaloid, piperine, which is a stimulant. This causes a flow of saliva and gastric juices and so is an aid to digestion. If distilled with steam, an essential oil is obtained which has the characteristic odour of pepper but is quite without pungency. The pungency is due to a resinous substance in the pepper, which is not volatile. It is easy to see, therefore, that if you like the aroma of pepper and not merely its pungency, you retain it best by using freshly ground peppercorns from the peppermill at the end of cooking. The perfect seasoning with freshly ground pepper is one of the most important operations in cooking.

When we speak of pepper we usually mean black pepper. To produce this the berries are picked green, and simply dried in the sun. They turn into the typical black or dark brown peppercorn we know so well.

White pepper is derived from the same plant as black pepper but instead of the berries being picked green and dried whole, the berries are allowed to ripen (they turn red). The skin and fleshy part is removed by first stacking to promote fermentation and then washing off. The corns are then dried. In these days white pepper may also have been made by rubbing off the outer layer of black pepper by machinery, though this is strictly not white but decorticated pepper.

White pepper is somewhat less aromatic than black pepper. Its main use is in white sauces to which black pepper gives an unpleasant speckled effect. It is beloved by many continental restaurateurs who are convinced that the flavour is better than that of black pepper (in Spain and Italy I have had many an argument on this point) and by some simply because it is more expensive. This is a question of personal preference. If you regard the flavour of black pepper as crude, then perhaps white is your choice.

MIGNONETTE PEPPER, also called shot pepper, is used in French cookery. It is a coarse-grained pepper made by grinding and sieving black or, more usually, white peppercorns. A coarse set peppermill can produce a roughly equivalent result.

The two species of the vine pepper called long pepper produce a commodity that looks like small hard black catkins, about half an inch long. They are minute dried fruits fused into one cone. Long peppers were once important in Europe, but today they are mostly grown and used in India, the Far East and the Pacific. The flavour of both species is very similar to black pepper, but is slightly sweeter. Long pepper may be listed as a curry or pickle ingredient under the Indian name of *pipel*, which has nothing whatever to do with the sacred *pipal* tree (*Ficus religiosa*) which is a type of wild fig.

CAPSICUM or RED PEPPERS of the potato-tomato family (which came from South America) give us chilli peppers, red peppers, sweet or bell peppers, paprika and cayenne pepper. Many species of capsicum grow wild in South America, particularly in Brazil, but one cannot be sure of the ancestor of the cultivated capsicum peppers as they were cultivated long before Columbus reached America. So, as is usual with plants in cultivation for a very long time, their origins are obscure. Most experts seem to think that all of the domesticated peppers are cultivated varieties of one original species.

Peppers were unknown outside of America before Columbus. Since today India alone produces over a quarter of a million tons of chillies each year, one wonders how they managed in former days.

It also seems odd that there is no clear cut distinction between the violently pungent chillies and the big fleshy sweet peppers we use as a vegetable. In fact, if one goes about the world looking at the hundreds of different peppers – fresh and dried – sold in markets, one realizes that the usual cook's classification of these peppers into chillies and sweet peppers is only made in northern countries where they do not grow and are by comparison little used. One finds peppers of all shapes and sizes, both hot and sweet, and with many variations of flavour. Some are suitable for drying and some are too fleshy. The ultimate recourse is to call them by their local names, and certainly to forget any idea one may have of classifying them by size and shape. It also becomes impossible to make a simple accurate translation from one language to another. However, from the point of view of the kitchen, provided one realizes that appearance can be misleading, it is possible to group peppers roughly into their uses.

CHILLIES are pungent varieties of capsicum, cultivated in hot countries in suitable areas throughout the world. They vary greatly in shape and size (from tiny, round chillies the size of a little finger to giant varieties almost a foot long) and in pungency (from mild to volcanic). When ripe, they are usually red, but may be yellow, cream or even purple-black. They are healthy in moderate amounts, being a digestive stimulant and rich in vitamin C, but hot ones can raise blisters and cause inflammation and painful swelling of the throat and tongue. In particular, seeds or bits of chilli can be harmful, and in the countries where they are much eaten are usually, unless mild, carefully ground or pulverized. Habitual chilli eaters, however, soon acquire immunity, as travellers in South India or Mexico will realize. Here the babies are (almost) given chillies as comforters.

Chillies are the flavouring *par excellence* of the hot, poor countries, but they are used in very discreet amounts in Western cooking as even the outer casings, usually milder than the seeds and core, are too hot for many people. Some varieties are exceptionally hot (particularly the small chillies known as bird-peppers); even some individual chillies in an otherwise mild batch may be exceptional. As one cannot always judge chillies by appearance, one must learn their pungency only by painful trial and error.

FRESH GREEN CHILLIES (unripe) are available in the markets of most hot countries, and even in Britain and the United States they are available in West Indian, Indian or *émigré* shops. They should be firm and green, and not wilted or beginning to change colour. They may be very pungent or mild and have usually a delicious capsicum flavour in addition to their hotness. Though not usually entering into European cooking, they are excellent broken and dabbed on to a grilled steak or, if the outer part is scraped to a pulp with a knife, can add a bite and flavour to many dishes, such as sautéed potatoes or even mayonnaise. This, if one likes hot dishes, is a field open to experiment. Green chillies are preferable to dried chillies in most pickles and would no doubt have become traditional in

Western kitchens, as in the East, had they been easily available.

When necessary for Indian and Southeast Asian dishes, fresh green peppers cannot really be replaced by dried chillies. A particularly delicious use of green chilli is to grind it to a paste with coconut and green coriander, adjusted with salt and lemon juice. This makes a common Indian chutney. *See* Coriander.

FRESH RIPE CHILLIES are usually red or orange and should have been ripened on the bush. These are the chillies from which to make chilli sauce or paste. It is true that one can buy Tabasco sauce and many brands of real chilli sauce (as well as piquant tomato sauce masquerading under the chilli name), but none is as good (with the exception of Tabasco, which is a separate speciality) as home-made chilli sauce. This can be made by cooking fresh red chillies with salt, vinegar, sugar, garlic and spices to one's individual taste. The pulp must, of course, be rubbed through a sieve to remove seeds and skin.

There are also many other types of red chilli preparations, particularly from Southeast Asia. Indonesian food, for instance, is usually accompanied by chilli *sambals* and other blistering preparations. Some are moderately mild and sweet, while others should be marked with a skull and crossbones. One might also mention the small fat pickled red chillies from the West Indies, which are too fierce for most people. Milk, ice-cream and yogurt are useful remedies for 'chilli burns'.

Ripe chillies dry very easily either in the sun or a warm oven. Whole, they are used in pickles or are put into dishes (e.g. *zarzuela*) to add pungency. They are not, of course, eaten and can be removed if the desired pungency is reached before the dish is ready.

CHILLI POWDER is used for an almost endless number of purposes in the kitchen, in dishes ranging from cheese straws, *chili con carne* and *tamales* to the thousands of dishes that come under the loose heading of curries. The flavour of chilli powder can be strong or slight and of varying fierceness. It should not be confused with paprika.

The best chilli powder is home ground. The dried chillies should first be lightly roasted by stirring them in a frying pan over heat until they turn dark red, fume slightly (this may make the eyes smart) but are not on any account burnt. After cooking, they may be ground in a blender mill and sieved.

Commercial chilli powders as sold in North America are often mixtures containing oregano, chocolate, cumin and other flavourings. They are intended for Mexican dishes, chilli beans etc. Brands vary, formulae are secret and people have strong opinions as to which brand is best. Strictly speaking, it is incorrect to call these mixtures 'chilli'.

CAYENNE PEPPER is a particular type of ground red chilli pepper supposed to have come originally from Cayenne in French Guiana, though more probably the name came from *Tupi*, the *lingua franca* of the Amazon basin and the South American coast. Old recipes indicate that the seeds were removed from the hot red chillies and the pods ground up with a little flour and salt into a paste. The paste was dried in small cakes and lightly baked before being ground into a powder. The usual distinction, if any, between cayenne and chilli powder, is that the latter is coarser. Cayenne is for use in the pepper pot at the table for those who like it with such foods as oysters, but finely sifted chilli powder is often better.

NEPAL PEPPER is ground chilli pepper of a variety which is yellow, aromatic and less pungent than cayenne. In the Himalayas, the peppers are dried on the roofs of the houses.

CHILLI ESSENCES are easily prepared by macerating chillies in alcohol or alcoholic solutions. Small chillies are often macerated in sherry and the liquid used for spicing soup at table. This was a common practice in every Indian Army Officers' Mess in the days of British India, since many officers accustomed to curry found soup insipid. Other recipes infused chilli in fine brandy. Some of these concoctions were so hot that, literally, more than one drop caused torture. Chilli essence is, however, a convenient way of introducing a bite, and the best ready-to-hand macerating liquid is probably vodka. The quantity of alcohol is so small that it contributes little to the flavour. The extra-hot essences are not recommended because it is easier to control the exact dosage when using weak solutions.

SWEET (or BELL) PEPPERS, which are larger than chillies and have little or no pungency, have been in common use in southern Europe and North America for a long time, but have only recently become popular in England. The plants will grow somewhat further north than chilli peppers and some varieties will withstand a trace of frost. The fruits vary in size and flavour, some being slightly pungent, especially in seeds and septae, others having had not only the pungency but most of the flavouring bred out of them. They are used green and both ripe and unripe. When ripe, they may be red, orange or yellow, according to variety.

Sweet peppers at best have a strong and unique capsicum flavour. While mostly used as a vegetable or salad fruit, they are also sometimes a flavouring. They are available canned or pickled. In general, sweet peppers suitable for vegetables are too fleshy to dry naturally, though this can be done artificially.

Paprika pepper (Hungarian pepper, Spanish pepper), the name of which comes from Hungary, is a bright red powder made from special varieties of pepper, pointed in shape, but free from the pungency of chilli. These are of European origin though they are now also grown in America. In order to reduce the pungency still further, the core and seeds are usually removed, so paprika is the powdered dry flesh.

Although paprika is the national spice of Hungary, an almost identical product is prepared a great deal in Spain (*pimentón*), as well as commercially in the United States and other countries. Unfortunately, there are many inferior paprikas sold, although it is no longer adulterated with red lead, as is said to have been the case at times in the past.

Good paprika should have a brilliant red colour, although the Spanish *pimientó* often turns towards the vermilion. If a dirty brown, it is probably stale. Good paprika is mild and sweet – though one can buy various grades of pungency – with a peculiar aroma and bitterness of its own. It is meant to be used in generous quantities and is very healthy on account of its high content of vitamin C. The little 'pepper pots' of paprika, as sometimes sold, are quite useless except for sprinkling as a decoration.

Paprika is essential for goulash, *paprikaş*, and for many other Hungarian dishes of meat and chicken, as well as Spanish food and various Spanish sausages (e.g. *sobresada*).

Spain, of all countries in western Europe, makes particular use of whole dried mild peppers. After all, they had them first and the climate is suitable for growing them. The pimiento from which *pimentón* is ground is top-shaped but fat. Special varieties are dried whole. One top-shaped variety is used for romesco sauce, while the variety known as *ñora* is a globular like a tomato, and is correct for instance in *bacalao a la vizcaina*. To substitute *guindillas* or worse, the *guindilla de Murcia* (type of bird pepper), for these special varieties would be disastrous, while to use *ñoras* instead of the real *romesco* peppers for a romesco sauce would produce an inferior flavour. Visitors to Spain should buy their own supply of the various peppers and keep them hanging in the kitchen. But beware! Stallholders in markets are not always good cooks and often give wrong information.

Pickling Spice

Pickling spice is usually based on black peppercorns, red chillies and some of the following spices: mustard seed, allspice, cloves, ginger, mace and coriander seed. The proportions vary in different recipes, and sometimes other spices are included.

Pine Nut

Indian Nuts (U.S.A.), Pignolias, Pine Kernels, Piñones

FR: Pignons
GER: Piniennüße
IT: Pignolo, Pinolo
SP: Piñas
BOT: Edible seeds of some eighteen species of Pinus
Ill. 17, Nos. 1, 1a, page 229

The classical pine nut, used in Mediterranean cooking, comes from the stone pine (*Pinus pinea*) found on the northern coasts of the Mediterranean, as well as the southern Atlantic coast of Spain and Portugal in the west, and to the east as far as the coasts of the Black Sea. Indeed, the stone pine with its beautiful umbrella-like head is one of the most characteristic pines of the Mediterranean. It is preserved and cultivated for nuts particularly on the west coast of Italy from just south of La Spezia to Anzio, and also on the Adriatic coast, in Spain and elsewhere. Where it has been introduced to other countries, it is mainly ornamental.

Cones are gathered during the winter from November onwards. They are then usually stored until the summer, when they are spread in the sun to open. The seeds can then be shaken out and cracked, and the kernels extracted. One usually buys pine nuts as extracted kernels.

Pine kernels have been used by Mediterranean peoples for a very long time. The shells of the nuts have even been found in the rubbish tips left by the Roman legions in Britain. The flavour of the nuts is very delicate, scarcely tasting of turpentine, and what little there is is usually dissipated on heating. They have then a delicious nutty taste. Pine nuts are used in a variety of Italian meat dishes, with game, in sweet-sour dishes, and in sweet dishes. They are also used with eggs and rice and in *pesto Genovese*. One may find them called for in recipes originating in any country from Spain to Egypt, but particularly in the Lebanon in stuffings for chicken, with minced meat, aubergines, tomatoes.

Although the nuts of the stone pine are classical in Mediterranean cooking, other pine nuts of varying quality from other species of pine are eaten all round the Northern hemisphere from Siberia, the Himalayas, China, Korea and Japan to the United States and Mexico. They vary considerably in size and appearance, and some have a markedly turpentine flavour.

Pistachio Nut

FR: Pistache
GER: Pistazienmandeln
IT: Pistacchio
SP: Alfóncigo, Pistacho
BOT: Pistacia vera
FAM: Anacardiaceae
Plate II, No. 12

The fruits of which the pistachio nut is the kernel are borne in clusters on small trees said to have originated in the mountains of southern Turkestan. They have been cultivated in Mediterranean and Middle Eastern countries for three or four thousand years. (Among the presents sent by Jacob to Joseph were pistachio nuts – Genesis XVIII, 11.) This pistachio likes a climate similar to that suitable for cultivating almonds and olives and today is grown in practically every country bordering the Mediterranean including southern France, Spain and Italy, as well as in Persia and Afghanistan. It is also grown in the south-western parts of the United States. There are many cultivated varieties and there are separate male and female trees.

The kernel of the pistachio nut is covered with thin brown-red skin, but the flesh of the kernel itself is bright green right through. In general, the greener the colour the better the quality. Pistachio nuts are not as well known as they might be outside the countries where they grow, probably because they are rather expensive compared to the other common nuts of commerce.

Ill. 15 Mints: 1 Eau-de-Cologne Mint, 2 Spearmint, 3 Peppermint, 4 Catmint, 5 Pennyroyal, 6 Calamint.

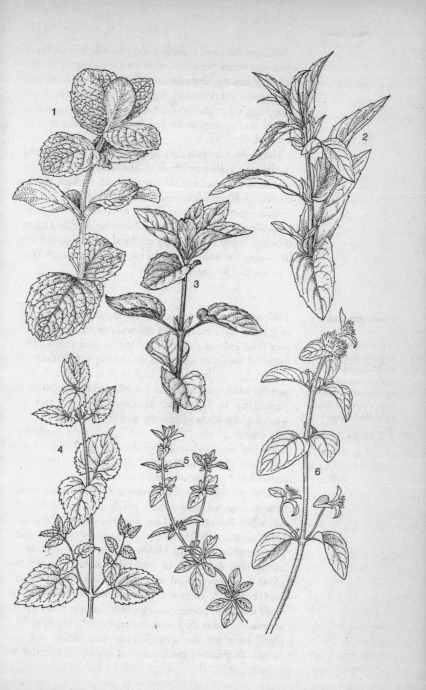

Without doubt, all travellers in the Middle East will have come on salted pistachios, their shells gaping open like little dry mussels. Pistachios are the green nuts in nougat and *locoum* (Turkish Delight). They are also used for decorating cakes and are (one hopes) the main colouring and flavouring in pistachio ice-cream, so popular in Italy and the United States.

The flavour of pistachio nuts is delicate. Extracts and essences are made from fresh good quality nuts. Pistachio nuts store well and a small quantity may be kept on the kitchen shelf for decoration or pounding into creams. Pistachio nuts are also included in certain meat and game recipes, particularly in Lebanese and other Middle Eastern cooking, but in this case they can be scarcely regarded as a flavouring for, although they look very pretty, their taste is swamped. (*See also* Mastic.)

Pomegranate

FR: Grenade
GER: Granatapfel
IT: Melagrana or Melagranata
SP: Granada
BOT: Punica granatum
FAM: Punicaceae

The pomegranate was probably the 'apple' of the Garden of Eden. It came from Persia and was cultivated there over four thousand years ago. The historical connotation of its botanical name, *Punica*, refers to the fact that it came to Roman Italy by way of Carthage in North Africa. Today pomegranates grow in warm dry climates the world over particularly in Spain and Morocco, all Mediterranean countries, the Levant and as far east as Pakistan and India. The beautiful vermilion-flowered bushes are a particular feature of the mud-walled gardens of the Middle East. There are also white-flowered and double varieties for decoration. Spiny varieties make a good hedge.

Good pomegranate fruits can only be got from good fruit varieties grown in places which have a cold winter and a hot dry summer. They are rather rare. The juice, either fresh, or boiled to a thick paste, is used in meat dishes over much of the Middle East. In Persia, it is commonly used in a delicious stew called *koreshe Fesenjan* in which meat is combined with a sweet-sour fruity taste. In the Lebanon, the juice, or a paste intended for meat stews, is made from sour pomegranates, rather than sweet ones. It is sometimes used in the famous aubergine dish, *Imam Bayildi*. Dried seeds are also sprinkled on sweet dishes and on *hummus* (a purée of chick peas and *tahina*) though this is mainly for decoration, but the seeds should be of the wild variety *dazu* common in the lower Himalayas and the seeds should be dried with the surrounding aril. This is the important sour and condiment called *anardana*. In India, dried seeds may be included in stuffing for *parathas*, in *pakoras*, and some curries. The syrup, *grenadine*, is made from pomegranate juice.

Poppy

FR: Coquelicot
GER: Mohn
INDIA: Cus-cus,
  Khush-khush,
  Khus-khus
IT: Papavero
SP: Ababa, Adormidera,
  Amapola
BOT: Papaver
  somniferum
FAM: Papaveraceae
Ill. 3, Nos. 1, 1a, page 54

Many kinds of poppy are grown for ornament, but though the leaves of the common cornfield poppy can be boiled as a spinach (slightly narcotic), and I have occasionally chewed the stems of the blue poppy (Sp: *Meconopsis*), which taste rather like lettuce stems, it is only the opium poppy that has real culinary importance.

The opium poppy is a native of the Middle East, and opium as a medicine was known to the Egyptians, Greeks and Romans and probably earlier, since its cultivation had reached Persia, India and China by A.D. 800. Opium consists of the gummy latex which oozes out of the green unripe seed pods when they are slit. It contains some twenty-four different alkaloids which are of interest to the doctor but not (one hopes) to the cook. Yet the seed of the opium poppy when ripe contains no alkaloid at all, and both the seed and the oil which can be expressed from it become important foods.

The opium poppy is an annual with large white, pink or lilac flowers. It is now found growing wild in many countries as an escape. It is common locally all round the Mediterranean and can even be seen in the eastern counties of Britain. Not only is the opium poppy cultivated in India, China and the Middle East but also in the Balkans, Germany and northern France and even a little in Britain.

There are many varieties of opium poppy and two quite different types of poppy seed (also called maw seed). The type commonly met with in Europe is like blue-grey shot, but the seed usually seen in India is much smaller and a creamy yellow. From the point of view of flavour, there is little difference.

In Europe and the Middle East, the main use of poppy seed is in confectionery. The flavour when baked is pleasantly nutty. The seeds are sprinkled on cakes and bread or included in various sweet stuffings. In India, poppy seed is known as *khus-khus* (not to be confused with the North African dish *cous-cous* or the Indian name for vetiver which is *khas-khas*). Poppy seed is used in curries where its function is partly for flavouring and partly to improve the texture and thicken the gravy. In India, starchy flours are never used for thickening curries.

Poppy seed is also an important source of oil. There is first a cold pressing which produces a clear edible oil known in France as *olivette*. Second pressings under heat produce a red oil, afterwards decolourized and used for paints and industrial purposes. As poppy oil is used by artists, supplies for the kitchen should not be obtained from the same shop from which you get the materials for your oil paintings.

Purslane
Pussley

ARABIC: Baqli
FR: Portulaca, Pourpier
GER: Kohlportulak,
    Portulak
INDIA: Kulfa
IT: Portulaca
SP: Verdolaga
BOT: Portulaca oleracea
    (Portulaca sativa)
FAM: Portulacaceae

Purslane is an annual, a sprawling plant with rosettes of thick fleshy leaves. It grows wild in India and has been eaten there for thousands of years: it is now established as a weed over most of North and South America as well. It is cultivated in the Middle East and to some extent in southern Europe. In England it is uncommon today, but was popular in the days of Elizabeth I.

Purslane needs a warm dry soil and full sun, and sowings made each month during the summer give a continuous supply. Make rows a foot apart with six inches between the plants in the row; gather the leaves like spinach as required. There are several varieties, some with golden leaves.

In the East, purslane is usually eaten cooked, but it is also an excellent salad plant used in France. In the Middle East one may find it in that mixed salad (containing bread) known as *fattoush*. Because purslane has thick fleshy leaves, it is sometimes pickled in vinegar, and there are many old English recipes.

Pyrethrum

FR: Pyrèthre
GER: Pyrethrum
IT: Piretro
SP: Piretro
BOT: Chrysanthemum
    cinerariaefolium

The word pyrethrum is loosely used for all single-flowered garden chrysanthemums and is also an insecticide. The insecticide comes mainly from three species, the one mentioned here which grows wild in Dalmatia (Yugoslavia) and two others – one coming from Persia and the other from the Caucasus. Roman cookery advocated a pinch of pyrethrum in rissoles. The pyrethrums are not poisonous,

FAM: Compositae
Ill. 9, No. 2, page 123

so if anyone grows them in the garden they may care to experiment. Other species of chrysanthemum have culinary uses in Japan, and even the large garden varieties can be used as a garnish for exotic salads or for decorating other foods.

Quassia
Bitter Ash

FR: Quassia amara
GER: Bitterholzbaum
    Quassia
IT: Quassia
SP: Cuasia
BOT: Quassia amara
    Jamaica quassia;
    Pacrasma excelsa
    (Picraena excelsa)
FAM: Simarubaceae
Ill. 5, No. 2, page 83

Quassia is, correctly, chips of the wood of a small tropical South American tree, though since the beginning of the nineteenth century it is more likely to be chips of the bitter ash, a much larger tree of the Caribbean Islands. The flavour in either case is intensely bitter. It is used in the preparation of apéritifs or as a substitute for hops. In brewing, these substances are often used instead of hops.

Quassia contains bitter glucosides and essential oils which are supposed to have tonic and digestive properties. This is why it is a common ingredient of the tonic wines and apéritifs used so much on the Continent to bolster flagging livers. Whether they do any good or not is a matter of opinion; anything bitter is popularly thought to be a tonic. In fact, anything must be bad if it enables one to drink and eat too much regularly. An occasional week's penance of nothing but raw oysters is considerably better for one's health and, in the long run, cheaper.

Rampion

FR: Raiponce
GER: Rapunzel-
    Glockenblume
IT: Raperonzolo
SP: Rapónchigo
BOT: Campanula
    rapunculus
    (Rapunculus verus)
FAM: Campanulaceae
Plate VI, Nos. 2, 5

The German name for this plant is known to many as it is also the name of the long-haired heroine in the Grimms' Fairy Story, *Rapunzel*. (Rampions were nicked from the witch's garden.) It was, as one might surmise, a plant well known in the past, though uncommon today, except in France and Switzerland.

The rampion is a native of Europe, North Africa and parts of Asia: in Britain, it is a local escape and is a close relative of the harebell or 'bluebell' of Scotland. The flowers are mauve, clustered in spikes, and there is a white radish-like root a foot long, but usually only half an inch thick. The seeds are the smallest of any vegetable, and for even sowing they are usually mixed with a little fine sand. Sow *in situ* in late spring, firm without covering and water frequently and carefully till they take hold. The plants grow to about two feet high and should have a four-inch space between each plant. A light rich soil is preferred, with some shade and plenty of water. Rampions are biennial. The roots can be lifted in early winter and stored in sand.

Both roots and leaves are used raw in salads. With a name like *Rapunzel* this is the salad for entertaining ballerinas, but don't confuse it with ramsons (wild garlic).

Ratafia

The origin of this word is uncertain perhaps Spanish or West Indian, but probably it is of Creole origin and is related to *tafia* (rum). To confuse the issue it means rather different things in different countries. In the Champagne country, ratafia is an apéritif of brandy diluted with un-fermented champagne grape juice. In England a ratafia is a bitter almond flavoured cordial or a small sweet biscuit also strongly flavoured with bitter almond.

A ratafia can, however, be spirit flavoured with any fruit or even herbs, the flavouring substances being extracted by soaking or maceration, almost always in brandy or grape spirit. Some liqueurs are ratafias, and many properly made essences might be called ratafias also. Strong alcohol is a powerful preservative as well as a solvent of substances which are not soluble in water.

In nineteenth-century cookery books, one finds many recipes for home-made ratafias, but these were the days before taxes had robbed the cook of the possibility of using brandy. There were ratafias of apricots, nectarines, peaches, blackcurrants, blackberries, angelica, oranges, gooseberries, orange-flowers, quince, raspberries, cherries, bitter almonds and roses. No doubt there were many more. These con-coctions contained supporting flavourings ranging from cinnamon, cardamom, cloves and nutmeg through vanilla, coriander, allspice, peach and apricot leaves to laurel leaves, sassafras, rosewater and even ambergris.

These preparations are clearly of great potential value to the cook. Faced with such exciting possibilities for flavour-ing cakes and creams, one can only suggest marching on the capital and requesting that the tax on brandy be reduced forthwith.

Resin

This is the gum that exudes from pine trees, when they are wounded. Various species are tapped like rubber trees, and the liquid resin is collected in pots. Amongst other uses this is the raw material for turpentine.

Resin is used to flavour the Greek wines called *retsina*. Some nine different species of pine grow in Greece, including the stone pine so characteristic of northern Mediterranean coasts. The resin from all species and some other resinous plants may be used in *retsina*, but the most common source (and also the most common pine) is the Aleppo or Jerusalem pine (*Pinus halepensis*).

Retsina itself is an acquired taste, and one is not very likely to acquire it outside Greece. For its proper enjoyment it requires the romantic atmosphere of the *taverna* and the flavour of grilled meat wound round with crispy entrails. There is a resin-flavoured liqueur known as *chaquesin*. (*See also* Mastic.)

Restharrow

FR: Bugrane
IT: Anonide
GER: Hauhechal
SP: Gatuña
BOT: Ononis spinosa
FAM: Leguminosea
Plate VI, No. 4

Common in Europe, especially on calcareous soils and on chalk in Britain, it is a rough hairy plant with dark green leaves and a tough creeping stem, often spiny. The flowers are like small, purple-red sweet peas.

Gerard says that 'the root is long, and runneth far abroad, very tough, and hard to be torn to pieces with the plough, insomuch that the oxen can hardly passe forward, but are constrained to stand still; whereupon it was called Res-Plough or Rest-Harrow'. He also says (it seems, quoting Dioscorides) that 'the tender sprigs or crops of this shrub before the thorns come forth, are preserved in pickle, and be very pleasant sauce to be eaten with meat as sallad'.

Rocambole

Sand Leek,
   Spanish Garlic
FR: Echalote d'Espagne,
   Rocambole
GER: Rockenbolle
   Schlangenknoblauch
IT: Aglio d'India,
   Aglio di Spagna,
   Aglio romano,
   Rocambola
SP: Rocambole
BOT: Allium

Rocambole is one of the onions, native to Europe and east to the Caucasus and Syria. It is found growing wild in dry places (a relative term here) on the coast of the north of England and parts of Scotland. Rocambole comes from the Danish *rocken bolle* meaning rock onion. Sand leek is another name that gives a clue to its habitat.

The flavour of rocambole is rather like mild garlic and is cultivated to some extent, though it is not as popular today as in the last century. In appearance the plant is very like the purple-skinned varieties of garlic but is easily distinguished because the flowers of rocambole are light purple, not white

scorodoprasum
FAM: Liliaceae
(Amaryllidaceae,
Alliaceae)

as are the flowers of garlic: also rocambole forms purple bulbils, that is, small aerial bulbs, which garlic does not. These bulbils may, of course, also be used for flavouring.

The rocambole is easy to grow in light soil either from the bulbils or by separating the root cloves. Good seed is rare. Bulbs can be lifted, dried, and stored in the same way as garlic. (*See* Onions, Garlic.)

Rocket
Rocket-gentle,
   Rocket-salad, Roka,
   Roman Rocket, Tira

FR: Roquette
GER: Ruke
IT: Rucola, Ruchetta,
   Rughetta
SP: Oruga
BOT: Eruca sativa
FAM: Cruciferae
Ill. 10, No. 1, page 136

Dame's Rocket, Damask
   Violet, Dame's Violet,
   Sweet Rocket,
   Vesper Flower
IT: Viola matronale
BOT: Hesperis matronalis

Eastern Rocket
IT: Erisimo
BOT: Sisymbrium
   orientale

London Rocket
BOT: Sisymbrium irio

Yellow Rocket
IT: Barbarea
BOT: Barbarea vulgaris

Lesser Yellow Rocket
BOT: Barbarea stricta

Wall Rocket
IT: Ruchetta Selvatica
BOT: Diplotaxis
   tenuifolia

Sea Rocket

This is an important plant commonly used to flavour green salads in Italy. The taste is pungent and interesting. It is a native of southern Europe and western Asia, but has run wild in North America. Wild rocket-salad can be found in waste places or as a weed on cultivated land. It has a yellowish flower, but can be easily recognized by its characteristic smell when bruised. The garden varieties are larger, one to two feet high and have creamy or whitish wallflower-like flowers and bigger, tenderer leaves. Rocket is an annual and is easily raised from seed. Although it will grow almost anywhere it is best grown quickly in rich moist soil, as otherwise the leaves are inclined to become tough. Cultivated varieties have a milder flavour than the wild plants.

Both the leaves and seed of rocket were used as a flavouring by the Romans, and it was common in Elizabethan England. Today, it is much used as a salad plant in the South of France, Italy and Egypt, but seems to have become neglected in more northern countries, which is a pity because it is one of the most interesting salad flavourings and is very easy to grow. The leaves are incorporated with lettuce or other green leaves, dressed with salt, oil and vinegar. Rocket salad is a common ingredient in the salad leaf mixtures which can be bought in Italian markets.

The name rocket is extended also to several other plants.

DAME'S ROCKET is a perennial, two to three feet high, with purple or white flowers, and native to Europe and western Asia. It is an escape in the United Kingdom and can be used in salads. EASTERN ROCKET, a relative of hedge mustard (*Sisymbrium officinale*), has established itself in Britain, although it is native to southern Europe and the Middle East. It became common on bomb sites in London, just as the LONDON ROCKET, also an escape in Britain,

IT: Cachile
BOT: Cakile maritima

South American
'Rocket'
IT: Araugia or fisianto
BOT: Araujia sericofera,
Physianthes albens

became established after the Great Fire of 1666. I have found no record of these last two rockets being used in salads, and they are mentioned only to avoid confusion.

YELLOW ROCKET, or common wintercress, is probably too bitter for salads, but is closely related to land cress or American cress (*see* Cress), which is, of course, grown as a salad. Another rarer species, the lesser yellow rocket, is also mentioned to avoid confusion.

WALL ROCKET is a close relative of the stinkweed (*Diplotaxis muralis*). Both of these plants have a strong smell when rubbed, but the wall rocket is used in the South of France as a flavouring herb in salads under the name *riquetta* (Nice), probably in confusion with the true salad rocket.

SEA ROCKET, which grows on the coasts of Europe as far north as southern England, is probably not eaten, although it is known in Italy as *ruchetta di mare*.

None of the above rockets is related to the South American ornamental, a so-called rocket also known as 'cruel plant'. Although this rocket belongs to a different family than the true rocket, *Araujia* and *Eruca* have the same etymological origin.

Rose

FR: Rose
GER: Rose
IT: Rosa
SP: Rosa
BOT: Rosa damascena
(the damask rose);
Rosa centifolia (the
cabbage rose); Rosa
gallica (Rose de
provins) etc.
FAM: Rosaceae
Plate VII, No. 4

There are perhaps more than ten thousand varieties of rose, but few are grown as sources of perfume and flavour. However, the petals of any scented rose can be used in the kitchen.

Fields of roses are cultivated for perfume in the South of France and in Bulgaria: in France, it is mainly types of cabbage rose; in Bulgaria, mostly the damask rose. Although Bulgaria is now so famous for rose oil (from the Valley of Roses), cultivation dates only from the early seventeenth century, while Persia, even at the time of Jesus Christ, was exporting rosewater to places as far away as China. Today rose oil is still produced in Persia by the ancient methods, and I have seen nothing more romantic than the Persian gardens in Meshed where rose oil (otto or attar of roses) is made in the old way for the great mosque. Armfuls of fresh petals are put into a copper cauldron with spring water, and the lid sealed with clay. A wood fire is lit under the cauldron, and the vapour conducted through hollow reed pipes and condensed in a second vessel cooled in the running water of the channel that irrigates the rose garden. The distillate is first milky: later, the pure rose oil rises to the top. It is a blow to romance that modern steam distillation in fact produces more delicate oils.

Rose oil is exceedingly expensive and so is frequently adulterated with palmarosa or rose geranium oil. As it is so strong, in cooking the much diluted rosewater or rose essence is used.

Drinks perfumed with roses have been made for centuries. The Romans put rose petals in their wine; the Persians made rose petal wine; in England, a rose liqueur was made in the twelfth century. Today we have Bulgarian rose liqueur, which is exceedingly sweet and scented to modern tastes (suited better to a harem than a dining-room), and a rose liquor from China (Pekin: *mooi quai dzao*) used as a flavouring in some pork dishes.

Rosewater is still used in sweet dishes in the East. Perhaps the most famous use of roses is in the rose petal jam so popular in the Balkans, Turkey, Bulgaria, Rumania and Persia. Honey is also flavoured by boiling water with the petals of roses and so also is Turkish *locoum*. Further east in India, a rose-flavoured candy (*gulkand*) is made by packing sugar crystals with the petals until they pick up the flavour. Here again it is in the sherbets and sweet dishes for which rosewater and rose essence are so essential. *Gulab jamuns* and *rasgullas* from India (*gulab*, a rose) are the most famous of these. Anyone embarking on mid-eastern or Indian sweet dishes really must have rosewater on the kitchen shelf.

In the West, we crystallize rose petals – but more for decoration than anything else, and André Simon's *Guide to Good Food and Wine* mentions the sprinkling of petals on top of the fruit before closing a cherry pie. If one does not in these days like highly perfumed sweet dishes, this was certainly not the case in the past, and Elizabethan recipes are full of the use of rosewater and musk.

Rose vinegar is sometimes made by infusing the petals or adding a few drops of an alcoholic extract of rose petals. Slightly rose-flavoured vinegar is particularly good for mixed green leaves.

Fresh rose petals can always be used as a decoration or

garnish, but stale roses are reminiscent of grandmother's *pot-pourri*.

Roselle
Red or Jamaica Sorrel

FR: Rozelle
GER: Rosellahanf or
    Karkadi
IT: Carcade
SP: Rosella
BOT: Hibiscus sabdariffa
FAM: Malvaceae

This annual hibiscus is bushy, four to five feet high and usually red. It is native to tropical Asia. The fleshy young calices surrounding the immature fruits are intensely acid and are used for flavouring jams, refreshing drinks and wine, or for making an excellent jelly or sauce which somewhat resembles cranberry. They are also dried. Roselle is important in India and Southeast Asia in curries and chutneys, and recently also in Cuba, Central America, California and Florida. It is generally becoming more popular.

Rosemary
Old Man

FR: Romarin,
    Rosmarin encens
GER: Rosmarein,
    Rosmarin
IT: Rosmarino,
    Ramerino
SP: Romero, Rosmario
BOT: Rosmarinus
    officinalis
FAM: Labiatae
Plate IV, No. 1

The word comes from *ros* (dew) and *marinus* (sea). Rosemary is a bush which grows wild in profusion round the Mediterranean (Spain, Italy, Dalmatia, Greece, North Africa, though only in isolated spots in Turkey, Lebanon and Egypt). It has now been taken to most countries which have a not too severe climate. This includes Britain, where it was introduced by the Romans, and the United States, where it is even cultivated commercially for the essential oil used in perfumery. In Britain, it thrives only in the south, and there it is already beginning to lose its finest savour, like many another aromatic plant moved from a warm dry climate to conditions that are really too wet for it. In northern parts of the United States, rosemary will also need winter protection.

Rosemary grows up to six feet high. It is an evergreen bush with pale blue flowers and spiky leathery leaves. It is very aromatic and the essential oil contains, amongst other things, camphor, an overtone one can recognize. The smell has also something reminiscent of pine needles on a hot day.

This is one of the most common aromatic wild plants of Mediterranean hillsides, especially in rocky limestone areas near the sea. In this climate, it flowers pretty much throughout the year. The finest flowers I ever saw were in Sardinia one November. Perhaps it is the most beautiful of all herbs, forming thickets with myrtle and arbutus, smilax and juniper.

Opinions on rosemary as a culinary herb are rather sharply divided, even in countries where it grows profusely. In Majorca, for instance (though not generally in Spain), the village people considered me mad to use it. On the other hand, in Italy it is one of the most common flavourings, especially for roast lamb and kid (*abbacchio* and *capretto al forno*). There, butchers will hand out free bunches of rosemary with the meat or prepare meat already tied up with it. It is discreetly used in French, Spanish or Greek cooking, but Italy stands rather alone in its passion for it.

There is no doubt that rosemary has a slight camphor taste which some people do not like. It is also a violent taste, one might call it a peasants' taste, and in Italy it is often used to excess. However, used with sense it is not only very good with grilled or roasted lamb and kid, but also with fish, shellfish, veal and even in strongly-flavoured chicken or rabbit dishes with garlic and wine.

As a garden plant, rosemary, as one might imagine, likes sun and a poor, dry, calcareous soil. It can be grown from cuttings or from rooted parts of an existing plant. When dried, it gradually loses its strength of flavour, and the needle-like leaves become easily detached from the stem – they are then not pleasant to find in the dish. But since rosemary is evergreen, one can get it fresh at all times of the year. It is almost always used in the whole sprig and rarely if ever chopped. In soups or stews it is best to add a large sprig and then remove it when the taste is sufficient, or it may be included in a bouquet garni. Rosemary is also available in these days as a powder. This may be convenient to people who live in a town, but, like all flavourings, it loses by powdering. For some reason fresh rosemary is not only difficult to get, but wildly expensive in London shops, which encourages the anti-social to whip sprigs from the park.

Rowan
Mountain Ash, Rodden

FR: Sorbe (berry)
GER: Eberesche,
  Vogelbeere (berry)
IT: Sorbo (not specific)

This well-known wild tree of northern Europe is also planted in gardens for its decorative orange berries. It is a close relative of the sorb apple or service tree and the whitebeams, and more distantly related to the hawthorn and azerole (Naples medlar). The word 'rowan' is of Scandinavian origin (*raum*, Norway; *rön*, Sweden).

SP: Fresno alpestre
BOT: Sorbus aucuparia
FAM: Rosaceae
Ill. 8, No. 3, page 114

The berries from this tree can be made into a delicious, astringent jelly which goes well with venison. The berries are boiled with enough water to cover until the juice is red and bitter. The juice is then strained through a jelly bag and boiled with sugar (between one and one and a half pounds per pint of liquid until it jells).

An old Northumbrian farmer's wife, one of the few superb English country cooks I have known, used rowan berries in many of her meat dishes. Readers may care to experiment with these sour, bitter and astringent berries, which yearly go to waste neglected.

Rue
Herb of Grace

FR: Rue odorante
GER: Gartenraute, Raute, Weinkraut, Weinraute
IT: Ruta
SP: Ruda
BOT: Ruta graveolens
FAM: Rutaceae
Plate IV, No. 5

This well-known member of the old-fashioned herb garden grows wild in southern Europe and in the Middle East. It is common in poor soil beside paths and amongst the flower terraces in Italy, from whence it was introduced to Britain by the Romans. It has sometimes gone wild in the United States.

Rue is a small bushy plant, one to three feet high, with blue-green leaves and small yellow flowers. It is easy to recognize by the strong and, to most people, nasty smell it gives off when rubbed between the fingers. There are several horticultural varieties, grown for decoration.

In the garden, rue is easily raised from seeds, cuttings or pieces of established plants replanted. Evergreen and perennial, it prefers sun, good drainage and plenty of room.

Rue is an interesting plant and has great importance in old folklore and country medicine all over Europe. Rue does in fact contain powerful medicinal substances, and these are extracted commercially. In small quantities, a leaf or two, it is a stimulant. Many people chew a leaf on a hot summer's day, but others are allergic to it and in large quantities it is dangerous. As it is popularly thought to induce abortion, there are sometimes accidents. The word rue comes from the Greek *ruta* (set free) which refers to its medicinal qualities. Both the leaves and seeds of rue were frequently used as a culinary herb by the Romans and in the Middle Ages. Its taste is powerful and bitter, but in tiny quantities, atomized by chopping, it is possible to use it as an unusual flavouring with fish or eggs and in cream cheese mixtures. It is also useful in vegetable juice cocktails. But a heavy hand with rue in meat stews (I remember an old lady who had it) is quite disastrous. Some stalwarts put the young shoots in salads.

Rue was one of the flavourings used in the old herb-flavoured mead known as sack. The classic modern use is in the Italian distilled grape spirit known as *grappa*. The sprig of green herb one often sees in the *grappa* bottle, labelled *Con ruta*, is rue, although usually of another less bitter Mediterranean species which the Italians call *ruta frangiata* (Bot: *Ruta chalepensis*). The flavour of *grappa*, especially when it has rue in it is, to many people, rather nasty; at least this assures that one does not drink too much of it. The guides of Cortina d'Ampezzo often give their clients a thimbleful on the vertical face of some Dolomite needle. It greatly aids the contemplation of eternity, and the rue is appropriate.

Saccharin

This is probably the best known of artificial sweetening substances. Chemically it is not a sugar, but a synthetic chemical benzoyl sulphonic amide or benzoic sulfinide made by treating toluene (a distillate of coal tar) with sulphuric acid. Saccharin was first discovered by chance in 1879, when a chemist working with these chemicals noticed his finger tasted sweet. Methods for producing it were patented in 1894. It is intensely sweet (estimates range to as much as seven times as sweet as cane sugar), but it has no food value and passes unchanged through the body. It is available commercially, most often in the form of tiny tablets, each being enough to sweeten a cup of coffee or tea. Some say that saccharin is harmful to the digestive system, and its taste is certainly inferior to that of sugar. It persists in the saliva, and gives a long-lasting and cloying sweetness in the mouth which sugar does not.*

Since the invention of saccharin, other non-sugar sweetening substances have been produced. Some of these, such as dulcin or sucrol and P-4000 (Verkade's compound) are not so virulently sweet as saccharin and do not persist to the same extent in the mouth, but they are toxic, at least in the opinion of the United States Food and Drug Administration.

Cyclamate sodium has the advantage that it withstands

* It has recently been noticed in some countries as potentially carcinogenic.

cooking, but is also under fire as potentially toxic. In general one should avoid using this sort of substance. One is in the hands of medical and health experts who not only hold conflicting opinions but cannot at the outset predict that a substance, whilst seemingly innocuous, will not have harmful effects when taken over a number of years. There are unfortunate people who cannot for health reasons avoid using artificial sweeteners. The solution for the future perhaps is to train our children to have less of a sweet tooth, and maybe we should stop replacing the less sweet milk sugar with sweet cane sugar in babies' bottles. (*See* Sugars.)

Safflower

Bastard Saffron,
  Carthamine Dye,
  Safflor, Saffron Thistle

FR: Carthame, Safran
  bâtard
GER: Färberdistel, Saflor
IT: Cartamo
  or falso zafferano
SP: Cártamo
BOT: Carthamus
  tinctorius
FAM: Compositae
Ill. 3, No. 3, page 54

The safflower is a native of India, and an important crop in many warm countries, It is grown in the South of France and is sufficiently hardy to survive in English gardens. The flowers are orange-red or yellow and contain carthamin, an important dyeing agent, used for colouring food, cloth and cosmetics (mixed with French chalk, it becomes rouge). In parts of Poland, the flowers are mixed into bread and other foods.

Safflower is also cultivated for its seed, from which an important edible oil is expressed. Of all of the salad oils, this one has one of the lowest percentages of cholesterol. The seeds are sometimes eaten by poor people, and even the leaves can be used as salad. Other wild species of safflower which grow in the Middle East and northern India have similar properties and local uses.

Saffron

FR: Safran
GER: Safran
IT: Zafferano
SP: Azafrán
INDIA: Kesar
BOT: Crocus sativus
FAM: Iridaceae
Ill. 18, No. 3, page 244

The saffron crocus must never be confused with the meadow saffron (*Colchicum autumnale*), which grows wild in Britain and is sometimes called 'naked ladies' because the leaves have withered before the flower comes out in autumn. The meadow saffron is exceedingly poisonous and is sometimes a nuisance to farmers because cattle are likely to die if they eat it. As Gerard says, 'the roots of all the sorts of mede saffrons are very hurtful to the stomacke, and being eaten they kill by choaking as mushromes do'.

The saffron we buy, sometimes called 'hay saffron' on account of its appearance, consists of the dried stigmas from

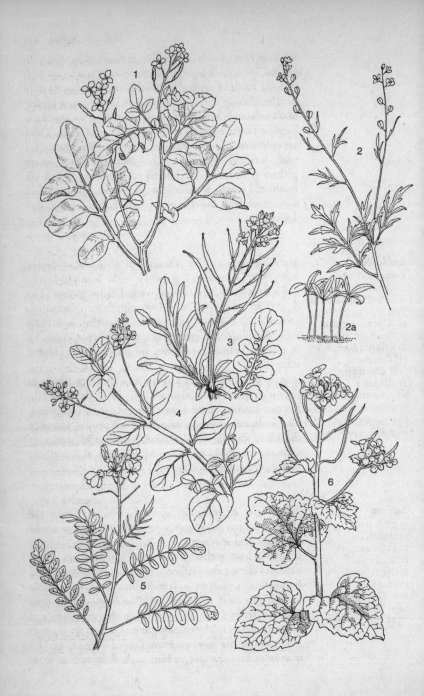

the flower of the saffron crocus. The saffron crocus is thought to have come originally from Greece and Asia Minor, but it has been cultivated from times beyond historical record. It was used in ancient Persia, was known at the time of Solomon (*circa* 960 B.C.) and was in great demand by the Phoenicians. It was also used by the ancient Greeks and Romans. Some people say that its use in *bouillabaisse* and Cornish saffron cakes is due to Phoenician influence, but a Greek colony at Marseilles followed the earlier Phoenician settlement, and the Phoenicians were after all a very, very long time ago. The introduction of saffron into Spain is usually attributed to the Arabs as late as A.D. 900, and if it was already grown in Britain at the time of the Phoenicians it seems to have died out, since it is recorded as coming into the country during the reign of Edward III (1327–1337). The story, as told by Hakluyt, is that a returning pilgrim carried a stolen corm hidden in his staff. At any rate it was about this time saffron growing was established at Saffron Walden (Essex, England) and it was cultivated there and in Cambridgeshire till the turn of this century after which it died out.

Today saffron is cultivated in most of the Mediterranean countries through the Levant and Persia to Kashmir and also in China. The amount of hand labour involved in collecting the three stigmas from each flower is prodigious, and estimates vary from between seventy-five thousand to a quarter of a million flowers as being necessary to produce one pound of saffron. As the world trade in saffron runs into many thousands of pounds, the number of flowers that must be handled to produce this is quite astronomical. Needless to say, saffron is exceedingly expensive but a pinch is enough for a large dish.

The saffron crocus is a typical crocus with blue or purple flowers which appear in the autumn (unlike Colchicum, it still has its leaves). It is easy to grow in almost any sunny well-drained position and will produce better saffron if it is not too well 'done'. Propagation is from corms planted in late summer, with four to six inches between plants. The

Ill. 16   Mustards and cresses: 1 Watercress, 2 Garden Cress, 2a Garden Cress Seed Leaves, 3 American Cress, 4 Brooklime, 5 Lady's Smock, 6 Garlic Mustard.

saffron should be picked the moment the plant opens. Most people, however, will buy their saffron. Unfortunately, because it is so expensive it is very often adulterated, and easiest of all to adulterate is the powder which is commonly sold in little packets on the continent. Good saffron should not be more than a year old, of a brilliant orange colour – not yellow, bleached or with white streaks – with a strong perfume and a pungent, bitter, medicinal, honey-like taste. In genuine saffron, the stigma expands immediately when a pinch is placed on the surface of warm water, and the colour easily diffuses out. Cheap saffron does not exist, so any bargain should be suspect.

Saffron contains characteristic essential oils, which give it flavour, as well as a high percentage of a yellow dye easily soluble in water. This makes it useless as a fabric dye but very suitable for cooking. Dishes require only very small quantities – a tiny pinch – both for colouring and flavour.

Saffron was much used in medieval cookery. Today, it is restricted to a few dishes, but its presence in these is essential. Saffron cakes and *bouillabaisse* have already been mentioned, but saffron is very commonly put into other soups and stews of fish (e.g. *zarzuela*) on the Mediterranean coasts of Spain and France as well as in sauces for shellfish, and even into that variation on *äioli* known as *rouille* (rust), which adds such a peppery garlic kick to fish soup on the French Riviera coast. Saffron is also essential in *risotto milanese* (with its delicately yellow-coloured rice), and is commonly put into Spanish *paella*, especially when this contains shellfish. In fact, it seems to combine particularly well with the flavours of garlic and fish. In Spain, however, saffron is used also with liver and goes into several sauces. It is also used to colour some liqueurs and various Eastern sweetmeats.

Many books on Eastern cooking use the word saffron when they mean turmeric, for saffron is not much used in India (except in rich mogul, Kashmiri or N. Indian cooking) or Southeast Asia on account of its high price. Turmeric has its own distinctive taste and cannot in any circumstances be used to replace real saffron in spite of the fact that the first *bouillabaisse* I ever tasted (served with a great deal of ceremony in a large restaurant in Marseilles) was 'done up' with turmeric. The result was like the worst possible fish curry.

Opinions are sharply divided on the question of saffron: people who are not used to it may find it unpleasant or too strong, masking the other flavours of the dish. If one wishes to have a yellow colour without the saffron taste, one may use safflower, sometimes called bastard or Mexican saffron, or even marigold petals.

Sage

FR: Sauge
GER: Echter Salbei,
  Edelsalbei,
  Gartensalbei, Scharlei
IT: Salvia
SP: Salvia
BOT: Salvia officinalis
FAM: Labiatae
Ill. 14, No. 2, page 189

Every gardener knows the genus *Salvia* (from the Latin *salvere* – *salvus*, save), which refers to its health keeping qualities. Sage, from French *sauge* in old books 'sawge' is only one of the very many species.

Garden sage is a native of the North Mediterranean coasts, and is common as a wild plant on the hills of Dalmatia, particularly round Rijeka (Fiume). Dried wild sage and sage honey are important exports from Yugoslavia. It is not quite clear when sage entered European cooking. The Romans certainly used it medicinally but it does not seem to have been used by them in the kitchen, though it was certainly well known all over Europe by the sixteenth century.

Sage is a variable species, and there are a large number of different varieties. Sages differ enormously in their flavour, and most of them should be regarded as decorative rather than culinary. The literature abounds with names such as pineapple sage, lavender sage, wormwood sage, Graham's and Gregg's sage (Mexico), Cyprus sage, red sage, ash-leaved sage (Morocco) and so on. For cooking purposes, the narrow-leaved sage, which bears blue flowers, or the broad-leaved sage, of which there are non-flowering varieties, are the best. In selecting herbs for the garden, one must be guided by one's own taste, because soil and climate influence flavour, and, for practical reasons, by what cuttings or plants can be obtained from friends or local nurserymen. It is, however, important to be alert to the fact that all sage is not equally good and to consider whether you have good sage in your garden: if not, change it.

As culinary sage is a plant of poor dry limestone areas, it thrives best in well-drained soil, though it can be grown almost anywhere if the climate is not too cold and wet for it. Propagation is usually by cuttings, often rooted by layering. Although the plant is perennial, it becomes woody and straggling, so it is best to layer and replant every few years. One or two bushes suffice in the average garden. Sage leaves dry well and are also suitable for quick freezing. As with many labiate herbs, the best flavour is developed just before flowering.

The flavour of sage is powerful, especially when grown in hot dry conditions, and contains overtones of camphor. Opinions are sharply divided on its culinary excellence, some hold that it is crude, others love it, and to lovers nothing is crude. Sage is one of the few herbs to stay through the decline of herbs in English cooking, but it has become almost limited to sage and onion stuffing for goose, with pork and in the stronger flavoured sausages, though not in the usual commercial sausages, perhaps because many children do not like it. In German cooking, sage is of note in its use with eels, both in soup and for wrapping round the pieces of eel to flavour them during cooking. The use of sage as a flavouring with eels extends down into Belgium. In French cooking, sage is used occasionally, but rarely as a dominant flavour. Italy on the other hand, has a great love of sage, and with rosemary and bay it is one of the common herbs handed out as a gift by the butchers. It is used particularly with liver and veal as in *saltimbocca* (in which thin slices of veal and ham are rolled up with a sage leaf, cooked in butter and finished with marsala) and also in many other dishes, with sausages and so on. Sage is also used fairly commonly on the Mediterranean for wrapping small birds, such as thrushes, before roasting, and meat for roasting is sometimes stuck with sprigs of sage or larded with the leaf. It is also threaded with meat on to kebab skewers and sometimes turns up in the excruciatingly powerful herb salads eaten by villagers in the Middle East. Some people, indeed, advocate sage shoots in salads as well as for flavouring broad beans and peas in the same way that savory is used in France. Personally, I like the flavour of sage in strongly aromatic meat dishes, but it is not subtle and goes better with a healthy outdoor appetite than in a more sophisticated context.

There are, throughout the world, many plants called sage such as 'sage brush' and the 'wild sage' of South

Africa, which are nothing to do with the family. Various species of sage are also used as teas or medicines across Asia from Europe to China. (*See* Clary.)

Salt

Cooking Salt
FR: Gros sel,
    Sel de cuisine
GER: Kochsalz
IT: Sale da cucina
SP: Sal gema,
    Sal de cocina

Table Salt
FR: Sel blanc, Sel de table
GER: Speisesalz,
    Tafelsalz
IT: Sale da tavola,
    Sale fino
SP: Sal de mesa

Sea Salt
FR: Sel de mer,
    Sel gris, Sel marin
GER: Meersalz
IT: Sale marino
SP: Sal de mar

Salt is the most fundamental of all the tastes in food, and it is a true taste detected in the mouth. The taste is due to the presence of monobasic anions and cations in the solution together, a statement that will mean more to those who did their chemistry homework than to cooks. In practice, saltiness is provided by sodium chloride (NaCl), because most other chlorides (e.g. calcium or potassium chloride) have unpleasant bitter tastes or are purgative or poisonous.

Sodium chloride is one of the minerals essential to animal life. It is the most important salt in the sea, and it accounts for the saltiness of blood. Most people take in eight or ten grams of salt every day, of which only one to one and a half grams comes naturally from the food; the rest is added. Food without salt is dull, as unfortunate people who are put on a salt free diet discover. Animals come for miles to salt licks, and travellers in the saltless regions, such as the Himalayas, will find salt a precious article of commerce.

The perfect salting of food is one of the most important acts of the good cook. 'French chefs feel satisfied if the foods they send from their kitchens with their final approval have the supreme flavour; and that nothing must be added to them, not even salt and pepper.'* Well, that is a counsel of perfection because it is well known that some people (alcoholics in particular) like more salt in their food than others, but certainly if more than a few guests reach for the salt the cook has been careless.

The final adjustment of salt should, where possible, be left to the end of cooking when the contents of the pan have reduced as far as they are going to. If a dish is adjusted before this point, the amount of salt will in most cases be too great for the final amount of liquid and the dish will be much too salty.

Dishes one cannot taste before cooking (it takes a courageous and rather foolhardy cook to taste raw pig's

* Quote from a letter from Arnaud Cazenade of Arnaud's Restaurant, New Orleans, Louisiana, to Lea and Perrins dated April 1930.

liver pâté) must have the salt measured, but everything possible should be tasted.

When salting dishes, indeed when flavouring them with anything, a very important scientific principle is involved which put very crudely is this: the more salt you have added, the greater must be the quantity added to achieve an increase in saltiness. Therefore, timid use of salt is no good, as the amounts required become less critical, not more critical, as one approaches the point of perfection. (See pages 29-31.)

If, however, a dish is over-salted by mistake, there is little to be done, unless it is possible to increase the volume so that the salt is diluted. Sugar is antagonistic to salt, but whether it can be used will depend on the dish. Some dishes require a very fine balance between salt and sugar to be adjusted, but usually one cannot add sugar to 'kill' salt.

Salt brings out the flavour of other things. It is of value in the water used to cook vegetables, because it makes the cooking water a little less ready to dissolve the mineral salts out of the vegetables. It raises the temperature at which water boils. Dry salt extracts water from meat or vegetables by osmosis which is one reason for salting vegetables before they are pickled. It is also a powerful preservative. When it is present, some organisms are completely stopped from growing, and others are very much slowed down. This is why salt is used for preserving meat, fish, bacon and vegetables. It also ensures that only the proper flavour-producing organisms develop in bacon, ham, cheese and fish products, as well as such lactic acid pickles as sour cucumbers and sauerkraut.

Because salt is never quite pure sodium chloride, there is some variation in the flavour and saltiness of salt from different sources. Considerable variation exists from country to country both in flavour and origin. Rock salt occurs in underground deposits usually formed by the drying up of ancient seas. It is crystalline, clear, white or pink from salts of iron. It can also contain traces of un-palatable soda or epsom salts and even, on occasions, poisonous salts of arsenic or barium.

By its very nature, rock salt is unpurified, but only that from safe deposits would be sold for human consumption. At its best, rock salt is regarded by many people as the finest flavoured of all salts. It must, of course, be ground for use at table in a wooden salt mill or pounded with a pestle and mortar.

COMMON KITCHEN SALT is usually obtained by pumping water into salt bearing underground strata and then pumping up the brine. This brine has then to be concentrated by evaporation until the salt crystallizes out. During the process of crystallization, the salt is to some extent purified. It is the common everyday salt in many countries, available in different degrees of coarseness, and in blocks and tablets.

TABLE SALT, though of the same origin, is ground fine, and specially treated to prevent caking. It is usually rather pure sodium chloride from which other salts having hygroscopic (water grabbing) characteristics have been removed. Starch, phosphate of lime and other substances which promote free running have usually been added. It is the least interesting in flavour.

SEA SALT is the common salt in many countries, and in others it may be bought in health food stores and good grocers. In its crude form it is often known as 'bay salt' because it is obtained by evaporating sea water in enclosed bays. Sea water itself contains a high percentage of sodium chloride and many trace elements ranging from iodine to silver and even gold, but it also contains considerable quantities of purgative, bad tasting and even poisonous salts. However, purification takes place during even the most primitive methods of evaporation, and the salt left has a good flavour and is recommended by many health experts.

SPICED SALTS are hallowed by tradition and were certainly sold in the last century and made at home for many centuries before. For illustration I quote the following (one of many recipes): '4 teaspoons of ground nutmeg and ground cloves; 2 teaspoons each of white pepper, powdered thyme, dried bay leaf, and mixed marjoram and rosemary; 1 teaspoon of cayenne pepper to give it punch.' This to be mixed with a pound of sea salt. It might be sensible to reduce the salt in such mixtures, as one can always add more salt to a dish if one wishes.

As salt is a powerful preservative, a physical help when flavourings must be ground with a pestle and mortar, and an ingredient of all savoury or meat dishes, it is a rather time saving device to prepare and keep variously flavoured salts in the kitchen. Garlic may be pounded with salt, although the flavour is never as good as fresh garlic, and celery seed, which is difficult to pound alone, maybe pounded with salt to make celery salt. These and various other flavoured salts (we might mention salt flavoured with hickory smoke) are available commercially in America and Britain. They are part of the new vogue for quick cookery, but celery salt and 'oriental' salt are excellent with gulls' or plovers' eggs.

Although it is a pity to rely on such products completely, and commercial products remove romance from cooking and destroy individuality, they can be useful on occasions. But it is also perfectly easy to make flavoured salts at home and then one is free to combine any flavours, and can give free rein to self expression. It is unrealistic to pretend that we are never in a hurry, and anything which helps towards cooking quickly without losing the personal touch is bound to be valuable.

VEGETABLE SALTS. These are various special salts of vegetable origin. The flavour of some of these is excellent. 'Mineral salts' are of course present naturally in vegetables and are essential to one's health.

Samphire

Peter's Cress, Rock
Samphire, Sea Fennel

FR: Bacile, Fenouil de
mer, Perce-pierres
GER: Meerfenchel
IT: Critmo, Finocchio
marino
SP: Hinojo marino
BOT: Crithmum
maritimum
FAM: Umbelliferae

The name samphire comes from the French *herbe de St Pierre* (St Peter's herb). It is an umbelliferous plant, with greenish-yellow flowers and can immediately be recognized by its fat succulent leaves with their strong characteristic smell. It is a plant of sea cliffs, rather local in Britain (though occasionally sold in markets), but common on the southern European Atlantic seaboard and in most Mediterranean countries and the Crimea. Samphire has a very strong aromatic and salty taste (it always reminds me of a mixture of celery and kerosene, but I am sure that this is a personal reaction). It used to be commonly pickled in England (there are accounts of maidens poisoned by samphire pickled in copper vats). Pickled samphire is still sold in markets in southern Europe; it is placed beside bowls of olives in Majorcan markets. Samphire is a rather overwhelming pickle, and one of which most people soon tire even if they like it at first. The plant is also sometimes used fresh in salads, or it may be eaten cooked in butter as a vegetable or garnish. It should not be confused with the so-called 'golden samphire' (*Inula crithmoides*), which is a close relative of elecampane (*Inula helenium*).

Sarsaparilla

FR: Salsepareille
GER: Sarsaparille
IT: Salsapariglia
SP: Zarzaparilla
BOT: Species of Smilax
FAM: Liliaceae
Ill. 5, No. 6, page 83

This comes from the root of several species of *Smilax*, most of them indigenous to the tropical jungles of Central America. Anyone who has tried to walk up a Riviera hillside will have probably been ripped by the thorns of the tangled, twining European *Smilax*, with its striking, arrow-like leaves. Most *Smilaxes*, though, are found in the Amazon and Central American forests. As they are climbing or trailing vines with viciously armed stems found in dense, humid forests, digging the roots is an unpleasant business. These contain a bitter principle, and when dried, they are used combined with other flavouring in the preparation of soft drinks and root beers. Although once considered a tonic, it is now regarded as useless.

One will, however, come upon soft drinks called sarsaparilla in many countries, and there are numerous substitutes for the real thing.

Sassafras

FR: Sassafras
GER: Sassafras
IT: Sassafrasso
SP: Sasafrás
BOT: Sassafras albidum
(Sassafras officinalis)
FAM: Lauraceae
Ill. 4, No. 4, page 70

The sassafras is a well-known North American wayside tree, native to the eastern parts of the continent from Canada to Florida and as far west as Kansas. The tree bears yellow-green flowers, which appear before the leaves. The fruits are dark blue with red stalks.

Although all parts of the sassafras tree are to some extent aromatic, the root bark is most rich in the essential sassafras oil. This root was chewed by the Indians and was noticed by the Spaniards on their first landing in Florida in 1512, being shortly afterwards hailed as a new medicine. Until the mid-nineteenth century, bark, leaves and buds were used in many American states as a tea substitute, and it is mentioned in older cookery books, mainly as a medicinal tea or cordial. The other contents of a recipe for sasssafras cordial is worth quoting as an illustration of the wide variety of flavouring ingredients handled by cooks in old time kitchens: sarsaparilla, gum arabic, white wine, juniper berries, pistachio nuts, lemon syrup, rosemary leaves, sweet marjoram, candied lemon and candied citron, sugar candy, muscatel raisins, sherry, and distilled grape spirit.

Because sassafras is used as a flavour in medicines, its taste is sometimes now described as 'medicinal'. It is the flavour basis of sassafras jelly to be eaten with meat, and the powdered dry leaves are used in Creole cookery to flavour and thicken soups and gravies. The young tender leaves may be used in salads.

Savory

FR: Sariette
GER: Bohnenkraut, Kölle
IT: Santoreggia
SP: Ajedrea de Jardin
BOT: Satureja hortensis
(summer savory),
Satureja montana
(winter savory),
Winter-Bergminze
SP: Sabroso
IT: Santoreggia selvatica
FAM: Labiatae
Ill. 14, Nos. 6, 7,
page 189

There are a number of species of savory, almost all coming from the Mediterranean area. The two listed here are the chief ones used in cooking, although in Spain another species, *Satureja thymbra*, more nearly akin to thyme in flavour, is used as a kitchen herb, and no doubt other wild savories are also used locally.

SUMMER SAVORY was used in cooking by the Romans, and they probably introduced it into Britain. It seems to be of earlier usage than sage. From Britain it went to America with the first settlers. The plant is a hardy annual, and once established will usually selfsow. Only a small clump is necessary, so broadcast and thin later to about six inches. The plant grows to roughly a foot high and straggles untidily. The flowers are pinkish mauve, small, and uninteresting; the leaves, narrow and elongated. The plant likes sun and light soil.

The flavour of savory is very biting, vaguely like thyme but more bitter and quite distinct. Its flavour is better before it flowers than afterwards. It dries well and keeps its flavour. It is used in sausages, stuffings and herb mixtures (sometimes in a bouquet garni), but its only traditional use is as a flavouring for beans and peas particularly in France, Switzerland and Germany. Some regard this as a mistake. When overdone it is certainly quite as barbarous as mint which the French consider an English mistake.

WINTER SAVORY is a shrubby perennial with purplish flowers, growing to about a foot high. Propagation is by rooted cuttings in spring. It likes poor soil and sun. The flavour is very like summer savory though, in most people's opinion, inferior. The essential oils are almost the same. In the past, it was used with trout.

Screwpine

Nicobar Bread-fruit,
Umbrella Tree

CEYLON, INDIA,
  MALAYA: Keora,
  Keori, Kevara,.
  Kewara, Kewda,
  Kewra, Keya, Rampe
IT: Pandano
BOT: Pandanus
  tectorius, Pandanus
  odoratissimus
FAM: Pandanaceae
Ill. 4, Nos. 2, 2a,
  page 70

One finds many references to screwpine or *kewra* in recipes from Southeast Asia. The trees are denizens of tropical swamps, forming umbrellas of aerial roots in the backwater canals of Kerala and similar unpleasantly humid swampy districts in Asia. Yet the male inflorescence has an exquisite perfume (a description might be roses with a dash of ether), so bewitching that people often throw the flowers into the village wells to scent the drinking water, a charming practice if not done to mask less pleasant odours.

Kewra is one of the scented flavours used with betel nut. However, as far as the cook outside the tropics is concerned, the flavour of *kewra* can only be obtained in made-up syrups, cordials or perfumed waters. These can be bought in Indian shops and used in sweet dishes, often in conjunction with rosewater, but also with other exotic flavourings such as sandalwood, khas-khas (vetiver) and musk. It is also often put into *biriani*. Screwpine is also dried and pieces are used in curry, particularly in Ceylon.

Sea Holly

Eringo

FR: Panicaut,
  Panicaut maritime
GER: Mannstreu,
  Stranddistel
IT: Eringio or
  Calcatreppola marina
SP: Cardo corredor,
  Eringe
BOT: Eryngium
  maritimum
FAM: Umbelliferae

This rather strange-looking prickly plant grows on sandy or stony situations close to the sea in Britain and other parts of Europe. It is covered with down, and the blue flower-heads do not look at all as if the plant belonged to the parsley family. It even requires a slight knowledge of botany to understand why it is so classified. Eringo was a quite important flavouring in the past, although it is seldom heard of today. The roots were lifted and parboiled, then dried or candied. It was harvested and sold for flavouring jelly, candy and other sweet dishes. Nowadays one will have to dig and process it oneself.

Sesame

Semsem

FR: Sésame, Teel, Till
GER: Indischer Sesam,
  Vanglo
IT: Sesamo
INDIA: Gingelly, Til
SP: Ajonjolí, Sésamo

Perhaps you have wondered why, in the story of Ali Baba, when Cassim forgot the magic pass word 'Open Sesame' he tried 'Open barley' and then other sorts of grain in a vain attempt to re-open the door of the treasure cave before the robbers returned.

A native of India, sesame is one of the world's most important oil seeds. It has been cultivated in the East for thousand of years. It was also used by the ancient Greeks,

BOT: Sesamum indicum
FAM: Pedaliaceae
Ill. 3, No. 2, page 54

Egyptians and Persians. Today, annual cultivation runs into three or four million acres. Although it has become spread all over the tropical and sub-tropical world, China and India still grow the lion's share, but sesame is also the main vegetable oil of Mexico. In China sesame oil is a flavouring and ground sesame is an ingredient in Japanese cooking.

The plant is an annual, growing from four to six feet high, either bushy or unbranched. The flowers are white or pink, and the seeds may be red, brown or black, but more usually they are a creamy white, depending on the variety.

Sesame seed is exceedingly oily; some modern strains contain nearly sixty per cent oil. The pure oil is almost without taste or smell and does not easily go rancid in hot countries, which is one reason for its popularity. Sesame oil is imported into Europe in large quantities, being one of the more important ingredients of margarine. It is also excellent as a cooking oil.

To the cook, however, the beautiful nutty taste of the seeds, especially after slight roasting, is of more importance. The seeds are used scattered on bread and cakes in much the same way as poppy seed, and with a somewhat similar result. In the Near East the sweetmeat known as *halva*, of which there are many types, is best known when made of ground sesame. It has that characteristic rich nutty taste.

Perhaps the most important sesame product of all, however, from the gastronomic point of view, is a paste made from the finely ground seeds and known as *tahina* in Greece, Cyprus, Lebanon, Jordan and Syria. *Tahina* is creamy or creamy-grey in colour, and has the texture, though not the taste, of runny peanut butter.

In the Levant, *tahina* is used as a basis for various salad dressings and to flavour a purée of chick peas (*hummus*), which is one of the staple Arab dishes of this region. Mixed with water and flavoured with garlic and lemon juice, *tahina* is a very frequent part of the *meze* (snacks with the apéritifs), a saucer of this delicious garlicky substance being

---

Ill. 17 Nuts: 1 Stone Pine, 1a Pine Nut Cone, 2 Cashew Nut, 3 Areca Nut, 4 Pistachio Nut, 5 Ginkgo Nut, 6 Peanut, 7 Candlenut.

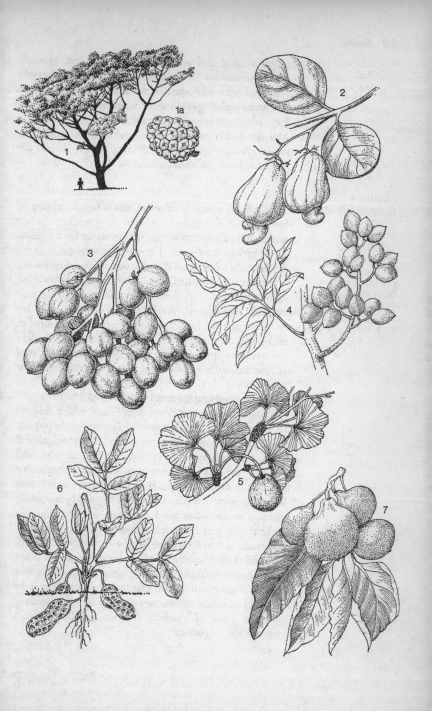

served with chunks of bread for dunking and, in many places, coming as a matter of course with the glass of arrack. I always keep it at home to serve with drinks and even in the preserves of gastronomic conservatism, France and Italy, *tahina* always proves popular. But one really might as well not bother to serve any dinner after it. A *meze* in suitable company is like an Antarctic sunset: 'it lasts for hours and hours and then becomes the dawn'.

Shallot

Eschalots, Spanish Garlic

FR: Echalote
GER: Schalotte
IT: Scalogna, Scalogno
SP: Ascalonia,
    Chalota Escalma
BOT: Allium cepa
FAM: Liliaceae Alliaceae,
    Amaryllidaceae
Ill. 1, No. 2, page 40

The shallot is a variety of onion which forms a cluster of bulbs instead of a single one. (Old books give it as a separate species *Allium ascalonicum*, the Roman name for a type of onion grown in Ascalon but there was confusion with another wild onion from Palestine which has a blue flower.)

Shallots are frost-hardy and easily grown from small bulbs planted to half their depth and at about six-inch intervals. By tradition, planting is done on the shortest day and lifting on the longest, but they can also be planted in spring and, in some wetter localities, in autumn. If lifted and properly dried off when the foliage begins to turn yellow, the bulbs will keep for a year and sometimes for two. Shallots are not grown from seed because we like to propagate from strains that do *not* go to seed.

Shallots are favoured in northern France, where they are an exceedingly important part of fine regional cooking. The flavour is more subtle than most other onions but varies considerably with variety, soil and climate, and different varieties are preferred in different districts. For instance, in Normandy the shallots resemble small onions with orange-brown skins and a mild flavour. In Burgundy markets on the other hand, they are elongated like big garlic cloves, grey, and with a strong aromatic pungency. Burgundians and Normans despise each others' shallots. One will make a better *coq au Chambertin*, the other a better *moules marinière*. Both, however, agree that other onions make a poor substitute and that shallots should never be browned as, unlike onions, they go bitter. English country-people will say, also rightly, that small shallots make a better pickle than onions.

Smoke

The flavour of smoke has become traditional in many foods, ranging from smoked salmon, bacon and ham, even to whisky and China tea. Moreover, whenever cooking is done over open fires, the flavour of smoke, even if unintentional, is likely to give special flavours which cannot be imitated in an electric rotisserie. Smoke is a flavour in all peasant cooking; the peculiar acrid smell of burning cowdung hangs in the air after a hot day in the Indian plains and gives its flavour to Indian village cooking. The aromatic smoke of burning myrtle and juniper perfumes the roast baby lamb to be eaten by the fire of some shepherd in the mountains of Sardinia. Grill meat or even cook it in a pan over a wood or charcoal fire, and the smoky flavour creeps in. It is, in fact, difficult to avoid it.

Deliberate smoking, as opposed to chance smoking from the cooking fire, was originally a part of curing. It dried and sealed the surface of meat or fish and, above all, kept away flies and maggots. In Africa today, one can still see what I imagine was the primitive process that led to smoking meat. When an animal is killed, any meat not to be eaten immediately is cut in strips and hung up to dry (a primitive *biltong*), but often so that it is touched by the heat and smoke of the camp fire, as this keeps away the flies. Flies not only lay eggs which hatch into maggots, but also carry putrefying bacteria on their feet and tongue.

Even so, in hot sunny climates smoking is usually coincidental, as drying is rapid; but in the damper parts of Europe smoking fish and meat was an essential part of preservation. Smoke holes were built behind kitchen fireplaces, or there were special smoke houses, sometimes temporary structures and sometimes permanent. Smoking was done over different woods, but oak and elm were the most common; in the United States hickory as well. Peat was used also in moorland areas; pine, if at all, only for finishing and depositing tar on the outside. Each fuel has its own characteristic smoky flavour. In these days, however, many commercial products are merely flavoured with smoke (pyroligneous acid) out of a bottle, and coloured with annatto (an edible vegetable dye). Smoking is easily done at home by making up a smoke box or barrel. The fish or salted meat is hung at the top, and smouldering sawdust is placed on a metal tray at the bottom. During World

War II, when stationed for long periods in Southeast Asia, where smoked foods are uncommon, some of us developed a craving for smoked fish which we were able to satisfy in this simple manner. Modern man is inclined to consider that such techniques, used by every peasant in the past, are somehow difficult. They are not, and in most cases are little work and surprisingly easy, a fact which has been rediscovered in America where smoke cooking of marinated duck and chicken is becoming a popular barbecue dish. A smoky flavour can also be introduced by using smoke-flavoured salt, e.g. salt flavoured with hickory smoke, or by smoked bacon or smoked sausage. It is, on the other hand, a careless cook who uses smoked bacon or sausage when unsmoked or 'green' bacon is called for.

Soda

Soda in the kitchen may mean bicarbonate or baking soda (sodium bicarbonate), or washing soda (sodium carbonate). The bicarbonate is changed to the carbonate (plus carbon dioxide gas) during cooking. Bicarbonate of soda also gives off carbon dioxide gas when mixed with an acid (e.g. sour milk), and these characteristics cause it to be used as a leavening and give it the name 'baking soda'. We are, however, concerned with taste, and thus with the taste of soda.

I once had a Kashmiri expedition-cook who carried a bag of washing soda to put in his tea. This turned the tea blood-red, and (in my opinion but not his) the result was disastrous. Old-fashioned soda bread and the girdle cakes of the north of England taste quite strongly of the baking soda used to leaven them. Soda bread is a robust country taste which I personally enjoy, perhaps only because it has happy childhood memories of splendid teas after skating on the local tarn.

Soda in meat dishes is rare, but the very strongly flavoured skinless 'sausages' of Rumania known as *mititei* are made of minced meat with garlic, salt, black pepper, a little caraway and bicarbonate of soda. Grilled over red hot charcoal they are a famous national speciality. The soda lightens and toughens the 'sausage' and gives it part of the very unusual flavour – worth trying if one likes strong new tastes at one's barbecue.

Sorrel

FR: Oseille
GER: Sauerampfer,
Sauerklee
IT: Acetosa
SP: Acedera
FAM: Polygonaceae
Ill. 7, Nos. 4, 5, page 103

Garden Sorrel
FR: Oseille de Belleville
GER: Großer
Sauerampfer
IT: Acetosa maggiore
SP: Acedera
BOT: Rumex acetosa

Round-Leaved Sorrel
FR: Oseille aux feuilles
rondes
GER: Rundblätteriger
Ampfer
IT: Acetosa romana,
Acetosa Tonda
SP: Acedera con hojas
redondas
BOT: Rumex scutatus
Ill. 7, No. 7, page 103

Spinach Dock,
Herb Patience
FR: Oseille-épinard,
Patience
GER: Englischer Spinal,
Gartenampfer
IT: Romice domestica or
Erba pazienza
SP: Romaza
BOT: Rumex patienta

Sheep Sorrel
FR: Petite oseille
GER: Kleiner
Sauerampfer
IT: Acetosa minore
SP: Acedera pequeña
BOT: Rumex acetosella
Ill. 7, No. 6, page 103

Curly Dock
FR: Patience frisée

Garden sorrels, round-leaved sorrel and spinach dock or herb patience are all derived from common wild sorrels. These three are commonly cultivated. Other species, such as sheep sorrel and curly dock, are sometimes used as greens. The broad-leaved dock is best reserved for nettle stings, as are the great water dock and others.

Sorrels are sour docks. The name sorrel is derived from an old Teutonic word for 'sour'. In the dock family, one finds also rhubarb, and the family is similar in many ways to that of the beets and spinach. The only sorrel of culinary interest which is not a dock is wood sorrel (q.v.).

The three species from which cultivated sorrels derive are all native to Europe and Asia, though now gone wild in North America. These vary in acidity and bitterness, and the cultivated varieties have large leaves and are in general less tough and acid than their wild ancestors.

Sorrel is known to have been eaten in ancient Egypt and by the Romans, who liked sorrel, as we do, to offset their rich food. Today sorrel is still used in Egypt and in many European countries, particularly France. In England it was popular in the Middle Ages (sorrel and herb patience were essential in the garden), but today it is known to only a few. This is a pity because sorrel is not only delicious and easy to grow but also, particularly in the case of herb patience, provides a flush of greens in early spring when fresh green-stuff of any kind is scarce. Gardeners should note that herb patience can grow to five feet tall, as opposed to the two feet of the other sorrels and so needs a little more space than the eighteen to twenty-four inches allowed between plants of the smaller species. Grow it from seed and plant out in spring in any soil in a sunny and moist position. Sorrel is perennial and hardy but should be prevented from flowering and renewed every four years or so. As only a few handfuls are needed at a time, a few plants suffice the average family.

Sorrel has a refreshing, somewhat bitter, sour, spinach-like leaf. It should always be cooked for a minimum time in order to preserve its fresh flavour, and it should be chopped only with a stainless steel knife and never cooked in an iron pan. (Iron with sorrel goes black and makes a nasty metallic taste.) It may be used raw in salads, but the leaves should be very young and tender. It is excellent as a purée

GER: Krauser Ampfer
IT: Romice crespa
   or Lapazio
SP: Acedera crespa
BOT: Rumex crispus

Broad-Leaved Dock
BOT: Rumex obtusifolius

Great Water Dock
BOT: Rumex
   hydrolapathum

melted in butter for a few minutes after being chopped raw, or blanched or lightly cooked in boiling salt water. This purée goes well with veal, pork, fish, eggs (especially in omelettes). Sorrel is also a superb sour flavouring for soups made with chicken stock, milk, lentils, tomatoes and cucumbers. Recipes will be found particularly from France, but I also have them from eastern Europe, Egypt, Sweden and elsewhere. Sorrel is also an ingredient of the herb mixtures used to stuff or cook with fish of many kinds ranging from sole and salmon to coarse fish and eels. Finally it is the basis for old English sour green sauces to be served with pork or goose.

Recipes using sorrel will be found in many books especially those dealing with French cooking. Elizabeth David's *Summer Cooking* and André Simon's *Guide to Good Food and Wine* contain sauce recipes. (*See* Wood Sorrel.)

Sour-milk Products

Buttermilk
FR: Lait battu,
   Lait de beurre
GER: Buttermilch
IT: Siero del latte
SP: Suero de manteca

Sour Cream
FR: Crème caillée
GER: Saure Sahne
IT: Panna acida
SP: Nata cuajada

Yogurt
FR: Yahourt, Yaourt,
   Yoghourth
GER: Joghurt
IT: Yogurt or Yoghurt
SP: Yajut

It is everybody's experience that milk and cream will turn sour, especially in warm weather, but it was not known that this was caused by bacteria until discovered by Pasteur only about one hundred years ago. As sour-milk products have been made under the most primitive conditions since time immemorial, it just shows that to be efficient in the kitchen one does not necessarily have to understand what one is doing – although it helps.

There are hundreds of different sorts of organism commonly present in milk, like weeds in a fertile field. Some are common in some parts of the world and not in others. These organisms float about on the dusty air of stalls and kitchens, settle on utensils, in water, on the coats of animals and on people. In a Balkan or Turkish farmhouse, where yogurt has been made for generations, it is more probable that the right bugs for yogurt are floating about than in a New York apartment. So kitchen directions involving bacteria which will work in one place will not necessarily do so in another. The right bacteria must be introduced.

To understand what is going on in making sour-milk products one must imagine not one kind of bacterium but a mixture of 'bugs' (bacteria, yeasts, fungi) in which each

kind causes different chemical changes. Some simply turn
milk sugars into lactic acid. Others produce cream- or
butter-flavoured substances, alcohol, and delicate fruity or
vinegary flavours. If these are well balanced the resulting
sour-milk product is delicious. But there are also less
favourable bacteria which attack the fats and proteins in
milk. These may at the same time be producing bitter,
rancid, fishy and putrid tastes, some of which we may like
in cheese, but which we do not want in sour cream. There
are also 'texture' processes which may be setting curd,
breaking it down or making it ropy or slimy. These, too,
are important in arriving at a correct result.

'Bugs' often depend for their nourishment on the
presence of other bugs in the mixture: they depend on the
others working first and then take a stage further the
processes started by them. Also, each 'bug' has its preferred
temperature at which it multiplies and works best, so by
controlling the temperature one can encourage one lot of
'bugs' at the expense of others. The chain of events becomes
incredibly complicated. In practical kitchen terms, one can
divide the milk-souring bacteria into two great classes;
those which act at room temperatures (in northern countries), and make ordinary sour milk and cream, and those
which work best at temperatures well above body temperature (a sort of high fever of 110°–120°F., 43·3°C.) and
create the yogurt and sour curds eaten in the hot countries
(the Balkans, Middle East and India).

So to produce sour-milk products of the very best quality
and flavour, it is necessary to start with the right mixture of
bacteria in the cream or milk and to incubate it at the right
temperatures. This can be done by taking boiled milk or
cream, innoculating it with the correct quantity of a starter
culture and leaving it in a warm place to 'prove'. It is best
to buy a starter culture to begin with – unless one has by
accident come on a good one – but afterwards it is only
necessary to hold back some of the previous brew as a
starter for the next.

It would save a great deal of trouble if one could buy
good sour milk, sour cream and yogurt. Unfortunately,
most commercial products are faked up with milk powder
and skimmed milk and bear little relation, either in flavour
or texture, to the real thing. Commercial yogurt, in

particular, is usually too acid, too slimy, too runny and thin in flavour. Such yogurt trades on the fact that most people have not eaten yogurt in its place of origin.

BUTTERMILK should be sour milk left over from butter-making after most of the fat has gone into the butter. It gives a special flavour to old-fashioned scones, griddle cakes, bread and oat cakes.

SOUR MILK (such as the *prostokvash* of northern Russia). This is ordinary sour milk. It will develop bad tastes if kept for long after it has soured. The best temperature to make it is 85°F. (29·5°C.) (warm room temperature).

SOUR CREAM, the *smytana* of Russia, is also much used in Germany, Hungary, Rumania, and other parts of eastern Europe. It should not be kept long after souring either, as bad flavours develop. The best incubating temperature is also 85°F. (29·5°C.), and the best flavour depends on aroma and flavour bacteria being present, as well as yeasts, to give an alcoholic touch. If made from pasteurized cream, it needs a starter containing strains of souring bacteria, which produce a slimy curd, as well as the flavour-producing organisms. It is used in *borsch*, with stuffed cucumber, paprika-flavoured dishes and other soups and sauces. Commercial yogurt is not a substitute.

Apart from clotted cream (Devonshire or Cornish cream), which has a slightly cooked flavour, many consider that cream should be either very fresh, deriving its flavour from cows fed on natural pasture (not on cake, hay or lays), or, failing that, be well matured, so that it is on the verge of going sour, and flavoured with bacterial products. Well-soured cream is delicious with almost anything.

If sour cream is impossible, a substitute can be made by adding lemon juice to fresh cream and stirring. It will thicken. But it is not as good as the real thing.

YOGURT. This is the Turkish name for a product common, with variations, all over the Balkans, Levant, Middle East, North Africa and India, as well as southern Russia. *Leben* (Egypt to Algeria), *laban* (Syria and Lebanon), *mazun, matzun, mazoon* (Armenia), *matsoni* (Georgia), *masturad, jodda* (Sicily), *gioddu* (Sardinia), *mast* (Iran) and *dahi* or *dahai* (Indian, and best from buffalo milk) are similar but not always identical products. They vary from a smooth, creamy, set curd to fermenting curd, smelling beery and full of bubbles. Sheeps' milk makes the finest yogurt, but cows' milk is more digestible. There are many ways of making it, but the best is to boil milk for ten minutes, allow to cool, innoculate (carefully under the skin of the milk) with a starter of either a bit of bought yogurt or yogurt culture and keep at about 110°F. (43°C.) for three to four hours till set. Then chill, but do not store for long in a refrigerator or it will become too sour. With the exception of tubercle and anthrax bacilli, all disease producing organisms are killed by the acid in yogurt, but as in almost all cases the milk has also been boiled during preparation, it is one of the safest foods in unhygienic countries, provided flies have not subsequently walked on it.

Yogurt is not only eaten but is used in the cooking of the entire region in which it is made and gives to dishes a characteristic flavour. Cows' milk yogurt is inclined to curdle when heated, but this can be prevented by a little flour or other stabilizer. Recipes containing yogurt vary from yogurt in cakes and sweets with chopped dried fruit and nuts (Armenian), to meat dishes of lamb and chicken and the raitas, curries and pilaus of India and Pakistan. It is also a dressing for salads, particularly of cucumber.

There are several other sour milk products well worth mentioning.

ACIDOPHILUS MILK. This rather modern preparation utilizes a particularly healthy acid-producing organism and is much used in Russia for health purposes.

CHAL, a product from Central Asia, is made from camels' milk.

DOUGH, a wonderful drink for hot weather, consists of yogurt beaten with salt and water. It is used extensively in Persia, where it is available gassed and bottled as a soft drink. In Lebanon it is *ayran* and in India *Lassi*.

KEFIR, originating in the Caucasus, is a fermentation product of cows' milk which is both sour and slightly alcoholic. Fermentation is started by peculiar dried grains known as kefir grains.

KUMISS, made by a combined lactic acid and alcoholic fermentation from mares' milk or mixed mares' and cows' milk, is from the southeastern U.S.S.R. As mares' milk contains more sugar than cows' milk, this drink is more alcoholic than kefir.

KYRINGA is a gassy alcoholic sour milk from eastern Central Asia.

Travellers are recommended to try these products, especially when the weather is unbearably hot. Speaking from experience, I have always given sour-milk products (after inspection) to my small children when travelling with them in the East. Yogurt with a skin on top is always safe, because removal of the skin takes care of the fly hazard. In Rumania during the war, I always breakfasted on sour milk from wayside stalls. They were none too clean, and I was solemnly warned against the practice by English and American diplomats. Time has proven them wrong though, and I now know that sour milk is, next to hot tea, the safest thing to drink in unhygienic areas, while sour-milk products in cooking are an excellent addition to the armoury of flavour.

Sourness

Sourness is a pure taste sensation detected in the mouth, and almost always due to an acid. Indeed the very word acid comes from the Latin *acidus*, meaning sour.

Acids and alkalis neutralize each other, so in theory one could remove acidity from sour dishes by adding soda. The result would be horrible because the salts formed would be bitter and medicinal. Thus from the point of view of taste, though not of chemistry, we regard acid sourness as neutralized by sweetness. In fact, adding sugar produces a sweet-sour combination liked by us perhaps because it spelled 'ripe fruit' to our monkey-like ancestors, the ripening of fruit being always characterized by an increase in the proportion of sweet sugars to acid. This is such a vital flavour combination that it has a section to itself. (*See* Sweet-Sour.)

Some common organic acids in food are acetic acid (vinegar), citric acid (lemons and citrus), malic acid (apples, sumac, and other fruits), tartaric and succinic acid (wine), lactic acid (sour milk). The mineral acids, sulphuric, phosphoric and hydrochloric (the last naturally present in our stomachs) are only used in commercial products, and then are safe only in great dilution. Some acids are stronger than others, and have to be in greater dilution to give comparable sensations of sourness. Mineral acids are stronger than organic acids, and acetic acid is stronger than citric or tartaric. On the other hand, the sourness of diluted strong acids more quickly goes from the palate than the stronger solutions of weak acids.

The following other properties of acids are useful to remember.

With bicarbonate of soda (baking soda) there is evolution of carbon dioxide gas (CO_2) which makes substances to which it is added fizz. This reaction is used in leavening.

An acid turns litmus paper red; an alkali, blue. Similarly, acid preserves and intensifies the colour of beetroot and red cabbage, while alkaline hard water turns them an unappetizing purple. But soft acid water yellows greens, while a pinch of soda improves their colour, as was known to the Romans. However, slight acidity tends to preserve vitamins, and alkaline water to destroy them.

Acids are chemically active substances and tend to first harden, but then to break down connective tissue, cell walls and fibres, so they are tenderizers, as when meat is marinated or cooked in wine, lemon juice or vinegar.

Acids are preservative. The precise degree of acidity is critical for the growth of micro-organisms. As a general rule, putrefying and disease organisms will not tolerate acid (just as many plants will not grow in acid soil), which is why lemon juice and vinegar are used for pickle, and yogurt or sour milk are safe in unhygienic countries. It is also why fewer precautions are necessary in bottling acid fruits than root vegetables.

Benzoic acid and boric acid have special preservative properties and are added to some foods in countries where they are permitted.

The formation of lactic acid in sour milk, yogurt, cheese, sauerkraut and sour cucumbers is due to bacteria, but even these are eventually stopped from multiplying when their critical degree of acidity is reached.

The adjustment of sourness is of great importance in cooking, but is frequently neglected. The sensation of sourness, like sweetness, is increased by heat and reduced by cold, so it is stronger in hot than in cold dishes. There are many naturally acid souring agents used to adjust sourness, and every country has at least one of these. Sourness, like salt, seems to be a basic taste necessity. Common souring agents are: vinegar, verjuice, sour milk, lemon juice, sour or unripe fruits (such as plums, pomegranates and apples), tamarind (India), sumac (Middle East), sorrel or wood sorrel (Europe), roselle (tropics) and powdered dried lime or lemon.

Of the pure acids, only citric and tartaric are used in the kitchen. Citric acid is extracted from lemons or made by fermenting glucose with special citric acid-producing bacteria.

Tartaric acid is made from cream of tartar (argol) which is precipitated from wine and forms a crust inside the casks. Cream of tartar is potassium hydrogen tartrate and is itself used in baking powder, home-made wines and yeast nutrients.

Southernwood
Lad's Love, Old Man

FR: Aurone
GER: Eberries
IT: Abrótano
SP: Abrotano
BOT: Artemisia abrotanum
FAM: Compositae
Ill. 9, No. 3, page 123

Southernwood is a strong-smelling bushy herb, commonly grown in gardens for ornamental purposes. Other *Artemisias* are wormwood, tarragon and mugwort. Southernwood is native to southern Europe and grows wild in Spain and Italy. It was first introduced into Britain in 1548. The smell is very strong and rather unpleasant. However, the young shoots are said to be used as a flavouring in Italy, particularly for cakes, but, although I have inquired about it, I have not yet come on this use myself.

It is also called *garde-robe* in France, as it protects clothes from fleas and moths.

Soy
Soya Bean

CANTONESE: Jeong yow
FR: Pois chinois, Soja, Soui, Soya
GER: Soja
IT: Soia
JAPAN: Shoyu
SP: Soja
BOT: Glycine max (Glycine soja)
FAM: Leguminosae
Ill. 3, No. 4, page 54

The soy bean is a native of Southeast Asia and one of the oldest crops, being already cultivated in China round 3000 B.C. In spite of this long history, it was quite unknown in Europe until the end of the seventeenth century and was only a curiosity until quite late in the nineteenth century. There are now thousands of varieties and millions of acres grown all over the world. The soy bean is undoubtedly the world's most important legume, being used not only as food but even as a raw material in industry. As a food the soy bean is extremely rich in both oil and protein. It is eaten as a fresh bean (it does not stand frost), as a dried bean and as a bean flour, and it is a source of a good cooking oil much used as a substitute for olive oil in Spain. Even a kind of milk is made from it. In the East, it is also fermented to make various kinds of curd and bean cheese. The soy product which concerns us is soy sauce.

Soy sauce is extremely important in China, Japan and any areas which have a sizable number of Chinese immigrants. It is thought to have been brought from China to Japan by a Bhuddist priest about A.D. 500. In the West it became well-known during the nineteenth century. It is one of the ingredients of Worcestershire sauce and Harvey's sauce. One can imagine that in an era where bottled ketchups and sauces were used extensively, soy sauce as a newcomer would be hailed with delight.

There are many types of soy sauce, and the methods of making it vary from place to place. In general it is made by fermenting a salted mixture of cooked soy beans and wheat or barley flour and then extracting the liquid. The result is a thin sauce with a salty, rather meaty flavour, usually dark brown in colour though it can range from black to pale straw. (See South East Asian Food – Brissenden.)

Soy sauce is essential in Far Eastern cooking and has been enthusiastically adopted in America, possibly diffusing from the Pacific coast. It is a common ingredient in marinades and barbecue sauces. This is a product which must be on the shelf of everyone interested in the cooking of eastern Asia, although continual heavy use is said to be bad for the liver.

Spice

FR: Aromate, Épice
GER: Gewürz
IT: Spezie
SP: Especia

This word has the same origin as 'species' and originally meant 'kinds of goods'. Today, by spice we mean usually the dried aromatic products mainly of tropical Southeast Asian origin, but there are a few from the New World or Africa.

There does not seem to be much point in taking an old word with historical connections and attempting to give it an exact modern definition. The following are commonly referred to as spices; black pepper and its relatives, white pepper, cubeb pepper, long pepper; nutmeg and mace, allspice, cardamom (seeds or fruits), cloves (buds), cinnamon and cassia (bark), dried ginger, turmeric (root) and so on.

Coriander, caraway, dill seed, cumin, saffron etc., might also be called spices by some, but temperate products which are grown in Europe are really in another category, since 'spices' implies that they were once brought from the East or the West Indies by ship. The French call them *Aromates*.

Spirits and Liqueurs

A large number of different spirits and liqueurs are used as flavourings in cooking, some commonly, others locally or as the particular secret of some chef. Although they have been made exceedingly expensive by taxation in many countries, usually only small quantities are required and miniature bottles make it possible for the cook to keep a large selection on the kitchen shelf, provided he can resist the temptation to drink them.

The contents of these bottles will have one thing in common: they are all strongly alcoholic and, unlike wines or even fortified wines, can be ignited if heated. This makes possible the spectacular operation of flaming, carried out in many restaurants as a far from gratuitous firework display. The real purpose of flaming is to burn off small quantities of fat which have mixed with the alcohol and make certain other changes in the flavour of the dish which are more easily experienced than described.

BRANDY is without doubt the most important spirit used in cooking. It is distilled from wine and varies greatly in quality and flavour depending on where it comes from, what type of grapes are used, how it is distilled, its age and so on. The best from France are cognac and armagnac. As brandy is above all a French spirit, and as it is used particularly in French cooking, it is obviously not going to be right to use, in a dish of French origin, a cheap colonial brandy which has often been made from muscat grapes and has retained their characteristic flavour. A certain amount of common sense is necessary in the choice. Even if one cannot afford a fine brandy, the so-called 'cooking brandy' is also best avoided.

Brandy is used as a traditional part of the flavouring in a large number of fish, shellfish, meat and fowl dishes originating particularly in France and Spain. Where used in other parts of the world, the dishes are most usually of French origin. One could find it in almost any type of dish: in savoury spreads such as *tapénade*; pâtés of liver, duck and game; in fish and shellfish soups (e.g. *zarzuela*, *bisque*); meat dishes (*tranches de mouton à la poitevine, daube de veau, estofade de boeuf, estofade de veau*); chicken (*coq au vin*); with game (pheasant, woodcock, etc.) as well as in a host of sweet dishes, often mixed with liqueurs.

MARC is another grape spirit, but is made from the fermented residues after the grapes have been pressed for wine. This is used as a flavouring in many regional dishes, especially in wine-producing areas. In these dishes, it sometimes replaces brandy.

OTHER FRUIT BRANDIES or *eaux-de-vie* are made by distilling fermented mashes of other fruits. The flavour of these is very unlike the taste of the fruits from which the spirit is made. These have great local importance in cooking and are used in regional dishes.

CALVADOS, a spirit distilled from cider and equivalent to the American apple-jack, is made particularly in Normandy and will occur in a number of Norman recipes often flamed, and particularly with chicken, tripe and apples. It gives a very characteristic flavour but where calvados is not available whisky has been recommended as the best substitute.

QUETSCH and MIRABELLE, distilled from two different kinds of plums, are used in certain regional dishes from northeastern France, where these spirits are made. Other fruit brandies from the same region, such as *framboise* made from raspberries, are also sometimes used.

KIRSCH, made from black cherries, is produced in the whole region of the Vosges, Black Forest and neighbouring Switzerland. This is one of the most important spirits used as a flavouring in sweet dishes, with fruit (particularly with pineapple, bananas and in fruit salads) and with chestnuts, in creams and confectionery; but it is also used with cheese (*fondue*) and in some meat and chicken dishes. Kirsch is dry, not sweet, and has a totally different flavour from the other cherry-based spirits such as maraschino.

WHISKY, distilled from grain, is not traditionally a common flavouring in cooking (the Scots prefer to drink it), but can produce some interesting results and has recently become popular with many chefs on the Continent in such dishes as *fagiano all' whisky* (Italy) and steak in whisky (Spain). Gin is sometimes used in England for flavouring a sweet sauce, and vodka can be used for flaming.

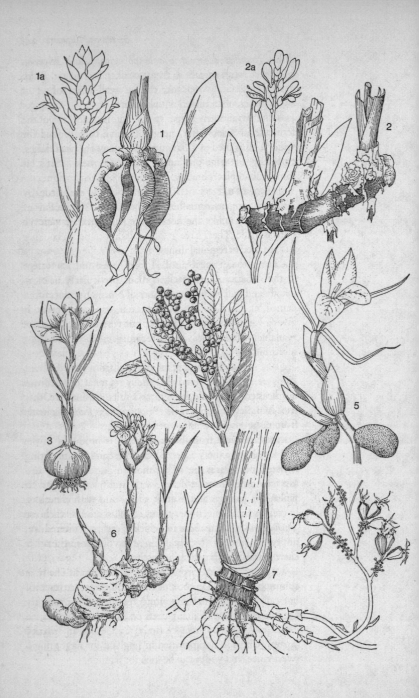

RUM, distilled from fermented sugar cane juice or molasses is a very important flavouring in cooking. Rums vary greatly in flavour from the very pale rums, of which the best known is Bacardi, to the dark strongly-flavoured rums such as those from Jamaica. Some are dry; others sweet. In savoury dishes rum is unusual, though found in some local recipes of Creole or Caribbean origin and also in Spain (*langostinos al ron*), but in cakes and sweet dishes it is a very well-known flavouring. The selection of the right rum is important, and it is certainly not sufficient for the cook to take any rum which comes to hand or to use rum flavour substitutes. It is worth becoming conscious of their variety.

All of the items dealt with so far, with the exception of gin, have their flavours derived from congenerics formed during fermentation and usually distilled from the alcohol or from other substances formed by chemical reaction during the ageing in the wood. In theory, at least, no other flavourings are added. In practice, at least so far as the cheaper brands are concerned, this is not always true, but it is the ideal. Gin is a frank exception, as it is always flavoured, usually with juniper and other aromatics.

There are, however, a host of liqueurs and other alcoholic drinks which depend on alcohol suitably flavoured and sugared. The alcohol may be derived from fermented grapes, grain, potatoes, or any other starchy or sugary substance, even from sawdust. The alcohol is highly purified and has very little taste of its own, save the slightly sweet burning taste of ethyl alcohol.

But alcohol and water together will dissolve many of the essential oils and ethers if fruits, aromatic seeds and herbs or spices are macerated in the liquid. Sometimes, these are again distilled, but otherwise they are just filtered and cleared to form a simple ratafia (q.v.). Colouring may be added and they are often sweetened with a sugar syrup. Most often, the exact formula is a trade secret. The main characteristic of these is that the flavour bears some resemblance to the materials from which the liqueur is made. For

Ill. 18 Spices: 1 Turmeric Root, 1a Turmeric Flower, 2 Galangal Root, 2a Galangal Flower, 3 Saffron, 4 Allspice, 5 Zedoary, 6 Ginger, 7 Cardamom.

instance, the uninitiated might guess from tasting that cherry brandy was flavoured with cherries, but would scarcely guess that kirsch was distilled from them.

MARASCHINO, a very sweet liqueur made originally from the marasca cherry on the Adriatic coast of Yugoslavia, has a unique flavour, very scented and quite unlike kirsch. A common flavouring in creams and sweet dishes and with fruit, it is quite clear and different in flavour from the dark red cherry brandies made particularly in England, Holland and Denmark. These have a more obvious cherry taste (with a dash of bitter almond from the stones and are less often used as flavourings).

ORANGE-FLAVOURED LIQUEURS are also important in cooking for flavouring both dishes and the orange-flavoured sauces to go with duck, etc. There are many of these orange-based liqueurs, varying considerably in flavour and sweetness, but all recognizably tasting of orange. While writing this book, I went through the interesting but rather sickly exercise of tasting a large number alongside each other, but the differences defy description. The most famous of these liqueurs are *Cointreau* and *Grand Marnier* as well as the various curaçaos named after the oranges from the Dutch island of that name off the coast of Venezuela, but now coming from many other places. But one may also note the Italian *Aurum* (gold), many liqueurs labelled '*Triple Sec*', a list of orange-flavoured liqueurs from Spain and, farther afield, *Unicum* from Hungary and *Van der Hum* from South Africa. They come in all colours from white (clear) to orange and even purple. Most of us will settle for *Grand Marnier* or *Cointreau*, but one may base the fame of one's cooking on something less obvious.

APRICOT-FLAVOURED LIQUEURS are probably next in importance to the orange liqueurs as flavourings. These, as far as I know, are used only in sweet dishes, though apricots as fruits are used in savoury dishes. There are many of these: *Capricot*, *Apricot brandy*, *Abricota*, *Abricotine*, and *Apry*. The famous *Barack* of Hungary is another apricot brandy but with no taste of apricots and, though one of my favourite spirits, is not as far as I know usually used as a flavouring.

There are also many other fruit-flavoured liqueurs, flavoured with every imaginable fruit, to choose from. Most of these will be used for sweet dishes only, if at all.

In cooking, other flavoured liqueurs may also be used, such as kümmel (flavoured with caraway and cumin), *crème de menthe* (peppermint) and the various kinds of *anis* or *anisette* (aniseed). Although it is not a liqueur, I shall also include the types of *pastis* – also flavoured with anise, star anise and fennel – which are useful in dishes where an unrecognizable touch of anise flavouring is required. There are also many apéritifs and other less known alcoholic drinks, such as *pineau des charentes*, which are used in special dishes.

Besides liqueurs which have an identifiable taste and are therefore fairly easy to place, there are also many liqueurs, flavoured with complicated mixtures of herbs and spices, which may be called for in particular dishes or with which one may experiment. The formula for most of these is secret. One may mention a few obvious ones, such as *Bénédictine*, *Chartreuse*, *Raspail*, *Goldwasser*, *Tia Maria*, *Izara* and *Trapistine*. Sometimes one will come on such ingredients in recipes, although their use as flavourings is rather the exception than the rule.

Star Anise
Badian Anise,
Chinese Anise

FR: Anis de la Chine,'
Anis étoile, Badiane
GER: Sternanis
IT: Anice stellato
SP: Badián, Badiana
BOT: Illicium verum
FAM: Magnoliaceae
Ill. 19, No. 5, page 253

Star anise is the star-shaped fruit of a small evergreen tree belonging to the magnolia family and native to China. The fruits are collected and dried before they are ripe. They have a strong flavour, rather similar to anise but slightly more bitter and pungent. The same essential oil, anethole, is present.

Star anise is grown in southern China and Indo-China and is said to have been first brought to Europe by an English sailor at the end of the sixteenth century.

It is used in the East as a spice. The oil, extracted by steam distillation, is much used in anise-flavoured drinks and commercial preparations instead of European aniseed.

Star anise can be bought in any good spice shop and must be on the shelf if one is interested in Chinese cooking, in which it is used particularly in pork and duck recipes, e.g. *Chiang Fou* (fragrant pork), *Hsiang Su Ya* (succulent duck), *ragoût de porc à la chinoise*, etc. (*See also* Anise, Chinese Five Spices.)

Stonecrop

FR: Orpin
GER: Fettkraut
SP: Chubarbas,
    Fabacrasas
BOT: Species of Sedum
FAM: Crassulaceae

Reflexed Stonecrop
FR: Grand orpin jaune,
    Orpin réfléchi
GER: Zuruckgebogenes
    Steinkraut
IT: Erba risetta,
    Sopravivolo dei muri
SP: Fabacrasa reflejada
BOT: Sedum reflexum
Plate VI, No. 7

The stonecrops, together with the house leek and wall-pennywort, belong to the family Crassulaceae. They have fleshy leaves and are well-known to most people from their habit of growing on old walls, roofs and damp rocks.

Of these, the reflexed stonecrop, also called the large yellow or crooked yellow stonecrop, is an excellent salad plant that was once used as a flavouring for soups, boiled like spinach or (as it is fleshy) pickled like samphire. The white stonecrop (*Sedum album*) can be used in the same way.

Some books also list the orpine stonecrop (*Sedum telephium*) of woods as a salad plant, but its other names, 'life everlasting' and 'long life', suggest correctly that the use of this plant was mainly medicinal.

The common stonecrop (*Sedum acre*), also known as wall pepper, wall ginger, bird bread and biting stonecrop, is not suitable for use as a flavouring, because of its exceedingly biting taste.

Sugar
Cane Sugar

FR: Sucre de canne
GER: Rohrzucker
IT: Saccarosio, Zucchero
SP: Azúcar de caña
Ill. 20, No. 1, page 268

Glucose
FR: Glucose, Sucre de
    raisin
GER: Glukose,
    Traubenzucker
IT: Glucosio
SP: Glucosa

Fructose
FR: Fructose, Lévulose,
    Sucre de fruit
GER: Frukose
IT: Fruttosio
SP: Fructosa

Malt Sugar
FR: Maltose, Sucre de
    malt

Although there are other substances with a sweet taste (*see* Saccharin, Sweetness) it is certain that if any natural foodstuff tastes sweet it will be due to the presence of a sugar. There are many sugars, each having different properties, and they occur in nature not only in plants but also in animals. They are carbohydrates: that is, they are built up from carbon combined with oxygen and hydrogen in the same ratio as in water.

The more important carbohydrates are classified as follows:

monosaccharides – glucose (grape sugar) and fructose (fruit sugar or laevulose);

disaccharides – sucrose (cane sugar or sucrose) which is ordinary sugar, maltose (malt sugar) and lactose (milk sugar);

polysaccharides – starch, dextrine (office gum), cellulose (indigestible vegetable cell wall) and glycogen (the animal starch in liver).

A point to notice is that these are in ascending order of complexity (mono = one, di = two, poly = many). Nature can build from simple to complex, but one can only break down from complex to simple in the kitchen. One

GER: Maltose,
Malzzucker
IT: Maltosio
SP: Azúcar de malta,
Maltosa

Lactose
FR: Lactose, Sucre de lait
GER: Laktose,
Milchzucker
IT: Lattosio
SP: Azúcar de leche,
Lactosa

Treacle
FR: Mélasse
GER: Melasse,
Zuckerdicksaft
IT: Melassa
SP: Melaza

Golden Syrup
FR: Mélasse raffinée,
Sirop de sucre
GER: Zucker sirup
IT: Melassa
SP: Melado

Molasses
FR: Doucette, Mélasse
GER: Melasse
IT: Melassa
SP: Mial de caña

Beet Sugar
FR: Sucre de betterave
GER: Rübenzucker
IT: Zucchero di bietola
SP: Azúcar de remolacha
Ill. 20, No. 3, page 268

Maple Sugar
FR: Sucre d'érable
GER: Ahornzucker
IT: Zucchero di acero
SP: Azúcar de arce
Ill. 20, No. 5, page 268

Palm Sugar
FR: Sucre de palme
GER: Palmzucker

can change starch to sugars, but cannot change sugars to starch. Sugars vary in their melting point, solubility in water and above all in their sweetness. If one gives ordinary cane sugar 100 marks for sweetness, the comparison would be as follows:

Fruit sugar (fructose)	173
Cane sugar (sucrose)	100
Grape sugar (glucose)	74
Malt sugar (maltose)	32
Milk sugar (lactose)	16

Thus, of these, fruit sugar is over ten times as sweet as milk sugar.

CANE SUGAR, SUCROSE or SACCHAROSE. Ordinary household sugar is almost pure sucrose or cane sugar. It is obtained from sugar cane and sugar beet, and possibly from sugar maple, sweet sorghum or palm juice. Sucrose also occurs in many fruits, particularly strawberries and pineapples, and in many root vegetables, such as carrots and beetroot. It is also in the nectar of flowers, though in honey it has been converted to simpler sugars by an enzyme in the bee's saliva.

Sucrose will dissolve completely in about one-third of its weight of water at room temperature. In hot water, more will dissolve than in cold, and syrup boils at a higher temperature than pure water. If sucrose is heated dry, it melts at 320°F. (160°C.), and when it cools again it will form the pale straw-coloured and glassy 'barley sugar'. But, if heating is continued, water from within the sugar crystals will boil away and the sugar will pass through the various stages of thread, ball and crack, familiar to the confectioner, and eventually at 356°F. (180°C.) will become caramel. If heated still further, it will become 'black jack'.

It is useful to know that if a few drops of pure hydrochloric acid are shaken up with cane sugar syrup and stood in a warm place for several days, the cane sugar will be converted to a mixture of equal quantities of grape and fruit sugars (glucose and fructose). By this reaction it is easy to make 'quick energy' soft drinks. A pinch of bicarbonate of soda or chalk will neutralize the acid.

GLUCOSE (also called dextrose or grape sugar). This occurs in large quantities in grapes and forms the hard

IT: Zucchero di palma
SP: Azúcar de palma
Ill. 20, No. 2, page 268

sugary nodules in dry raisins, hence its alternative name. In nature, glucose is often associated with fructose. It also forms some thirty per cent of honey, again mixed with fructose.

Commercial Glucose, which is available either purified as a powder or in the form of chips and thick syrups, is made by gently cooking starch or cane sugar with hydrochloric acid and subsequently neutralizing with chalk and purifying. Known also as starch sugar, corn sugar or corn syrup, the usual forms used in commercial confectionery are not pure glucose, but mixtures.

Liquid glucose is a heavy clear syrup containing water (eighteen per cent) and glucose (thirty-five per cent) with dextrin (forty-seven per cent). Dextrin is an intermediate product between starch and glucose, well known as cheap office glue. Liquid glucose is very useful in home sweet-making.

Solid glucose is in the form of chips. In making this, the conversion of starch to glucose has been more complete, though otherwise the process is the same. This contains glucose (seventy to eighty per cent), dextrin (six to eight per cent) and some water.

Glucose may be used for sweetening jam or candy. Though once regarded as an inferior substitute for cane sugar, it has now become hallowed as a source of quick energy. It is much less sweet than cane sugar, and so, if it is used to replace cane sugar in recipes, this must be taken into account.

FRUCTOSE (also called laevulose and fruit sugar) is like the glucose usually present in ripe fruit and honey, but as a pure substance it is not a usual culinary commodity. Fructose is very sweet, dissolves more easily in water than glucose, but ferments less rapidly.

MALT SUGAR (maltose). This, as the name suggests, is a sugar produced in malting. It is formed when the enzyme diastase, liberated from the germ, acts on starch. At the same time, dextrin is also formed. Malt sugar, therefore, is present to a considerable extent in malt extract; there is some also in honey. Malt sugar is important in baking and brewing and is fermented rapidly by yeasts. Perhaps its most useful quality in the kitchen is that it is not only exceedingly soluble in water, but is also hygroscopic, i.e., it tends to cling to water and to retain moisture. So if it is used in bread, in the form of malt extract, then the loaf keeps moist for longer.

LACTOSE or MILK SUGAR. This is the sugar of milk and is the least sweet of the common sugars. It is extracted from skimmed milk left over from butter making and is mainly of interest to the cook in that being the sugar of milk its reactions are important in cheesemaking and in sour or fermented milk products such as yogurt. It can be bought at druggists and is used in commercial confectionery.

SUGAR CANE. This plant is a giant grass ten to twelve feet high. It grows in clumps and has stems rather like bamboo, although solid. Inside a tough rind is an exceedingly fibrous centre full of sweet juice. It is this juice which contains the cane sugar.

In the countries where it grows, sugar cane is often chewed, but there are only certain varieties suitable for chewing. Most cane has a flat, intensely sweet taste. Unlike fruit, it does not contain sufficient acid or flavour (*see* Sweet-Sour). However, if fresh cane is put through a crusher with a few limes and fresh ginger, it makes a most delicious soft drink. This drink is made by street vendors in many parts of the tropics and should be tried (if one can find a clean stall).

Sugar cane is still the world's major source of sugar. Although it is not known in the wild state, it probably came originally from south and east Asia: the Chinese used it about 1000 B.C. It was already an important crop in India when Alexander the Great brought some to Europe (327 B.C.), and it reached Egypt about a thousand years later (A.D. 641) and Spain a hundred years after that (A.D. 755). The Portuguese took it to Madeira, Columbus took it to America on his third voyage, and it reached the Caribbean Islands in the early sixteenth century. Today, it is cultivated all over the world in suitable warm climates. It was once grown in southern Spain and Sicily, but it really prefers even warmer climates.

In evaluating old recipes, it must be appreciated that refined sugar is a modern commodity. Although it was used in Europe in the Middle Ages, it was still an expensive substance sold in small quantity by apothecaries, and it was not until well into the nineteenth century that it became really cheap. The old sweetening was usually honey.

The primitive method of preparing sugar can still be seen in many tropical peasant communities. The ripe cane is cut close to the ground, the bottom of the stem being richest in sugar. The dry leaves are stripped off, if they have not already been burned off whilst the cane was still standing. The trimmed canes are fed into a simple crusher consisting of two large cogs powered by oxen. The juice, which looks somewhat like dirty bathwater, is run into wide shallow pans set over a fire of the crushed cane stems. As the juice boils and evaporates, lime is added. The proteins in the juice coagulate, and the froth they form with the dirt is skimmed off. A thick, dark brown, semi-clear syrup remains from which the sugar begins to crystallize. This can be scooped out and some of the molasses allowed to drain from it. As it cools, it forms into a fudge-like mass of dark raw unpurified cane sugar. This is known as open-pan or *muscorado* sugar (from the Spanish) and was once exported from the West Indies. From India comes another variety of an even cruder flavour known as *gur*. It can be obtained from shops specializing in Indian spices and is an important flavouring in many Indian dishes, not only sweet dishes but vegetarian curries. The darkest commercial brown sugars are no real substitute.

Modern commercial cane sugar is made by the scientific separation of the pure crystalline cane sugar from the molasses, and various degrees of refining have been practised for a long time, the processes having probably been invented by the Arabs. The earliest type of white refined sugar was sugar loaf. Sugar loaves were known in England even in the early fourteenth century and persisted in Europe and America until well into the last century. Today one will still find them in common use in Persia. The refined sugar has been cooled in volcano-shaped moulds – like a sugar-loaf mountain. Before use, the cones must be broken up (there are special tools), a tedious job carried out in every Persian roadside tea house. Lump sugar is still called 'loaf sugar'.

Ill. 19   Spices: 1 Curry Leaf, 2 Cinnamon, 3 Black Pepper, 4 Long Pepper, 5 Star Anise, 6 Clove, 7 Nutmeg.

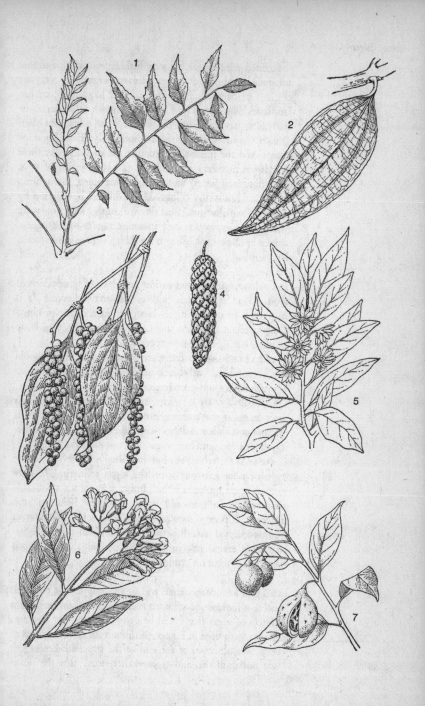

Refined white sugar has very little flavour but an almost unadulaterated sweet taste. Brown sugars of varying degrees of colour are less refined and have more or less 'molasses' flavour. These may be known as demerara or barbados, having come originally from what was then British Guiana and Barbados respectively. Foot sugar or 'foots' was the sugar that settled in the casks. Today these words are not very meaningful, except in terms of light brown sugar (pieces) and dark brown sugar. Sometimes sugars are artificially coloured, and this can be detected by washing with water. Real brown sugar will not wash white. It is, however, best to judge sugars by tasting, as names become misleading once their original connotation has vanished.

In cooking, one also uses various treacles and syrups derived from sugar cane, each with a distinctive flavour. It is important to use the right ones in recipes. These products contain about half cane sugar, the balance being made up of other sugars which do not crystallize.

TREACLE itself is a transparent brown syrup and should not be confused with black or West Indian treacle, which is much darker and stronger.

GOLDEN SYRUP is milder in flavour, and comes from a later stage in the refining process. About a third of it is sucrose and almost half non-crystallizing sugars. It is sometimes imitated with cane sugar, glucose and flavourings.

MOLASSES, which is often confused with treacle, is the much cruder left-over from the sugar refinery. The taste of beet sugar molasses is foul, but cane molasses is palatable and is used in rum and other products. Being rich in minerals, it is an important health food said to counteract the undoubted harmful effects of too much refined sugar. It is used extensively in American cooking. Black strap is the English term for crude black molasses.

SUGAR BEET. Sugar cane will grow only in hot climates, and so a number of attempts were made in Europe to find sources of sugar that could be grown locally. For instance, carrots were tried in France. Although sugar in the roots of beets was observed at the end of the sixteenth century, it was not until the mid-eighteenth century that the possibility of beet as a source of sugar began to be considered in Germany. At the beginning of the nineteenth century (when Napoleon was feeling the effects of the British naval blockade), considerable interest was taken in France, but after Waterloo interest faded until it was revived again some fifteen or twenty years later. Since the mid-nineteenth century, sugar beet has become of greater and greater importance in the agricultural pattern of northern countries as a source of sugar.

Extraction of the sugar from beet is done in the winter when the roots are mature. They are washed, pulped and heated in water to dissolve out the sugar. The solution is treated with lime and carbon dioxide gas to precipitate impurities, and then the liquid is evaporated and the sugar crystals removed by centrifuge.

The purified white beet sugar is pure sucrose or cane sugar (which is why we should perhaps drop the name cane sugar in favour of sucrose), and it is not possible by any ordinary means to tell whether the white sugar you buy has come originally from cane or beet. They are chemically the same. We do not, however, get any open-pan or brown sugars from beet for although sugar beet molasses has commercial uses, its taste is horrible and all traces of it must be removed.

MAPLE SUGAR. The sugar maple is a handsome tree of the deciduous forests of northeastern America, from Canada down through Connecticut and west to Ohio. As long ago as 1673, explorers in these regions observed that the Indians were making a crude sugar from the sap of this and other species of maple. The sap tapped from the trees in late winter was concentrated by being thrown on to hot stones. More water was extracted by removing the ice formed when the liquid froze in the winter. The early settlers improved the process, boiling down the sap to a thick syrup and then dropping it into snow in what is known as the 'sugaring-off' process. It was then crystallized in moulds. Nowadays, a hole is bored in the tree trunk and a spile inserted. The loss of sap, which flows freely, does not seem to harm the tree. The concentration is carried out in evaporators and the sugar extracted.

Production of maple sugar reached its peak in 1869, but has since declined. Maple sugar is said to have a better flavour than cane or beet sugar. Outside America, maple syrup is better known than maple sugar, and this has a distinctive taste, though it is frequently flavoured or adulterated. (In America, a maple syrup label which includes a maple leaf indicates an unadulterated product.) American cookery books contain many delicious old recipes based on it, and it is used at breakfast and lunch with waffles or griddle cakes, alone or with bacon, sausages or scrapple.

PALM SUGAR. Sugars are prepared from a number of palms, of which the wild date palm, the coconut palm, the toddy palm, the palmyra palm and the Gomuti palm are the most common. The date palm is tapped like a maple, but unlike the maple this stunts the palm and the tree cannot be tapped every year. Other palms are tapped by cutting off the tip of the shoot that bears the flowers and later the nuts. This means climbing the tree and hanging an earthen or bamboo pot underneath to catch the drips. Also, in the tropics, it means collecting the sap at least twice a day as it otherwise ferments rapidly to produce toddy. In these days, preservatives are sometimes put into the pots to prevent this. Palm sugar is usually a country preparation equivalent to open-pan cane sugar, very dark brown and strong in flavour. It can be bought in shops specializing in oriental goods, usually under the Indian name, *jaggery*. Often it is in the form of a ball wrapped in leaves. This is a very old product of India and will often feature in Indian recipes. Because the sap of palms contains more non-sucrose sugars than other sources, and as the refining is inefficient, palm sugar is apt to remain permanently sticky.

SWEET SORGHUM is a large grass, a plant of the tropics and one of the many varieties of sorghum. These plants include broomcorn, kafir corn (Africa), *kaoliang* (China), *durra* (India) and many others. Most sorghums are cultivated for grain and they are one of the first plants man took into cultivation. Sweet sorghum is unsuitable for the production of sugar, but an important syrup is made from the juice and thus, it deserves mention.

Sumac
Sicilian Sumac, Sumach

Sumacs are known to gardeners as decorative plants, but the leaves of some species are grown as a source of tannin

ARABIC: Sammak
FR: Sumac
GER: Färberbaum,
Sumach
IT: Sommacco
SP: Zumaque
BOT: Rhus corioria
FAM: Anacardinaceae
Ill. 7, No. 2, page 103

for the leather industry. One of these, Sicilian sumac (grown commercially in Sicily and southern Italy), has sour seeds which are used extensively in Middle Eastern cooking. This sumac grows wild there on the rocky mountains, away from the coast, and the higher up it grows the better the quality. Almost all houses in the Lebanon would keep a stock of sumac seeds. They are either ground to a red-purple powder or used whole, in which case they are broken, soaked in water for fifteen to twenty minutes and then squeezed out thoroughly to extract the juice.

Sumac is sour, with a pleasantly astringent taste. It was used by the Romans (lemons had not yet arrived in Europe), and they called it Syrian sumac.

Today sumac is used in the Middle East to make a sour drink, much recommended for 'gyppy tummy'. However, its great importance is as a souring agent in Arab recipes in which it is preferred to lemon. The extracted juice is used in salads, the ground powder in dishes such as that spicy fish stew, *samak el harrah*, much as tamarind is used as a souring agent in Indian curries. (Do not confuse the Arab word *sammak* = sumac, with *samak* = fish.)

Sumac ought to be better known. It can sometimes be bought in the form of a red powder from shops that specialize in Lebanese or Jewish food. I have used it myself, ever since I discovered it some years ago, for it has a rounded fruity sourness (due to malic acid as in sour apples) without the distinctiveness of vinegar or the brutality of tamarind or lemon.

The scarlet sumac (*Rhus glabra*), a roadside shrub in North America, bears clusters of bright red berries in August (the poison sumac produces strings of white berries) which were used by the American Indians to make a sour drink. It seems probable that this sumac could also be used to prepare the Lebanese dishes and has the ancient connection between the Phoenicians and America anything to do with its use in both places? Do not confuse this species with another American sumac, the various species of the genus *Toxicodendron*, which is poisonous to the touch. These are smooth bushes with green-white berries and are found in swamps.

For recipes, see Mrs Kahayat's *Food from the Arab World*.

Sunflower

FR: Girasol, Hélianth
   annuel, Soleil,
   Tournesol
GER: Sonnenblume
IT: Girasole
SP: Girasol, Helianto,
   Mirasol
BOT: Helianthus annuus
FAM: Compositae

Probably sunflowers came originally from Peru, but they have been cultivated for so long that their origin is in doubt. They are grown as a crop, particularly in Russia, Bulgaria, Hungary and Rumania, as well as in the Argentine and Africa. The seeds contain some forty per cent of oil which has become well known of late because it is a highly 'unsaturated' oil and so is considered possibly to provide some protection against arterial disease. The oil is fine, almost tasteless and of a light yellow colour. It is excellent as a cooking and salad oil. The buds of the sunflower may be used in salads and the seeds roasted in their husks, salted and eaten by the handful like peanuts.

Sweetness

Although a few salts of metals (such as lead and beryllium), and some synthetic substances (such as saccharin) have a sweet taste, we normally associate sweetness with sugars, either refined or in sweet fruits and honey. In nature, sweetness is usually associated with ripe fruit, because sugars are formed in the fruits as they ripen. Sweetness is a true taste, as it is detected in the mouth and not in the nose, and is particularly liked by most animals, children, and often again by old people.

The perfect adjustment of sweetness is as important as any other operation in cooking, although it is often neglected due to the ease with which extra sugar can be added at table. In sweetening dishes it is as well to remember that while salty and bitter tastes are more pronounced in cold than in hot dishes, with sweetness and sourness the converse is true. In dishes such as jellies which are tasted for flavour when hot, a slight over-sweetness is necessary so that they will be correct when cold. Ices must taste very sweet before they are frozen.

Sweet Cicely

Anise Chervil,
   Giant Sweet Chervil,
   Spanish Chervil

FR: Cerfeuil d'Espagne,
   Cerfeuil musqué,
   Cerfeuil odorant

Sweet cicely is an old-fashioned herb found wild in nothern Europe, including northern England and southern Scotland. It is a stout umbelliferous plant, growing usually about three feet high but sometimes reaching five feet. It has white flowers, large, lacy, downy leaves, hollow stems and a smell and flavour between anise and liquorice. It is perennial and can be grown from seed or by root division.

GER: Englischer
    (Spanischer) Kerble,
    Wohlreichende
    Süßdolde
IT: Mirride odorosa
SP: Perifollo
BOT: Myrrhis odorata
FAM: Umbelliferae
Ill. 6, No. 5, page 97

Partial shade is preferable. One or two plants would be more than enough in a garden. It is sufficiently decorative to be used in an ornamental border.

Opinions are sharply divided on sweet cicely. Some would not give it house room, but others regard it as useful, particularly because it is available over such a long period: from early spring, right through the summer, and well into winter when other herbs are becoming scarce.

Sweet cicely has a tap root which, when boiled, can be eaten as a salad, dressed with oil and vinegar. The fruits are large and, when green, are also recommended to be eaten with oil and vinegar (Gerard's *Herbal*). For people who like an anise flavour, sweet cicely can be used in sweet dishes or with fruit, and it is used in flavouring liqueurs.

Sweet-Sour

The combination of sweetness and sourness (acids with sugars) occurs in nature in almost all of the best fruits. Indeed fruits which do not have this 'antagonism' are usually flat and uninteresting. Being so fundamental a quality and one fairly simple to measure, it is often the main scientific criterion of breeders when they wish to evaluate new varieties of fruit or tomatoes. It may not be true to say that a tomato with both plenty of acid and plenty of sugar is always good eating, but it is safe to say that if it lacks these elements it is certainly not.

The combination of acidity and sweetness in fruit dishes we accept as such an everyday matter that it passes without remark. Indeed, we simply regard it as sweetening something which is over-sour, and usually the balance is tipped well on the side of sweetness. However, if 'sweet and sour' is mentioned in connection with meat or fish dishes, many people think only of Chinese food. It is true that savoury sweet-sour combinations are important in the East, but for a long time back, certainly in Roman times, they have also been important in the West. Italy, Germany, Austria, Scandinavia and Holland have many sweet-sour dishes, and in the Middle East they are popular too, especially in Persia where there are many combinations of meat with fruit.

We have, of course, been speaking about a dominant effect, but the combination is also important as a background. It is a common practice with some cooks to make dishes a trace sweet with sugar and then adjust back to 'neutrality' with lemon juice. They say that this enhances the flavour of the whole. It is a matter of opinion. There are certainly many meat dishes containing naturally sweet vegetables, such as onions or carrots, which need to be adjusted with a few drops of lemon juice, and this is certainly a sweet-sour background.

Finally, I must mention the delicious effect of mixing sweet-sour combinations in the mouth rather than in the dish. A spoonful of sour cream in bortsch would be an example of this, as would be serving a sour sauce with a sweet or slightly sweet dish.

Sweet Woodruff

Asperula, Quinsywort, Sweetgrass
FR: Glycérie
GER: Waldmeister
IT: Asperula, Stellina odorosa
SP: Aspérula olorosa
BOT: Galium odoratum (Asperula odorata)
FAM: Rubiaceae
Ill. 5, No. 4, page 83

This is a perennial herb with white flowers, native to Europe and common wild in England in damp woods on chalk. Another English wild plant, squinancy wort, (*Asperula cynanchica*) is confused with it in some books ('squinancy' is an old, obsolete form of 'quinsy').

When crushed, woodruff gives off an aroma of new-mown hay and it is traditional in a variety of 'cups'. It is the flavouring for the German *Maitrunk* (May drink) or *Waldmeister Bowle*, made by infusing the young shoots in Rhenish wine and adding brandy and sugar to taste. In France, it is infused in champagne, in Switzerland in cognac or Benedictine and in the United States there is 'May wine punch' (wine, brandy and Benedictine, once more). People say that woodruff helps to make a party lively, but herbalists say it is mildly anaesthetic. In northern Europe, it is used in certain kinds of sausage. Since sweet woodruff will increase rapidly if established in shady corners or under trees, it is a doubly good plant to have in a garden.

Tabasco

Tabasco sauce, that famous and exceedingly pungent thin red pepper sauce, is made from a small Mexican variety of chilli which was brought into Louisiana in 1868 by a soldier returning from the wars. It has many uses on the bar, at table and in the kitchen, and is one of the important commercial sauces.

Tamarind
Indian Date

FR: Tamarin
GER: Tamarinde
IT: Tamarindo
SP: Tamarindo
BOT: Tamarindus indica
FAM: Leguminosae
Ill. 7, Nos. 1, 1a, page 103

Tamarind is probably a native of tropical east Africa, but possibly also of southern Asia. It certainly grows wild all over India and has been used there for a very long time, hence its alternative name. It was also used by the Arabs and, to some extent, in Europe during the Middle Ages. Supplies at that time came mostly from India.

The tamarind tree when fully grown is quite large, and sometimes reaches heights of eight feet, although it is usually smaller. The tree bears pods six to eight inches long, which become dark brown when they are ripe. The pulp surrounding the seeds contains some twelve per cent of tartaric acid, so that although it also contains sugar it is intensely sour.

Commercial tamarind, as available in Indian shops, consists of the partly dried, broken and sticky mass of pods without the seeds. It always contains fibrous material. If this is macerated in hot water, an intensely sour brown juice can be squeezed out. This juice is the common souring agent used in Indian curries. Tamarind keeps almost indefinitely and must always be on the shelf of people who like real curries, as other souring agents will never produce quite the same results. Today tamarind is grown throughout the tropics, including the West Indies, and is used commercially as a basis for fruit drinks. It is mildly laxative.

Tansy

FR: Barbotine,
Herbe amère,
Herbe aux vers,
Tanaisie
GER: Drusenkraut,
Rainfarn, Wurmkraut
IT: Tanaceto
or Ariceto or Erba
amara
SP: Argentina,
Balsimita menor,
Tanaceto
BOT: Chrysanthemum
vulgare (Tanacetum
vulgare)
FAM: Compositae

Tansy is a native of Europe, including Britain, and is also common wild in the eastern United States. The plant is usually two to three feet tall with golden yellow, button-like flowers and fern-like leaves. There are decorative garden varieties, and tansy is cultivated as a commercial crop in a few places, notably in the United States.

This was a commonly used wild and cottage garden herb of medieval Europe, though it is little used in cooking today. The flavour is strong and, to many, rather unpleasant. It is very easy to grow by root division or from seed.

A 'tansy' is a kind of custard, baked or boiled and flavoured predominantly with tansy leaves. Chopped tansy leaves also flavour tansy cake and tansy pudding, dishes, in the past, especially associated with Easter. Various reasons are put forward for this, yet nobody has put forward the theory that people liked it. However, tansy frequently

FAM: Compositae
Plate V, No. 1

appears in recipes from the sixteenth and seventeenth centuries, and Izaak Walton mentions it in a recipe for minnows. Some authorities recommend it for omelettes, stuffings, freshwater fish and meat pies, as well as for salads. It is also reputed to be one of the many herbs in chartreuse, but this liqueur is credited with every herb in the calendar.

Tarragon

FR: Estragon
GER: Dragon, Estragon
IT: Dragoncello or
    Estragone
SP: Estragon, Tarragon,
    Tarragona
BOT: Artemesia
    dracunculus
FAM: Compositae
Ill. 9, No. 1, page 123

Tarragon is one of the great culinary herbs, botanically related to wormwood, southernwood and mugwort. It is a bushy perennial, three feet high, with narrow leaves and small shot-like grey-green flowers. It requires well-drained soil and sun or partial shade. In winter, it should be cut down and covered with litter to protect it against frost, or it may be lifted in autumn and kept in a cold frame for a winter supply. Beds should be renewed every three or four years, as, especially if grown in the wrong soil, the flavour tends to go off.

True 'French' tarragon rarely, if ever, sets viable seed so it must be grown from cuttings or by root division. Good strains are often difficult to get. Seed is always from the very inferior Russian tarragon (*Artemesia dracunculoides*), which has paler leaves and a very different taste, more pungent and with little of the delicate and special flavour for which French tarragon is desired. Russian tarragon is commonly used in Persia as a salad plant with grilled meat.

Tarragon is particularly used in dishes of French origin, but, even in the markets of France, the supply is irregular and Russian tarragon has crept in. In Italy, it is rare except in and around Sienna.

The flavour of French tarragon is impossible to describe in terms of anything else, but most people know it from tarragon vinegar so perhaps we should start with that. Tarragon vinegar can be bought, but one can make it by stuffing a bottle with the fresh herb, gathered just before it flowers, and filling it with white wine vinegar. After two months it is ready for decanting, but it is better to leave the herb in the bottle both for its appearance and because it produces a better flavour. Tarragon vinegar has many uses, especially in salad dressings and mayonnaise. It is also important in mixed mustards.

Tarragon can be dried, but it usually then acquires haylike overtones. It can be quick frozen or bottled by simply packing the leaves into jars, sealing and sterilizing.

Tarragon vinegar and the fresh herb are essential for *sauce Béarnaise*. It is, of course, also essential in all French dishes *à l'estragon*, e.g. *poulet à l'estragon* and *oeufs en gelée à l'estragon*. It is usual as part of a fines herbes mixture for omelettes, as well as being an ingredient of many sauces (*verte*, *ravigote*, *messine*), butters, purées with cream and cream soups. It may also be used, with sole, chicken, eggs and salads. Although the flavour of tarragon is elusive, it is strong and diffuses quickly through dishes, especially hot ones. As it is used mainly in delicate dishes, it must be added with good judgement. Tarragon also flavours various liqueurs and is used in perfumery.

Another plant, *Tagetes lucida*, has a flavour somewhat like tarragon and is sometimes used as a substitute.

Thyme

Garden Thyme
FR: Thym
GER: Römischer
  Quendel, Thymian
IT: Timo
SP: Tomillo
BOT: Thymus vulgaris
FAM: Labiatae
Ill. 14, No. 1, page 189

Continental Wild Thyme
FR: Serpolet
GER: Feldthymian,
  Quendel
IT: Serpillo
SP: Serpoleto
BOT: Thymus serpyllum

Common Wild Thyme
BOT: Thymus drucei
Plate IV, No. 4 and
  Ill. 14, No. 3, page 189

Larger Wild Thyme
BOT: Thymus
  pulegioides

Thymes are powerfully aromatic and contain more or less of an essential oil called thymol, which is a disinfectant. Thus, thyme is a preservative. It dries well, retaining most of its flavour and developing none of the 'hay' off-flavour which comes to many other dried herbs. In fact, species coming from hot dry climates are very nearly desiccated when living. Thyme can also be quick frozen.

Thyme is one of the great European culinary herbs. It was used by the ancient Greeks (the word itself comes from the Greek *thymon*) and probably earlier. There are many species coming from an area including Europe and western Asia, North Africa and the Canary Islands.

Garden thyme comes originally from southern Europe and the Mediterranean, and there are many cultivated varieties (e.g., broad-leaved 'English' thyme and narrow-leaved 'French' thyme) with varying flavours. It grows wild in the dry hills of southern Europe, for instance in the mountains along the Riviera, and here it is incomparably more aromatic than the same species grown in gardens in Britain. (When I lived in Liguria, I always gathered my own thyme on the mountains, but experience forced me to taste and smell the plants as I gathered them, since the best could not always be recognized by sight.) In other areas, such as Spain, the flavour may again be different.

Typically, wild Mediterranean thyme is a small bushy plant with woody stems, tiny grey-green leaves and purple flowers. When growing wild in very dry conditions, the leaves are exceedingly sparse, and the habit of the plant straggly. Thyme is easy to grow from seeds or from pieces of plant with a bit of root attached. It prefers sun and dry conditions in light calcareous soil. In damp clay it can be difficult and will not have such a good aroma. Thyme is perennial, but some people advocate replanting every few years.

What most cookery books call 'wild thyme' can rarely be found wild in Britain, but is found in continental Europe. The common English wild thyme (of Shakespeare's banks) is the *Thymus drucei*, and there is a larger wild thyme found on chalk downs in the south of England. All of these have a thyme flavour, but to most tastes are inferior to garden thyme.

Of the many cultivated and decorative thymes, are lemon thyme, orange thyme and, from Corsica and Sardinia, caraway thyme (*Thymus herba-barona*). Their taste follows their descriptive names, and lemon thyme is of particular value in the kitchen, where it serves the same purpose as regular garden thyme or may be mixed with it. Other species and varieties are mainly decorative. A good herb garden should include several types, and cooks must follow their own sense of taste in selection.

In European cooking, thyme is an exceedingly important herb. Like sage, it is commonly used in stuffings, but there any similarity ends, for although both are powerful herbs, pungent and warming, sage always has a certain crudity which thyme at its best has not. It is, with bay and parsley, an essential part of a bouquet garni and, therefore, enters into the background flavouring of innumerable dishes. It goes into many soups, with vegetables (such as tomatoes, potatoes, courgettes, aubergines and sweet peppers); with fish, into court bouillon and stuffings; but most of all it mingles with wine, onion, garlic and brandy as a part of the flavouring of countless savoury meat, game and fowl dishes, especially those cooked slowly for a long time in an earthenware crock or casserole. In this sort of dish, thyme seems to contribute a deep aromatic quality, and without it cooking would be greatly the poorer. To quote a few examples: with beef (*boeuf à la bourguignonne, à la mode, en daube, estofade de boeuf*) and with oxtail and shin, though more rarely with veal; in various stews of mutton (*navarin*), and with pork and wild boar, particularly in the marinades (*carré de porc provençale*); with duck and goose (*oie en cassoulet, canard braisé*), with chicken and guinea fowl (*coq au vin, pintade en daube*); with rabbit and hare (*lapin en gibelotte, civet de lièvre*); in terrines and in salmis of wild duck, woodcock, plover, teal and so on. Often thyme is mixed with marjoram. In Italy, thyme is used somewhat less than in France, sweet marjoram and more violent species of *Origanum* often fulfilling much the same function. Thyme has many other uses: for instance, it is often used in the pickle to flavour olives, and it is said to be one of the herbs used in *Bénédictine*. In conclusion, I must repeat that there is a world of difference between thyme gathered on a Mediterranean hillside and the dried thyme of shops. Close attention to such detail is essential for cooks who wish to rise above the common rut.

Tomato

FR: Tomate
GER: Tomate
IT: Pomodoro
SP: Tomate
BOT: Lycopersicon
    esculentum
FAM: Solanaceae

The tomato is a fruit and vegetable and an important flavouring as well. It is probably native to the northwestern part of South America (Peru and Ecuador), but long before Columbus discovered America, it had been taken to Mexico and domesticated. It was brought to Europe by the Spaniards, who apparently used it, but elsewhere in Europe it was, to begin with, often regarded as a curiosity, even as poisonous. Perhaps this was because it so obviously belongs to the same family as the poisonous deadly nightshade, and, actually, the green parts of the plant are poisonous.

Today, the tomato is grown in practically every country in the world, in both tropical and temperate climates, but there are an enormous number of varieties and flavour varies considerably as also does the water content. Unfortunately, the most profitable commercial varieties, which look good and stand up to transportation, have often an inferior flavour. In foreign markets and out of the way places, one will sometimes find miserable looking little tomatoes, all wrinkled and oddly shaped, which have an incomparable flavour. So tomatoes, as other fruit, should not be bought by eye. Particular varieties of tomato, such as the plum-shaped tomato much grown in Italy (though of British origin) are suitable for particular purposes, such as canning or conversion into tomato purée.

In the Mediterranean countries, there are also a number of important preserved tomato products, and tomatoes are halved and spread out in the sun to dry, after which they are preserved in olive oil. These dried tomatoes develop a special flavour which fresh tomatoes cannot imitate. During the winter, the market stalls of some Mediterranean countries sell a very rough tomato purée preserved under oil and commonly sold in old wine bottles. This has a rather smoky taste which comes through quite distinctly in local food, so dishes made at home with more sophisticated ingredients do not always taste exactly as they do in their own country. Canned tomatoes also have a special taste of their own, and these are much used by cooks in Italy. Commercial tomato purée again has a different flavour. So, it is very important in following Mediterranean recipes to use the correct tomato ingredient. Tomato ketchup is often called for, particularly in modern recipes.

Truffle

Italian White Truffle,
  Piedmont Truffle,
  Italian Truffle,
  Grey Truffle
FR: Truffe des magnats,
  Truffe Piemontaise
GER: Piemontesiche
  Trüffel
IT: Tartufo bianco
  (d'alba)
BOT: Tuber magnatum
  (tycoon's truffle)
Plate VIII, No. 8

Black, French or
  Périgord Truffle
FR: Rabasse (Provence),
  Truffe de France,
  Truffe des gourmets,
  Truffe du Périgord,
  Truffe noir,
  Truffe vraie

Truffles are the underground fruit of some fungi; to be unscientific, they are like subterranean puff balls growing one or two feet down and in the vicinity of trees or herbs particular to the kind of truffle in question. Because of this association, truffles cannot be cultivated as we cultivate mushrooms. The best that can be done is to introduce truffles into plantations of trees where they have not grown before.

Because truffles are entirely underground, they have to be found by smell, by dogs or pigs. Pigs are less favoured, in part because they are wayward creatures and will root for other delicacies besides truffles, but most of all because they gobble up the truffles if the owner is not quick enough to get there first. Dogs on the other hand are obedient, have a keen nose and do not like eating truffles. They find them through no natural inclination, but only because they have been trained and are rewarded with pieces of biscuit carried by the truffle hunter in his pocket. Truffle dogs are usually intelligent mongrels who obviously enjoy the sport, and good 'truffle hounds' are worth hundreds of pounds. When

GER: Perigord-Trüffel
IT: Tartufo di Norcia,
Tartufo nero dolce
SP: Trufa del Périgord,
Turma de tierra
BOT: Tuber
melanosporum
Plate VIII, No. 7

Summer, English, Bath
or Red Truffle
BOT: Tuber aestivum

Winter Truffle
BOT: Tuber brumale

Terfez or Sand Truffle
IT: Terfezie
ARABIC: Terfez (North
Africa)
LEBANESE: Kama,
Kamaieh
BOT: Terfezia leonis and
other species of Terfezia

Pig or 'White' Truffle
BOT: Choiromyces
meandriformis

Hart's Truffle
BOT: Elaphomyces
granulatus

a dog has found a truffle, he begins frantically digging and is then helped by the truffle hunter, who uses a small pick. So powerful is the aroma that, once digging has proceeded a little way, it is usually possible for the truffle hunter to smell the truffle himself.

The two best kinds of truffle are the Italian white truffle and the French black or Périgord truffle. These are two of the most expensive foods known to man. As the flavour varies greatly according to locality, the truffles from some regions are very much more expensive than from others, so poor truffles are frequently brought into the markets of the best areas in order to deceive.

There is an unending dispute between the French and Italians as to which is the better truffle, the white or the black. To express an opinion in this matter is a certain way to get a black eye. The famous French gastronome Brillat-Savarin did, apparently, on one occasion say that he considered the white Piedmont truffle superior. He must have been a brave man. Perhaps it is for this reason that many Italians consider him the 'unquestioned arbiter in materia gastronomica'. There is only one way to decide this argument: start a gastronomic holiday in Piedmont in November and then proceed to Périgeux (if you have any money left) as the season for black truffles conveniently starts after the white is over.

The ITALIAN WHITE TRUFFLE centre is Alba, about forty miles southeast of Turin, but it is found in the foothills of the ranges that border the south side of the Lombardy plain and the north side of the Apennines as far south as Modena. It is also found in France and Yugoslavia. The season begins in October with a 'truffle fair' in Alba and extends onwards into the winter, until snow usually puts an end to the sport.

The truffles are located by the trained dogs, usually near the edge of a field which has suitable hedge trees, but I once saw a big one accidentally ploughed up. So valuable are white truffles that great secrecy is observed by the hunters. Truffle maps are passed from father to son or bequeathed as potential riches, and the digging is often done at dead of night, a damp time when the dogs can certainly smell better and when the hunters can search the special places, unobserved by rivals.

At the beginning of the season, the price of truffles in Alba may start at as much as fifty pounds per pound – about fifteen dollars for a fungus the size of a walnut.

The white truffle looks like a chalky-yellow misshapen new potato and is usually about that size, although giant specimens are occasionally found. The perfume is so strong that a single specimen brought into the kitchen will reach the sleepy gastronome in his bedroom up four flights of stairs and cause him to salivate. The smell is unique, quite unlike that of other fungus. Some say it is reminiscent of garlic, others that it is more like the rich smell of escaping gas. In fact, the perfume cannot be accurately described, but is delicious. As for the taste, this is not the important factor, but it is slightly peppery.

Italian white truffles are usually sliced raw directly onto the dish when it comes to table. A special slicer that produces razor-thin sections is used. The truffle's function is to perfume risotto, pâté, salads, meat dishes and that rather sickening Piedmont speciality called *bagna cauda* (*see* Anchovies). Cheese 'fundua' is another dish, to which white truffles are added in Piedmont.

Old recipes for cooking white truffles date back to the Romans, but besides being impossibly expensive in these days, such recipes ignore the fact that white truffles have more perfume than flavour and are far better raw than cooked.

Because the price is so high, and truffles attach their perfume to anything they are kept with (they will penetrate and flavour an egg overnight) it is common to pass off inferior Yugoslav truffles, puff balls, (and even potatoes) in the market. There are shops in Italy which will send truffles by air mail, anywhere. One small one is quite enough for a party. White truffles are also canned, but in the process there is a great loss of aroma and the result is probably not worth the high price.

The FRENCH or BLACK TRUFFLE centre is Périgeux, a town some eighty-five miles north east of Bordeaux, on the western edge of the Massif Central; but black truffles

---

Ill. 20 Sweetening Agents and Ajowan: 1 Sugar Cane, 2 Sugar Palm, 3 Sugar Beet, 4 Ajowan, 5 Sugar Maple Leaves with Keys.

are also found locally all round the southern foothills of the Massif, and up the Rhône valley in the hills on either side as far as Burgundy. They are also found in Italy and in other parts of southern Europe. However, truffles from other parts of France and Italy are less delicate than those from Périgord. The season is from November to March.

The black truffle is coal black and covered with small knobs, which makes it difficult to clean. It is more plentiful than the white and the annual production in France alone, though less than it used to be, runs into millions of pounds. Like the white truffle, it has a strong perfume and almost no taste. It can be eaten raw, but (unlike the white) it is more frequently eaten cooked. The best-known use of truffles is, of course, in pâté, but there are many other mouth-watering ways of cooking them in France, of which a good selection can be found in the *Larousse Gastronomique*. Black truffles and even the peelings (since black truffles are also expensive) are available in cans. It may be that there are some rare brands which retain the aroma of the fresh fungus, but in most cases canned truffles are only fit to be used for the sake of appearances. More-over, from personal observation, I know that the truffles that go into the can are usually of poor quality or even of other inferior black species, of which vast quantities, look-ing like sacks of coal, are gathered for the commercial pâté and sausage industry.

The SUMMER TRUFFLE is a common European truffle, one of the few also found in England, particularly at the edge of beechwoods on chalk downs. At one time they were collected in the south of England and, as with other types of truffle, dogs were used to find them. Any dog with a good nose can be trained for this purpose by the usual find and reward technique, but, obviously, if the dog is to know the smell of what it is expected to find, you cannot train a dog without first securing a truffle of the species. Thus, it is difficult to restart truffle hunting once it has died out.

The summer truffle is black with large pyramidal warts. The inside is usually brown with yellowish white veins. The aroma is much less than the Piedmont or Périgord truffles and tends to vanish altogether when it is cooked. It can be found in late summer or autumn and is from one to four inches in diameter. Although it is nothing more than a good edible fungus, it has plenty of snob value, due to its noble relatives.

The WINTER TRUFFLE is smaller and is also found in England as well as on the Continent. In many people's opinion it comes next in excellence after the Périgord truffle. It grows in the same woods as the summer truffle, but is found later in the season (November and December). The warts on the surface are smaller, the colour of the flesh is black or violet-brown when ripe, and it is veined. The aroma is much more powerful than that of the summer truffle, but becomes unpleasant when the truffle is old.

Other species of truffle are also edible and are used on the Continent, *Tuber mesentericum*, *Tuber macrosporum*, and *Tuber borchii* being examples of these. They are similar to inferior forms already described and are all true truffles. They possibly go into tins.

The TERFEZIAS are fungi related to the truffles and to be distinguished from them only by botanists. They grow to some extent in southern Europe, but are very plentiful in North Africa and the Middle East, where travellers are likely to come across them. They are abundant in the Syrian desert, in places like Palmyra and also in the Libyan desert. Although usually pale in colour, dark varieties are also found, and these are regarded as superior. They are somewhat tasteless when compared with the true truffles, but are still excellent when cooked in local ways or eaten raw as salad. Visitors to Beirut or Damascus should try them. They are easy to find as they grow near the surface and cause a slight mound in the sand which gives away their presence. They are also sold in local markets.

The PIG TRUFFLE should not be called the 'white truffle' because it may be confused with the Italian white truffle. Also, it is not a true truffle, but as it has a strong perfume, gastronomically it may be classified as one of them. It grows on the European continent and in England, usually under oak trees and often only half buried in the ground. Being white or creamy brown, it is very easily seen, and may be found without a dog. The size is anything from a golf ball to a child's football. It is like an irregular potato, with flesh creamy or light brown and can be eaten raw, cut in slices, used as a flavouring or dried. It is one of the better truffle-like mushrooms of Europe.

In general, all truly underground tuber-shaped fungi are edible unless they are foul smelling (e.g. species of *Rhizopogon*). A very few species, e.g. *Choiromyces terfezioides* and *Balsamia vulgaris*, contain an acrid substance which will cause vomiting. They taste nasty, but none of them is lethal.

HART'S TRUFFLE is a very common, tiny, European, truffle-like fungus found shallowly underground, often under moss, in forests in wintertime. The outside is brown and covered in minute warts, giving it a granulated appearance. The flesh is pink, later turning dark brown, and it has a strong smell. This is inedible and is mentioned because those hunting truffles are likely to see it.

The section on truffles would not be complete without mention of the common *Scleroderma* (*Scleroderma aurantium*) an exceedingly common fungus of the northern hemisphere, North and South Africa. This fungus is a relative of the puff balls. It grows on the surface of the ground, but is occasionally half buried. It can be found in summer and autumn on dry sunny heaths and in open woods and has a very thick leathery skin. With age, the skin turns from dirty white to yellowish-brown and becomes rough and scaly. Inside, it is at first white-pink, then turning to blue-black veined with white fibres.

This fungus is often listed as poisonous, but, in fact, it is quite harmless when young or when older *in small quantities*. It has a strong, to me nasty, smell and somewhat truffle-like taste. It is frequently used, especially in eastern Europe, as a truffle substitute in sausages and pâté. It may be sliced and dried. It also finds its way into tins marked truffles, no doubt by mistake.

There are other rather similar species which are regarded as poisonous, but none of them is deadly. Another near relative of the puff balls, which grows all over the world and is used as a truffle substitute when young is the dark brown, smooth, ball-like fungus, *Pisolithus arenarius*. Small quantities of this are all that is required to flavour a dish. All types with thick tough skins should be peeled before use.

Anyone wishing to pursue this subject who invests in an illustrated book on fungi, should make sure that the book includes the truffles, since many fungi books deal only with the Basidiomycetes and so do not include morels or truffles. The above descriptions apply to Europe and the Mediterranean region. One cannot guarantee that in other parts of the world there are no poisonous truffles, or equally, no excellent ones that have not been mentioned. Because truffles are difficult to find, the subject is rather an obscure one, and it is possible that there are truffles which have never been discovered.

Turmeric
Indian Saffron

FR: Curcuma, Safran
  des Indes,
  Terre-mérite
GER: Gelbwurz
INDIA: Haldi, Huldie,
  Safran des Indes
IT: Curcuma
SP: Cúrcuma
BOT: Curcuma longa
FAM: Zingiberaceae
Plate I, No. 14 and
  Ill. 18, Nos. 1, 1a,
  page 244

Ground turmeric is well-known as a yellow powder used in 'piccalilli'. The plant is native to Southeast Asia, from Vietnam to the humid hilly areas of South India. Today, it is grown in tropical places throughout the world. It is perennial with large lily-like leaves and pale yellow flowers clustered in dense spikes. Like its relation ginger, the rhizome provides the spice, but turmeric rhizomes are round (in section), not flattened, and when halved show a brilliant orange colour. The rhizomes are boiled and then dried in the sun for about two weeks, after which the outer skin is polished off. As far as I know, fresh turmeric is not used in cooking. Although whole turmeric is commonly sold in Eastern bazaars, this is one of the few spices one could buy ready-ground; it is sufficiently cheap to be unadulterated and is difficult to grind at home.

Turmeric is one of the spices that found its way from India, overland through Arabia, into Europe. It was used as a dyestuff, but is not a very satisfactory dye because the colour is not fast, though the saffron robes of holy men in the East are often dyed with it. It is the cheapest and most common yellow dye available. The colour is sparingly soluble in water (though readily so in spirits), but in commerce turmeric is used a good deal for colouring food, particularly mustard and pickles. It is a usual ingredient in curries and curry powder and is much used in Indian cooking for colouring sweet dishes. It cannot, however, be used as a substitute for saffron or as a flavourless colouring like annatto, because it has a peculiar 'spice cupboard' taste of its own.

Turmeric is often mistranslated 'saffron' in books on Indian cookery, although the only thing they have in common is their yellow colour. Conversely the result of substituting turmeric for saffron, e.g. in *bouillabaisse*, is disastrous. (*See* Saffron.)

Vanilla

FR: Vanille
GER: Vanille
IT: Vaniglia
SP: Vainilla
BOT: Vanilla planifolia
FAM: Orchidaceae
Plate I, No. 12 and
   Ill. 4, No. 5, page 70

Vanilla is the pod of a climbing orchid, originating in the humid forests of tropical America. It was brought to Europe by the Spanish, who had found it already used by the Aztecs as a flavouring for chocolate. In modern plantations, the vanilla orchid is trained up posts or trees. The long, yellow pods are picked unripe, and fresh pods have no vanilla flavour. This develops only as a result of internal chemical activity (by enzymes) during a curing process. Curing is done in various ways but always involves 'sweating' in airtight boxes.

The best cured vanilla pods are dark brown, tough, somewhat flexible and covered with a frosting of crystals of aromatic vanillin. Since real vanilla is expensive, and a frosting is rather easy to fake, the best guide to the amateur buyer is a good shop and a fair price. One should be suspicious of cheap vanilla pods.

As a flavouring, vanilla pods are definitely superior to essence. Pods may be used many times over, even after warming or steeping in creams or custard, provided they are afterwards washed and re-dried. Since, however, vanilla flavour is almost always used in sweet dishes, the easiest technique is to keep several pods in a jar of sugar, which will then absorb the aroma. If the jar is continually refilled with sugar, the pods will perfume it for a long time.

Vanilla is grown in Mexico, Guiana, Puerto Rico, Guadalupe and Dominica, Madagascar, the Seychelles, the Comoro Islands, Réunion, Tahiti and other places with suitable climate. Pompona or West Indian vanilla comes from another species, *Vanilla pompona*. Do not confuse with the garden heliotrope (*Heliotropium arborescens, Heliotropium peruviana*), which has vanilla-scented flowers, known to many people as vanilla flowers and used in perfumery.

The best vanilla essence is made by extracting crushed vanilla pods with alcohol. Synthetic vanillin can be made from a substance present in clove oil (eugenol). Like most synthetic substances, it lacks the depth of the natural flavouring. Cheap vanilla essence may also, in countries where it is allowed, contain coumarin.

Vanilla flavouring is used in countless commercial products, in liqueurs and for poodle-faking cheap brandy and whisky.

Verbena
Lemon Scented Verbena

FR: Citronelle, Verveine, Verveine odorante
GER: Verbene, Zitronenstrauch
IT: Cedrina
SP: Vervena, Yerba de la princesa
BOT: Verbena tryphilla
FAM: Verbenaceae
Ill. 9, No. 6, page 123

Verbena should not be confused with vervain, although they are both of the same family. Most of the Verbenaceae are tropical plants: lemon scented verbena is no exception and is native to South America. It was brought to Europe by the Spaniards and is cultivated to some extent as a source of oil for perfume, although cheaper sources of the oil such as lemon grass are more commonly used.

Lemon verbena is easily grown from seeds or cuttings in any warm, sunny part of the garden. Although in hot countries it can grow up to four to five feet, in colder climates and more adverse circumstances the height will be much less. One or two plants will be sufficient in a family herb plot, or it can be grown in pots in a sunny window. Being strongly perfumed with lemon, it could substitute for lemon grass in recipes from Southeast Asia. It is also used as a source of an aromatic lemon flavour in sweet dishes, fruit salads, and soft drinks, but it must be used with care, because to many people it is reminiscent of scented soap.

Verjuice

FR: Verjus
GER: Obstsaft, Traubensaft
IT: Agresto
SP: Agraz

Verjuice, literally from the French *vert* (green) and *jus* (juice) is the juice of unripe fruit and was once a common souring substance, though little used today.

In England, it was made from sour green apples, preferably crab apples. The small amount of sugar present in such juice was allowed to ferment by standing a day or so, after which scum was removed and salt added. Sometimes it was concentrated by boiling. Such verjuice would keep well, due to its high acidity and salt content. Very sour fresh cider which has not yet vinegared may be substituted for it.

In France, verjuice was made by a similar process from the juice of sour green grapes, and there were special varieties for the purpose. Today, verjuice is mainly used in the preparation of mixed mustards, but is almost always a made-up and not a natural product. (*See* Mustards.) It should not be confused with must which is the unfermented juice of ripe grapes, though sometimes verjuice means the juice of ripe white grapes (*Perdreaux au verjus*). (In many grape-growing areas, green grapes are occasionally used in meat dishes. I have come on them sometimes and they are excellent.)

Vermouth

FR: Vermout
GER: Wermut
IT: Vermut
SP: Vermut

'Vermouth' comes from the German *wermut*: wormwood. Although these flavoured and fortified apéritif wines are imitated in many parts of the world, the modern centre for vermouths is southern France and northern Italy. Vermouths vary from dry to intensely sweet and from white or straw-coloured to red or brown. They also vary enormously in flavour according to the marker. Vermouth is always more or less bitter, and wormwood is the basic flavouring, but other flavouring agents such as angelica root, anise, calamus, cinnamon, cloves, coriander, camomile, bitter orange peel, peppermint, orris, quassia, quinine, gentian, nutmeg and so on are used as well. As with many apéritifs and liqueurs exact quantities and details of its making are commercial secrets.

Vermouths are used as a flavouring in some dishes. Fish, particularly sole, is sometimes cooked in vermouth or served with a sauce flavoured with it.

Vervain

FR: Herbe sacrée
  Verveine officinale
GER: Eisenkraut
IT: Verbena
SP: Verbena
BOT: Verbena officinalis
FAM: Verbenaceae
Ill. 9, No. 5, page 123

This is one of those herbs which, since the days of ancient Persia has been recorded as having magical, medicinal and culinary uses. Vervain is sometimes called verbena (and confused with it) and is often mentioned in old herbals. The dried leaves were used to make teas, but probably the purpose of this was entirely medicinal. Since, however, it was supposed to be particularly effective in love potions, there may be occasions when the cook would like to try it. Vervain is said to be good for the kidneys and the liver; it is also a frequent ingredient in home-made liqueurs. In North America, the common wild vervain is another species (*Verbena hastata*), also medicinal.

Vinegar
IT: Aceto

The word vinegar comes from the French *vin aigre* meaning 'sour wine'. There is also an old word 'alegar' or 'algar' meaning sour ale, now out of general use. Today, we call all such sour liquids vinegar, with a descriptive adjective; thus, wine vinegar, malt vinegar, cider vinegar and so on.

Vinegar has been used for at least five thousand years and probably for much longer, because it develops through an entirely natural process. Yeasts are always present in the air so, under natural conditions, a liquid containing sugar (such as fruit juice, malt liquor or honey water) will ferment with the formation of alcohol. Once alcohol has been formed, unless the liquid is closely corked, bacteria take over and oxidize the alcohol to acetic acid. The result is the sour liquid known as vinegar. The bacteria, in oxidizing the alcohol, use oxygen, which is why vinegar forms only from wine uncorked and exposed to the air.

If vinegar is left opened, the acetic acid in it will, in turn, be attacked by micro-organisms and further broken down, unless the concentration of acid is over a certain strength. Just as spirits or fortified wines will not sour, so also artificially strengthened vinegar will not deteriorate. Dilute vinegar may, so when making pickles of watery vegetables one must be sure to start with a really strong vinegar or extract some of the water first.

The strength of acetic acid in vinegar varies considerably. Wine vinegar is the strongest natural vinegar with about six and one half per cent acid; malt vinegar and cider vinegar are less strong with between four and five per cent acid. Distilled or fortified vinegars, on the other hand, go up to about twelve per cent.

Though acetic acid has some flavour as well as sourness, the special taste of good vinegars is due to small quantities of other substances, mainly volatile esters, having fruity or other interesting aromas. These substances are also present in the original wine (malt or cider) from which the vinegar was made, so good vinegar comes from good wine. The selection of a fine vinegar, especially for use in salads and delicate sauces, is very important and is frequently not given sufficient consideration.

WINE VINEGAR may be either white or red, being made from either white or red wine. In wine-growing countries, most vinegar is made from wine (or is claimed to be) and varies in quality. Because vinegar is wine vinegar, it is not necessarily good. In many places, it is customary for people to make their own by pouring left-over wine into a bottle and leaving it till it turns sour. Sometimes such hit or miss methods make very good vinegar, but as often as not the result is rank and raw.

Commercial wine vinegar is made by dripping wine through open casks loosely filled with wicker work or wood shavings to provide plenty of surface. On this surface the wine and bacteria are exposed to the oxygen in the air. The bacteria proliferate, turn the alcohol to acetic acid, and during the process heat is produced; the faster the reaction goes, the hotter it gets. Heat tends to drive off the more delicate volatile aromas, and, therefore, fast vinegar processes, though cheaper to operate, produce inferior vinegars.

The superior vinegars are produced by the Orléans and Boerhaave slow processes. Oak vats with air holes at the top are kept half filled with wine and a film of the bacteria, known as 'mother of vinegar', forms on the top (this also contains tiny nematode worms which help in the process). The temperature is kept at about 70°F. (21°C.). The alcohol tends to move to the top of the cask and the acetic acid to the bottom, so that vinegar can be drawn weekly from the bottom and more wine added to replace it. The slow processes, cool and quiet, preserve in the vinegars the flavours of the wines from which they are made. Fine wine vinegars made by the slow processes are expensive, but a good wine vinegar is always worth paying for. It is far superior to lemon juice or malt vinegar as a dressing for salads and rarely causes digestive upsets, which lemon juice, though much publicized by health food experts, can do.

MALT VINEGAR. In England and northern Europe, vinegars are traditionally made from beer and are called malt vinegars. Malt, or malt and grain mixed together, is heated with water and then fermented to make a crude kind of beer known as 'gyle'. Bacteria act on this alcoholic liquid as it drips through the vats filled with basket work or beech shavings. The malt vinegar, after being matured for several months, contains about six per cent acid and is then diluted to the strength required for sale. Malt vinegar is usually coloured and has quite a different flavour from wine vinegar. It is better for some purposes, for instance, in recipes for English pickles. For international cooking, one should keep several kinds of vinegar in the kitchen, using malt vinegar for recipes of English origin and wine vinegar for recipes from southern Europe, unless one is quite certain from personal experience that a change from tradition is preferable. One cannot say that one kind of vinegar is better than another, only that it is different.

CIDER VINEGAR is made from cider and has a strong particular taste of its own. It is rather popular in America, but cannot be indiscriminately substituted for wine or malt vinegar. There is, however, quite a lot of evidence to suggest that cider vinegar is an exceedingly healthy substance in the diet. Cider vinegar in water is the basis of a whole school of naturalistic medicine which started in America and has spread elsewhere.

DISTILLED VINEGARS are popular in the north of England and in Scotland. (What Scotsman can resist distillation!) They are colourless and are made by carefully distilling natural vinegar in a vacuum. Although much stronger than natural vinegar, some of the aroma of the original is retained. Because distilled vinegar is strong, it is useful for making pickles.

SPIRIT VINEGAR is made by distilling before all the alcohol has been converted to acetic acid. It therefore contains a small quantity of alcohol, which makes the flavour rather different.

OTHER VINEGARS can be made from mead, fruit wine or any fermented liquors. Vinegars rather naturally tend to follow the drink of the country in which they are made, and so in Japan and China one will find vinegar made from rice wine. *Yamabukizu* is a sweet-sour Japanese vinegar used for seasoning rice (substitute a small cup of white vinegar sweetened with three teaspoons of sugar). Another interesting vinegar is produced from wine made from the fruit of the cashew nut.

Ill. 17, No. 2, page 229

FLAVOURED VINEGARS are often made with fruits, flower petals, herbs or spices. These may be made at home, but some are on sale in shops. Tarragon vinegar is the most usual. Herb vinegars are made simply by macerating the herb or spice in vinegar and, afterwards, straining if necessary.

SYNTHETIC AND INFERIOR VINEGARS. There are some really nasty vinegars about. They may be made from synthetic acetic acid suitably diluted with water, either colourless or coloured with caramel.

More commonly, cheap vinegar is made by the natural process, but starting from cheap ingredients like wood pulp. Unless the product has been carefully purified, traces of harmful chemicals are possibly present, so cheap vinegars should be avoided not only for their poor flavour but also for reasons of health.

Violet

FR: Violette
GER: Veilchen
IT: Viola mammola
SP: Violeta
BOT: Viola odorata
FAM: Violaceae
Plate VII, No. 6

The flavour of sweet violets, which may be extracted by infusing the flowers, is sometimes used for flavouring creams, ices and liqueurs. It is the main flavouring for very sweet, violet-coloured liqueur, *parfait amour*. Violet flowers are preserved in sugar as crystallized violets, used mainly for decoration, but are sometimes crushed as a flavouring. The fresh flowers and the leaves are harmless and may decorate salads or garnish meat dishes, particularly veal. One violet salad is made with endive, celery, parsley, olive, and violets dressed with olive oil, salt, pepper, wine and vinegar.

Viper's Bugloss

FR: Vipérine
GER: Natterkopf
IT: Viperino
SP: Buglosa
BOT: Echium vulgare
FAM: Boraginaceae
Plate V, No. 7

Viper's bugloss is a common flower found on chalky soil in Europe, including the south of Britain. It is a hairy biennial growing to about two and a half feet high. The flowers are blue, although the buds are pink. This plant is in many ways similar to borage and can be used for the same purposes (particularly in iced cups), although it does not have such a pronounced cucumber flavour. Blue is not a common natural food colour, but it is sometimes useful to know a few blue flowers which are edible and can be used for decoration. Viper's bugloss is in this category with wild chicory, violets and borage.

White Deadnettle
Blind, Dumbor Bee

This is an exceedingly common hedgerow and waste-land plant in continental Europe and Britain, except in Ireland

Nettle, White
  Archangel
FR: Lamier, Ortie
GER: Taubnessel
IT: Lamio, Ortica bianca
SP: Ortiga muerta roja
BOT: Lamium album
FAM: Labiatae
Ill. 13, No. 4, page 168

Purple Deadnettle
FR: Lamier rouge,
  Ortie rouge
GER: Rote Taubnessel
IT: Lamio purpureo
SP: Ortiga muerta roja
BOT: Lamium
  purpureum

and northern Scotland. Like the other deadnettles, it looks rather like a nettle at a casual glance, but it does not sting and does not belong to the nettle family. It has white flowers and the same square stem as many labiates.

The white deadnettle has very little of the strong aromatic quality associated with this family, but it is edible and is used in soups or as a vegetable (although it is not eaten by cattle). It is said to be sometimes cultivated in France, but is such a common weed that cultivation seems scarcely necessary.

It is mentioned in Madame Prunier's *Fish Cookery* as an ingredient in eel recipes (*Anguille à la flamande*), though one learns from her that her chef usually substitutes mint and sorrel.

Linnaeus, the great Swedish naturalist, recorded that a close relative and, if possible, even more common garden weed, the purple or red deadnettle was boiled and eaten as a vegetable in his country.

Wine

Wines give a characteristic flavour to the cooking of France, Italy, Spain, Portugal and Greece; but although wine has been made in the Levant and Middle East since time immemorial, it does not enter commonly into the modern cooking of the Arab countries, Turkey or Persia.

It is perhaps rather surprising that a relatively small amount of wine cooked slowly in meat dishes creates a characteristic and strong flavour quite different from that of the original wine. The alcohol contained in the wine will have vanished early in the cooking, because alcohol has a lower boiling point than water and will have vapourized and gone away in the steam. What one has is a unique flavour, basic to dishes such as *coq au vin* or *boeuf à la bourguignonne*. Anyone who has lived for a time in one of the European wine countries will have no doubt become used to adding wine to the cooking as a matter of daily habit, casually and without thinking twice about it. Those who are not so fortunate – who live in countries where wine is regarded as a luxury or a 'booze' instead of a necessary part of a meal – will be unused to having wine always available in the kitchen. For these people, using wine presents some problems, apart from expense, because few dishes call for a whole bottle of wine and it goes sour rather quickly, once it is opened. (The reason for this is explained in full under Vinegar.) But wine will not go sour if it is kept out of contact with the air, for the bacteria that cause wine to sour need oxygen. One solution to the problem is to keep left-over wine away from the air by pouring a little good cooking oil on the surface.

Both red and white wines are used in cooking, and the quality of the wine is of prime importance. The flavour of the wine and its acidity or sweetness influence the flavour of the dish, and some acid wines tend to toughen meat. There is another factor in that some wines break and become 'thin' during cooking. Experience is the only guide, since most people cannot afford to use a fine-named wine for cooking (for instance, a whole bottle of Chambertin) and must depend on whatever *vin ordinaire* is supplied by the local wine merchants. It is obvious, however, that, in the absence of indications to the contrary, a wine of the type produced in the district where the dish originates is the correct one to use. One would not use a claret for a dish originating in Burgundy. Some recipes call for very particular wines. For instance when wines are used in English cooking, they are often those which have come from districts close to sea ports, such as Cadiz (Jerez) and Oporto. This is perhaps why both port and sherry are used so much in English dishes, though rarely on the Continent. There is often this strong link between history, geography and the ingredients used in cooking.

Madeira is used to flavour consommé and aspic. This wine correctly comes from the Portuguese island of that name, situated north of the Canary Islands, and was more popular in the past than it is today. It is a fortified wine and, like port and sherry, can be kept for a couple of weeks after the bottle is opened. It comes in various degrees of sweetness, varying according to the grape used. The four principal varieties are Sercial, Bual, Verdelho and Malmsey, of which Sercial is the driest and the best to use in such dishes as *jambon au Madère*.

Marsala is another fortified wine, usually rather sweet, and tasting partly of caramelized sugar. This wine comes correctly from the area around the port of Marsala at the most westerly tip of Sicily. It is used a great deal in Italian cooking and anyone who has a liking for Italian food must keep a bottle of Marsala in the kitchen cupboard. As some of the cheaper Marsalas are quite horrible and as only small quantities are required, it is better to buy a fairly good one and not go for the cheapest thing on the market. Marsala, like Madeira, is made in varying degrees of strength and sweetness and the same rules apply to its use in cooking as do to Madeira.

Port comes from the hinterland about fifty miles from Oporto, although today it is imitated in many parts of the world. This is indispensable in English cooking for dishes such as jugged hare and Cumberland sauce.

Rice wines of various kinds are much used in the cooking of China and Japan, as they have a slightly sherry-like flavour; in Europe it is usual to substitute dry sherry, although rice wines are available in specialist shops. The Chinese flavour-combination of fish stock, grated turnip, ginger and rice wine (dry sherry) is excellent.

Wood Sorrel
Shamrock

FR: Alléluia, Oxadile blanche, Petit oseille, Surette
GER: Sauerklee
IT: Acetosella
SP: Acederilla, Oxadile blanca
BOT: Oxalis acetosella
FAM: Oxalidaceae

A common wild plant of woods and damp shady places, it has white flowers streaked with fine purplish lines. The leaves are clover-shaped, light sensitive, and hinged; and they close against the stem at night or in bad weather. Some say that this is the true shamrock, the national emblem of Ireland, but the Irish usually nominate another plant for this distinction.

The wood sorrel contains a great deal of oxalic acid, about an ounce in ten pounds of leaves. (*Oxalis* is from the Greek for sour or acid and *acetosella* is from the Latin *acetum*, vinegar.) Oxalic acid is poisonous in quantity (we know it as a chemical used for removing ink stains) and cattle grazing in woods on wood sorrel can become ill; it can even kill sheep. Oxalic acid or its salts also occur in rhubarb leaves, as is well-known. Less well-known is that it occurs in spinach, garden sorrel, and many other vegetables. Thus, one can safely eat wood sorrel in the quantity one would use for a salad or sauce. It can replace garden sorrel in salads or in soup, and Gerard, the famous Elizabethan herbalist, says that it makes 'a better greene sauce than any other herbe whatsoever'. Since wood sorrel is also decorative, it makes a useful dual-purpose plant to grow in the garden.

**Worcestershire
Sauce**
Worcester Sauce

This bottled commercial sauce is so famous and so world-wide in its use in every country outside the Iron Curtain that it deserves to be mentioned. The story of its origin is probably this. About 1837, the year Queen Victoria came to the throne, a retired governor of Bengal went to his local druggists in Worcester, one of several shops belonging to two pharmacists by name Lea and Perrins, and ordered that a recipe he had brought back from India be made up. This was done, but it did not pass muster with the ex-governor, and he rejected it. The matter was forgotten until some years later when Mr Lea and Mr Perrins were turning out the cellar and the barrel came to light. On tasting it they found it was now quite superlative. Unlike O. Henry's tale of the Apollinaris water, they still had the recipe, and began to make it up for local consumption. The sauce so rapidly became popular that ten years later it was used in the household of many noble families, and the druggists had even begun to export it. Its fame was quickly spread around the world by the pursers of the early steamships. For instance, in June 1843, it was recorded that 'The cabin of THE GREAT WESTERN had been regularly supplied with Lea and Perrins' Worcestershire Sauce which is adapted for every variety of dish – from turtle to beef, from salmon to steaks, to all of which it gives a famous relish. I have great pleasure in recommending this excellent sauce to captains and passengers as the best accompaniment of its kind for any voyage.' Not only does Worcestershire sauce come into most bar cures for a hangover, but it helps to soften the sight of salt pork when one is seasick.

Worcestershire sauce is now manufactured in many countries and the same old recipe is used. Indeed, the Lea and Perrins factory in Worcester still uses the same splendid Victorian cast iron and wood machinery which, together, with vaults full of barrels of maturing sauce, convey the atmosphere of a winery, belied only by the smell of vinegar and spices.

Worcestershire sauce is a thin piquant sauce of a general type popular in the days of the East India Company. It is based on vinegar, soy and molasses and contains the juice of salt anchovies together with red chilli, ginger, shallots and garlic; in all, over twenty different tropical fruits and spices. It is not a cooked sauce but is a product of maceration and is matured in oak hogsheads for a long period as it was in the pharmacists' cellar.

Probably the greatest international use of 'Worcester' is in bars for flavouring tomato juice and, as already mentioned, for reviving people with a hangover (e.g. prairie oyster). But a look through old correspondence shows that Worcestershire has been used by a surprising number of great chefs as one of their 'secrets'. It is clear that whilst nothing is worse than the excessive use of Worcestershire sauce to disguise bad cooking, it is a valuable flavouring when used with skill and moderation. There is someone to advocate its use in almost any dish: soups, fish, shellfish, meat and game and poultry, eggs, cheese, salad dressings and sauces. Cooks do better to steer clear of made-up flavourings, but an item which has been popular and unchanged for over a century and is used by chefs in so many countries must be an exception. Indeed, one could almost say that it has graduated as a basic natural ingredient.

Wormwood

FR: Absinthe, Armoise amère, Génépi
GER: Absinth, Hilligbitter, Wermut, Wurmkraut
IT: Assenzio
SP: Ajenjo
BOT: Artemisia absinthium
FAM: Compositae
Plate V, No. 3

Wormwood is a close relative of tarragon (*Artimisia dracunculus*), southernwood (*Artimisia abrotanum*) and mugwort (*Artemisia vulgaris*). It grows wild occasionally in Britain and, from there, right through Europe and Asia to Kashmir and beyond. It is a bitter aromatic herb with grey foliage covered with fine hairs and yellow flowers. It has been used for thousands of years as a medicine (to cure worms) and in the preparation of various apéritifs and herb wines. Even today, it is often difficult to say exactly where medicine begins and drinking for enjoyment leaves off, especially in the Mediterranean countries, where it is still customary to prop up congested livers and flagging appetites with semi-medicinal drinks (always alcoholic, of course) which, even if they do no direct harm, are guilty of putting off the evil day to a yet more evil one. Possibly the worst result is that people even get to like these semi-medicines. Wormwood is a common ingredient in many of them as well as more pleasant drinks. It gives the name to vermouth via the German, *Wermut*; Old English, Wermod; and finally wormwood.

Modern vermouths contain many ingredients, and their exact formula is usually a trade secret, but in the less developed parts of Europe it is still common to find wine in which sprigs of wormwood have been steeped (in the Carpathians, for instance) and botanically-minded gastronomes, who find this plant on a walk or grow it in their garden, can try putting a large sprig in a bottle of vodka. It will impart a bitter flavour which some vodka drinkers like. A Polish friend of mine even purloined pressed leaves of wormwood from my collection.

The essential oil of wormwood is produced in France and the United States by steam distillation. In concentrated form, wormwood is a narcotic poison and so should be used in moderation. The alarming effects from its use in absinthe are only too obvious in some of the villages in southern France.

There are many other species of wormwood, indeed ten species grow on the Riviera coast alone, nearly all in the mountains. Roman wormwood (*Artemisia pontica*) is one of these and is also commonly used in vermouths. (*See* Southernwood.)

Mugwort (*artemesia vulgaris*), a common hedgerow weed in parts of Britain, is s m times used in the stuffing for goose in old English country recipes. In Germany it is known as Beifuss, Ganse-(goose), Johannis – or Besenkraut and used with game, wildfowl, eels, and even stewed veal, also for sauces and in salads. In Spain Artemesias are used in such diverse dishes as onion and vegetable soups, with eels and carp, with roast pork and duck, goose, and as a sauce.

These are the sort of herbs which can add an individual tang to cooking if used well below the level of recognition.

Yarrow. *See* Milfoil.

Yeast

Most people know bakers' yeast as a cheesy-looking substance smelling of beer. It is, in fact, composed of millions of yeast plants, small single-celled plants which multiply by budding when grown in a suitable warm sugary medium such as fruit juice. Yeasts are very tiny, though larger than bacteria and are usually oval in shape during their 'vegetative phase'. They produce 'spores' when a tough resting stage is needed to survive adverse circumstances.

Yeasts produce enzymes which act on simple sugars to make carbon dioxide gas and alcohol. This is the normal process that goes on in wine making and in leavening bread and various cakes, to which this process adds a distinctive flavour. There are, however, a vast number of different kinds of yeast, and they create different flavours in the liquids they ferment. In making home-made wine, it is better not to use bakers' yeast, as suggested in the old recipes, but to find one of the true wine yeasts, cultures of which are now available in specialist shops. These yeasts are naturally present on the grapes from various parts of the world, and their flavour is superior. One must also always beware of rogue wild yeasts which are in the kitchen air and can get into home-made wine and spoil it completely.

Zedoary

FR: Zédoaire
GER: Zitwerwurzel
IT: Zedoaria
SP: Cedoaria
BOT: Curcuma zedoaria
FAM: Zingiberaceae
Ill. 18, No. 5, page 244

The plant is very similar to turmeric and is a native of Southeast Asia. In the jungles of South India, I have found many plants superficially resembling turmeric or ginger, but with variously smelling rhizomes. The flavour of the rhizome of zedoary, which is large and fleshy, is somewhat like ginger but with a slight camphor undertone. In Southeast Asia, it is used as a spice, the tubers being first cut in slices and dried. In Singapore, it is known as *kunchor*, and in Indonesia as *Kentjur* or *KentJoer* (Dutch).

Appendix: Plants by Families

Index